Sunday Miscellany

A selection from 1995 – 2000

SUNDAY MISCELLANY

A selection from 1995 – 2000

Edited by Marie Heaney

In association with RTÉ

TOWN
HOUSE
DUBLIN

First published in 2000 by

Town House and Country House Ltd

Trinity House, Charleston Road

Ranelagh, Dublin 6

ISBN: 186059-134-5

A CIP catalogue record for this book is available from the British Library

Typesetting: Typeform Repro

Cover design: Jason Ellams

Frontispiece image: 'A Girl Reading', Patrick MacDowell, reproduced by the kind permission of The National Gallery of Ireland

Printed in England by Cox & Wyman Ltd.

CONTENTS

A SENSE OF PLACE 37

A SENSE OF HUMOUR

A SENSE OF PRESENCE

A SENSE OF THE PAST

FOREWORD

It's Sunday morning, you're at home, the radio is on... suddenly you're captivated by a voice, a story, a memory or an evocative piece of music. And then you're hooked – as many before you have been – by *Sunday Miscellany*.

When I took over the production of the programme in 1995, I must admit I was nervous. After all, the popular RTÉ series had been running for almost thirty years, so where would I start?

But as soon as I began to read my first batch of scripts, I realised the amount of talent that was out there, and suspected that I'd never reach the end of the pile – how right I was! Burning the midnight oil, sitting at my kitchen table, poring over a stack of scripts has become a constant feature of my life since then. And I still get a rush of excitement when I come across a script that seems to jump off the page...

Meeting the contributors, working with them, and giving studio direction as they read their own scripts certainly provides plenty of variety. Then comes the challenging task of finding a piece of music that echoes the tone of each story, sometimes hours of listening until you finally come across that elusive piece which sounds just right. After that, the job of shaping the programme, piecing together a jigsaw of different stories, moods, accents and music. And the result? A kind of serendipity, I suppose, where, as a listener, you never know what's coming next. So, hopefully, you'll hear something that makes you smile, or moves you, sets you thinking or takes you to a place you've never been before...

As for that ever-increasing pile of scripts, I'm still amazed by the numbers of people (many of whom have never been published or broadcast before) who submit stories for *Sunday Miscellany*. I've personally enjoyed encouraging newcomers – about three hundred have been introduced over the last five years – and some remarkable talent has emerged.

So in this collection you'll meet the well-loved and the new, from every part of the country. And even though you cannot hear the voices, Marie Heaney's skilful selection recaptures the pleasure of the programme and provides you with the opportunity to re-experience those pieces that have vanished into the air.

Finally, to all who have featured on *Sunday Miscellany* over the last five years, to colleagues Liz Sweeney and Laurence Foster who have taken up the reins during my holidays, and to the programme assistant Máire Ní Fhrighil who has been a tower of strength, a very special word of thanks.

Martha McCarron
Producer, Sunday Miscellany

INTRODUCTION

For thousands of listeners, the signature tune for *Sunday Miscellany* heralds the start of a journey that takes them through time and space, introduces them to a cast of memorable characters and involves them in adventures far removed from their Sunday morning routine. It is this happy mix of the past and the present, the ordinary and the fabulous, the humorous and the moving that gives the programme its perennial appeal.

In compiling *Sunday Miscellany: A Selection from 1995 – 2000,* I have tried to conserve this element of surprise, while ordering the material in a way that gives a necessary coherence to a collection such as this.

A number of balancing acts were involved. How to select over one hundred and fifty pieces from the six hundred submitted? How to arrange the material once it was selected? How to best represent the contributors – the less well-known as well as the familiar?

As regards the actual selection of scripts, my prime concern was that they worked as pieces of *writing*. In this my criteria were a little different from that of the producer of the radio programme. What works well on air may not work well on the page. Colloquialisms, local sayings, delivery and the timbre of the individual voice, all the things that bring a radio script alive, cannot or may not work in print. The result is that some pieces that were memorable as radio may not be included in the anthology whilst the obverse may also be true.

There were at least three possible ways of arranging the pieces: alphabetically, chronologically or thematically. I opted for the third way as the one that would give a unifying shape to the anthology. It had, however, inherent difficulties, the first being that creating themes could work against the essential element of surprise. It also meant arbitrarily placing some contributions in one category when their complexity was such that they fitted into other categories, or none. To overcome these difficulties I devised headings that were as broad and inclusive as possible and, within these capacious categories, I juxtaposed the pieces to give the maximum variation of subject and tone.

One of the trickiest aspects of the selection process was to strike a balance between the rival claims of the occasional or one-off contributors, and the well-known ones. This dilemma resolved itself naturally, for it transpired that the best-known contributors were often experienced writers as well as broadcasters and it was the excellence of their writing as much as the familiarity of their voices that occasioned more than one entry in the anthology.

In keeping with the philosophy of the radio programme, I included as many new voices as possible to add variety and new perspectives to the collection. As with the regular contributors, it was the quality of their writing coupled with the originality of their material that ensured their inclusion in the book.

Sunday Miscellany: A Selection from 1995 – 2000 will be an invaluable resource for the many devotees of the radio programme because it gives permanence to a form that is, of its nature, evanescent. Through it listeners-turned-readers can recover half-remembered pieces, relish familiar voices, discover new ones and re-experience the pleasure of a good story well-told.

But *Sunday Miscellany: A Selection from 1995 – 2000* is more than just a companion volume to a much-loved programme. It stands on its own as a unique compendium of some of the most personal and most heart-felt writing that has appeared in this country over the past five years.

Marie Heaney

A Sense of Occasion

WITH THE GRACE OF AN EAGLE
Carol Slowey

I always arrived early at the Leisure Centre for my night class. The forty minutes' wait before the lesson I passed sitting on the very back bench of the spectators' gallery of the swimming pool, watching serious solo swimmers doggedly swimming length after length in the single lanes, knots of youngsters seeing how far they could go before the guard blew a warning whistle, and patient fathers and mothers with tiny little children in inflated arm bands and rubber rings. I watched the traffic up and down past the spectators' gallery too, youths with hold-alls and squash bats, white crowds of judo devotees, the security man on a slow wander. An odd time someone would join me in the spectators' gallery, carefully making their way down the giant steps to the front, to lean over the rails and communicate to someone in the pool, or open a book and prepare to wait.

One night as I was sitting in my usual place – I heard a lot of noise coming from the changing rooms below – a noise like the excitement of young people in a crowd. After a while a man emerged from the changing rooms and took up a position at the entrance, from which he seemed to be directing something that was going on inside. The noise gradually became subdued, and then, as though cutting some invisible ribbon, the man stepped to one side to release a crowd of about thirty young boys. They came surging forward with a wild joy, shouting and running and jumping towards the pool. All except one, a great fat boy, taller than the others too, who walked among them like an Emperor, sailed slowly through them like a large ship surrounded by bobbing small craft. I felt a wave of pity. Oh, let them not be unkind to him, I thought. I watched him as he made his way with slow heavy state along the side of the pool, past the pool attendant's umpire's chair, past the darker water in the deep diving pool to the ladder to the diving board. I saw him slowly mount the steps, and plod heavily to the end of the board. There he stood gathering concentration, collecting himself like someone preparing for prayer. He seemed to be alone in the pool, and the pool silent. Slowly he raised his arms. Another moment and he rose with the grace of an eagle into the air and slowly, beautifully, dove into the pool. I was spellbound. A moment later and he appeared from under the water in the pool. He climbed out. Heavy and sodden, he made his way to the diving board again. I watched him again, and again, over and over: the same heavy plod to the end of the board, the same stillness, the same silence, the same slow raising of his arms to rise into the air and dive.

For me, it was like coming upon a phrase of music that catches at your heart, leaves you so that you don't know whether you feel happy or sad, wishing you could hear it again.

GO BACK TO YOUR MOTHER
Paul Andrews

When a bishop asks a question from the altar, I'm not sure that he expects an honest answer. The Archbishop of Paris – we are talking about 1913 – was all set to ordain my Uncle Frank as a sub-deacon. He was standing at the altar of Saint Sulpice, the seminary on the left bank of the Seine. Frank was a thin, dark, clever boy from Cork, as pious as they come, and deep. He *thought* about things. The ceremony in Saint Sulpice was important. Becoming a sub-deacon involved the promise of celibacy. As seminarians used to say, 'This is the day we lock on the iron pants and throw away the key'. The liturgy was framed in formal Latin, but each candidate was called before the bishop beforehand to speak for himself.

'Frank Mulcahy,' he asked, 'are you seeking ordination of your own free will, and without pressure from anyone?'

Frank thought for a moment. In the preparations for the formal ceremony, this exchange had been unrehearsed, taken for granted. The bishop had asked a reasonable question and Frank gave a straight answer. 'It wasn't really my idea, my Lord. It was my mother's.'

A shocked pause. 'Then go back to your mother,' said the bishop calmly. Frank packed his bags, went back to Cork, and found his vocation as a businessman. He married my father's sister, who gave him two remarkable much-loved children. The boy, also Frank, died as a missionary in a Brazilian shanty town. The daughter died before her time as the mother of twelve children.

Later in life Frank would read Gibbon's *Decline and Fall of the Roman Empire*, then, disturbed and fascinated, read it again; and a third time. Family legend has it that by the end of the third reading he had lost his faith, to which, as a matter of interest, he returned at the end of his life. Those who knew him throughout his life remembered a happy man. On the brink of manhood he had discovered just in time, the distinction between his mother's dreams for him, and his own.

FREE AS THE WIND
Annette Black

Hurricane Fran came raging out of the Caribbean, lashing the coasts of the North and South Carolinas and before finally blowing itself out, venting its dying fury on southern Virginia. Off the coast the waves rolled twenty feet high, their eerie whiteness challenging the morbid darkness of the blacked-out coastline, while inland the winds swept across the peninsula formed by the York and James rivers. Swept across the very soil where General Washington, commander of the American Armies, outmanoeuvred the British forces, but even before that, the very place where the first Virginian colonists stepped on American soil and set about taming the wilderness and its native American inhabitants.

The morning after Hurricane Fran dawned bright and fresh, the September sun still high in the cloudless sky, its heat intense even at that early hour in the morning. I left Yorktown quiet and still in its Sunday slumber and set off on foot across the battlefields. The gently rolling countryside looked fresh and green after the storm, belying its bloody history. These battlefields once resounding with artillery fire and musket retorts, once littered with bodies of young men dressed in their scarlet and blue uniforms, were now littered with uprooted trees and other debris. The blue, blue waters of Chesapeake Bay twinkled and glittered in the background and somehow I felt that it was the spirits of the Indians who once owned these lands that had visited in the unseen wind.

It was the spirit of the Indians that the colonists sought to break – although the colonists themselves were the victims of many a bloody massacre, the Indians were wiped from the face of their beloved hunting grounds. With unrepenting belief in their righteousness, the colonists liked to catch young Indian boys and train them to be useful lackeys of the empire. But it was the Irish-born scientist Robert Boyle who founded a school, Brafferton Buildings, to train the wild ones in the fineries of civilisation. Young braves from several tribes were brought together – strange to one another, strange to the English language, unused to the strictures of the scratchy coarse uniform, unused to being locked up and pinned down.

One young brave escaped each night to run free in the woods surrounding the school, setting ever-increasing endurance tests, living only for the nights when his body and spirit could run wild and free, hearing the call of the marshes, the sea and his ancient homelands.

After dark he used a smuggled rope to climb down from his third floor room and then he ran bare-breasted and barefooted through the trees, perhaps hearing in the sounds of the night the rhythmic beat of his tribal tom-toms.

One night he ran and ran until he fell exhausted preferring the call of his ancestors to a life of service with the English invaders.

Perhaps it was in the hurricane winds blowing without constraint that his spirit returned and perhaps that is why the earth smelled so sweet and fresh to me, that September morning.

MOUNTAIN TURF
Brian Leyden

'I'm going to the mountain to cut turf,' my father announced in the pub. The idea caused a bit of a stir. We were, after all, living in the coal mining village of Arigna. The smell of turf smoke in the air might be a special feature of life in the west of Ireland but not in Arigna; in its place we had the thick smog and reek of native coal fires.

'Have you rights?' someone asked.

'Nobody goes near the mountain any more,' my father said. 'I'll cut turf on the first bank I come to.'

A discussion started; about the great men long ago, and all the turf they saved. Men who had blackened the mountain with turf. But that generation was dead and buried and it was doubtful if there was even a proper turf cutting *sléan* left in the village. Might a garden spade be used instead, or a hay knife? It was agreed there was a right way to strip a turfbank. And cutting turf in neat level benches, or 'spits', was an art in itself. And you had to take into account the quality of the turf on different parts of the mountain. Indeed, so much turf was saved in theory by the coal-miners sitting around the bar, the owner, Mick Flynn said, 'Someone open the back door or this turf will never dry'.

But my father was as good as his word, and after dinner – a mid-day affair in our house – we tackled an ass and cart, the ass being a lot easier borrowed and more of an all-purpose vehicle for the terrain than the big red trucks used to haul coal from the mines.

I was about ten years old at the time and it was a new experience for me, as our ass and cart expedition set out. We left the surfaced road and turned up the steep incline of the bog lane. There was a loud fart from the ass when the strain came on the tackle. 'He's switching over to the reserve tank,' my father said.

After the green pasture fields, hedged with yellow flowering gorse, we met drifts of lovely white bog cotton, rock and heather. A mountain hare ran a wide circle along the horizon and made a proper fool out of our dog, who returned panting but in high spirits. Dogs take after their owners, and we were all happy to be going to the mountain more for adventure than reward.

We were amazed when we found that a neighbour had slipped away from the pub and reached the mountain ahead of us. His jacket was off, and he had laid claim to the first turf-bank next to the lane. Two days later he would have the place fenced off more securely than Fort Knox.

We continued as far as Noone's worked-out mine, where the coal and slate dark road ended. In a clear blue sky the larks disputed. 'Go back... go back... go back,' a disgruntled grouse seemed to say when it broke cover and flew from the turk-bank we finally singled out as ours. Tools and tea-making things were unloaded. The cart was heeled-up and the ass tethered. My father lit a Woodbine, and used the match to burn off the old heather. Smoke rose like a rebel uprising.

When he finished his cigarette he cut the first layer of poor, wiggy turf. The second spit was better, good, black turf he said, that would dry as hard as a goat's knee.

I made a make-shift barrow from ends of timber, a sheet of galvanised iron, bent six-inch nails and a bicycle wheel. We christened it the moon-buggy, and while my father cut the turf in a hound's-tooth tweed pattern, it was my job to barrow away the wet, buttery new sods of turf for scattering.

It wasn't long before Tommy Tivnan arrived in a spruce white shirt, a *sléan* across his shoulder, whistling 'When I first said I loved only you, Maggie'. He waved to us and set to work on the opposite turf-bank.

The next man that landed with a spade was Johnny Guihen. He summered cattle on the mountain between Rockhill pit at one end and Derrinavoggy pit at the other. He knew where all the air shafts going down to the mines were along the route, and warned me of the danger. Then he told me where to find an old clamp of turf, which we used to build a fire. We boiled water in a battered saucepan. Tommy Tivnan brought over his sandwiches. We drank tea that tasted of turf-smoke, and ate soggy egg and tomato sandwiches seasoned with salt from a twist of newspaper. We relished every morsel with sharp, open-air appetites. Then Bernie Gilhooley appeared, and stuck his arm in the cold mineral-brown waters of the bog hole for ten minutes to soothe his arthritis.

I'm sure we burned more turf than we saved that day, sitting around the fire in its ring of stones drinking tea. But we would make regular trips to the mountain after that; to finish the cutting and the scattering; to foot or rackle the turf in little pyramids, crowned with a level sod along the top to keep off the rain; to gather the turf in clamps and to build it into reeks; to haul the turf home in loads with the ass and cart – with more loud reports from the ass going down hill when the strain came on the breeching.

And out of the drudgery and pleasure of saving the turf that summer, my memory fixes on that first day, and those coal-miners who gathered around our fire, resolved to claim their acre of turf. Pitmen whose work kept them underground for so much of their lives, hunkering down along with Father under a blue sky, liberated again to a sweet mountain breeze.

'BLEDDY WASTE A TIME'
Pat Boran

My father, Nicholas Boran, died in February 1999 and, as anyone who's suffered the loss of a family member knows, you feel it in unpredictable but sometimes, also, in delightful ways.

A countryman, from a small farm background in County Kilkenny, my father somehow ended up marrying a townie and settling into married life in a big old three-storey house in Portlaoise, twenty miles or so to the north. But there were quite a few townie things he never developed a feel for. Such as backing horses. Until just over two years ago, my family lived right in the middle of the main street of Portlaoise, so it wasn't all that strange that our front windows looked directly at Paddy Power Bookmaker's across the way. Despite its proximity, however, to the best of my knowledge my father never went in there, except to bring us over in turns to place a few pence on the Grand National when we were kids. Gambling for my father was, like pop music and going to the pictures, 'a bleddy waste a time'.

And so then how strange that only a couple of months after his death, the house which was knocked down during his long illness was replaced with a brand new building, the first tenant of which is Paddy Power, the bookmaker.

A couple of weeks later, down visiting for a day, I made a point of going there to place my own small bet as if, in some way, the story of that house and my father might be completed.

After standing opposite for a few minutes to survey the concrete facade and new signboard, I steeled myself, crossed the street and entered.

Inside, the decor was unrecognisable – television screens lined up against one wall; newspaper betting pages tacked on to a notice board that ran the length of the other; three girls behind a high counter, all of them wearing spotless white shirts and intent on their business. And, of course, a number of faces I recognised from years of looking out my bedroom window were there. And a number were missing.

And then I looked up. And my heart almost stopped.

'I know what you'll be putting your money on,' said a man I half recognised.

But I was completely unable to answer him. For I had just then seen that running in the 2.00 at Newbury, the first horse on the card in fact, its name currently blazing from every second television screen in the room, was a horse called Borani. *Borani*, the Borans! It was an unmistakable sign. Of something.

I staggered to the counter, ransacking my pockets. It was two minutes to two. I had only ten pounds and odd pence. If I'd had a thousand I would have put it on that horse. The name Boran is unusual, to say the least. Borani I have never come across. And that this horse should be running now, in this one race I had decided to bet on, and here on the site of the very place where my father had brought the name from country to town, from single man to married couple, from singular to plural. Borani... My God, my whole family was involved.

My heart was pounding. My mouth was dry. My legs were literally shaking.

'And they're off!'

Almost as soon as I heard the words I knew what was about to happen, but I tried to keep it back, tried to keep it in some part of my mind where I wouldn't have to acknowledge it.

But long before they entered the final furlong, it became clear that not only would Borani not win the 2.00 at Newbury, he would not even be placed. Judging by his pace he may not even finish.

'Good money,' my father whispered deep in my ear, evidently enjoying himself.

And we both said it together then, 'Bleddy waste a time.'

HUMPBACK WHALES
Neil Cleminson

The sea slid by; silently. Quicksilver – grey and oily smooth. Our outboard chugged gently. Barely turning over. The small inflatable left a tiny wake. We were trying to use stealth. We'd failed so far with a direct approach.

It was cold. Very cold. A low veil of mist merged with the sea two or three hundred yards away. It was hard to be certain. There was no horizon. We were slipping through a timeless grey-out. The only tinge of colour from what seemed to be shards of old glass. Ethereal green they floated. Motionless. Dotting the water. It was ancient ice.

We were listening. Listening for their breath. We'd heard them every ten minutes or so. They seemed to be getting closer.

And then one broke the surface. Frighteningly near. Absolutely immense. Its mighty exhalation was deafening. Like the first long whistling whoosh of steam from a giant locomotive. I could see right down its nostrils. I could smell its breath. Pungent and fishy. A fountain of spout still lingered high above our heads. In a slow graceful arch, first its dorsal fin and finally the tail flukes, individually patterned like a fingerprint, dipped out of sight. We'd had a close encounter with a humpback whale. Fifty feet long and a ton for every foot.

Al lowered the camera, turned and smiled. Raised his thumb. He'd got it on film. And you could trust Al Giddings. He was one of the world's best underwater cameramen. We'd last been together six months earlier, much further south in the Pacific. Humpbacks winter in warmer, sapphire-coloured waters. They give birth in January around the Hawaiian Islands. Al had filmed the mothers and their two-ton babies for me. We'd heard and recorded their haunting songs. Under water you can feel their songs. The pulses of sound vibrate in the cavities of your head and chest. Their music seems to come from inside your own body.

Now we were in Alaska. In Glacier Bay where the ice retreats faster than anywhere else on earth. Great chunks crashed down from white cliffs into the eroding sea. The waters here teemed with tiny life. A dilute soup of plankton, fish fry and shrimp. The humpback whales' summer diet. Next day we found them feeding. The whales swim upwards in a slow spiral, rising from the depths, blowing bubbles, making an airy cylindrical net. It concentrates the prey in the centre near the surface. We filmed as the final bubble completed a perfect circle twenty yards wide. Two seconds later, right in the middle a massive mouth broke clear of the water. The shoal herded together; gone in one gulp.

We were on our way back to our mother-boat when another ship sailed slowly through the sound. A vast, white cruise liner, picking its way through the small bergs. There was no-one on deck. It looked ghostly. Like the *Marie Celeste*. Two hundred yards directly behind it, a giant shape broke the surface. The whale breached three times. That was enough to film a display that's rarely seen. All fifty tons lifting clear of the water.

So where were all the passengers? We found out a few days later. The cruise tourists from California and British Columbia had had their whale watch from a lounge seat on closed circuit TV. They told us they *always* watched nature programmes on television!

INSECT ADORNMENTS
Gordon D'Arcy

Some years ago I found myself unusually graced by an insect. It was a cold New Year's night and I was attending the celebration in a draughty hall in County Waterford. A massive blow-heater, brought in to raise the temperature to a comfortable level, had stirred a tortoiseshell butterfly out of hibernation in the rafters and it fluttered conspicuously above the heads of the revellers. Eventually the band struck up and dancing commenced. To my astonishment, the colourful butterfly spiralled down to settle on the lapel of my suit, wings open and quivering flirtatiously. There it sat, as though pinned like a collector's specimen, for most of the dance eliciting comment from everyone who noticed it. The metallic blue suit (I cringe to think of it now) which I was wearing had proved attractive, though not quite as I had planned.

A similar but even more remarkable incident occurred in the lazy heat of a January morning in West Africa. I was attending Sunday mass in a little Portuguese church on the island of Bubaque of the coast of Guinea-Bissau. The pew in front of me was already full of beautifully clad black women from the village awaiting the start of the ceremony. While I was admiring their wonderfully braided hair, in most cases bunned-up at the back and held in place with an ornate hair slide, an enormous insect (at least four inches long, I guessed) flew in the open door and settled on the hair-bun of the woman directly in front. It chose the only head of hair not pinned up with a slide, rather simply trussed in a black silk cloth. There the bright green mantis sat quite still – as though trained by some eccentric fashion designer. Mercifully, the woman was quite oblivious to her living trinket but another woman beside me reached across and picked it up without her knowing. She removed it gently but assuredly, revealing a domestic familiarity with other such monsters, and lobbed it rhythmically towards the open door. In fact it did not make it to the outside. I watched it fly briefly then cling to the fine door veil which was billowing in the warm breeze. It then crawled to the pelmet where it sat dignified and dramatic against the dark wall, its spring-loaded pincers drawn up in front, praying like the rest of us.

BEE COLLECTING
Don Heenan

It looked like a cloud of smoke but I recognised its unmistakable noise. The air was alive with whirling, droning bodies which abruptly interrupted my afternoon walk in the leafy lanes of Warwickshire. It was a prime swarm of more than twenty thousand bees intent on establishing a new home. The swarm was centred on a privet hedge where it was methodically alighting. A nucleus of bees the size of a football was already clinging to the bush with many more forming a flying cumulus around it. My immediate thought was of how I could get them home, where, as it was mid May, I had a hive prepared for such an opportunity. But I had no means of capturing or carrying them.

The bee-keepers' mantra says 'A swarm in May is worth a load of hay', so I was determined not to lose this windfall which could produce a hundredweight of honey by August.

I took a decision and stepped into the swarm where I spent the next hour in their world. Completely enveloped by them, I proceeded with a plan of capture. I cupped my left hand under the cluster and swept a ball of bees into it with the other. They quickly spread over my wrist and arm in an almost liquid manner. I shook a branch causing a second batch to pour on top of the first. They too spread like melting butter. By now, as I stood in the midst of the swirling deafening mass, I had bees on my face, in my hair and inside my shirt. After a few more manipulations, I had transferred most of the bees onto my hand which was now well covered up to the elbow.

Then came the crucial moment. As I shook another twig, I saw the queen among the tumbling bodies. She hastily ran between my fingers to join the burgeoning cluster suspended under my arm. I knew then that the swarm was mine. The bees did not, of course, share my claim since they do not recognise the principle of ownership.

I stood motionless for another fifteen minutes allowing the remaining bees to join their queen. They seemed content to accept me as a substitute for the privet. They tolerated me, not because they understood what I was doing, but because I did nothing to interfere with their instinctive behaviour pattern.

When I was sure that I had gathered most of the clustered bees, I started for home knowing that the flying bees would follow me. By now my hand and arm were completely enveloped. The swarm was a huge triangular mass of seething bodies. The mechanics of clustering bees is intriguing, with several thousand individuals, each clinging to its neighbour, building up to a shape which appears solid yet is very fluid in character. My arm was getting very tired as I had to hold it horizontally throughout.

I walked the two miles home very slowly to where I had a prepared hive. With my free hand I placed a sloping board up to the entrance. With a sharp downward movement I dumped the swarm onto it. A few scouts went in and soon reappeared at the entrance. They stood with their heads down facing inwards, tails in the air, their wings fanning to waft their 'welcome' scent to their comrades, who then began to move inside.

I saw the queen run over the backs of her workers to install herself in the new quarters. I knew then that the process was complete and that their swarming drive had been satisfied. Their homing instinct would erase all information about their previous residence and would now guide them infallibly to this new location.

My walk home generated a little excitement among the neighbours, one of whom ran home for a camera. Occasionally, when we take out our box of photographs we encounter a couple of dog-eared snaps which remind us of the time when I was handsomely rewarded for my successful impersonation of a privet bush.

In case you have a question, the answer is yes, twice, and both stings were as a result of my carelessness.

EASTER
Pat Donlon

I sometimes find myself muttering that centuries old chant 'ah, things were different then'. But they *were* different. Even Easter smelt and sounded different. The strange silence of Good Friday – my father swearing that even the birds stopped singing between twelve and three o' clock – followed by the bells of Easter day: St Patrick's cathedral, Christchurch, St Nicholas of Myra… Did sounds travel farther then, or could I really have heard them all together? And then the smells…

There is a cold smell to Easter that is linked forever in my memories to furious activity as my mother in a temper of spring-cleaning attacked everything in sight. Floors were scrubbed with great cakes of Sunlight soap, to be polished with Mansion polish – and the only relief for a skulking child was to be allowed skate around with old cloths tied to shoes. There were seemingly endless days of this fierce activity, as tired curtains and cushion covers were laundered and mangled, leaving home a curiously denuded and comfortless place. This daytime activity was matched by the sound of the sewing machine whirring and clacking late into the night as old dresses were remodelled and new ones created, for custom dictated that we wear something new to Mass on Easter Sunday. One Easter we went shopping to Pims or Maceys to buy my first shop-bought outfit, a blue 'costume' with a dark velvet collar. Nothing since has matched the excitement and feeling of sophistication, never mind that its pleated skirt started down at my ankles (you'll grow into it) and ended up loathed and well above my knees as I feared I would never grow out of it.

I was a particular fan of *Girl's Crystal* and *Girl* comics, devouring their contents. *Girl* had a feature I loved as it fed my fantasy of being creative. It was headed 'Mother Tells You How' and starred a paragon mother, Superwoman's ancestor, and her perfect family of husband, clever daughter Judy and baby Robin. Each week Mother instructed in some crafty enterprise usually inspired by the seasons. For some reason Easter exercised her greatly and Mother told how to bake a Simnel cake, make an Easter bonnet, create a clever brooch for your Easter outfit, make Easter decorations, greeting cards, and Easter novelties – novelties for goodness sake! All of these were shown to my dubious mother, who sniffed in derision at such nonsense and wondered out loud if all that reading was really good for me, and what in the name of all that's good and holy was a Simnel cake, and by the way have you done your homework? But I hankered after all these things and years later when my own daughters arrived, baked my first Simnel cake and loved the symbolism of the eleven golden marzipan eggs, one for each of the disciples excluding Judas. And I learned the reason why such a cake full of eggs should celebrate Easter, for eggs were forbidden during Lent and brought to church to be blessed on Easter Sunday as a symbol of rebirth and resurrection. Best of all I added to that old cold smell of Easter new smells of cinnamon, almonds and marzipan.

AT HOME WITH DIOR
Frances Donoghue

In the autumn of 1947 the fashion house of Dior lit up Europe's post-war austerity with something called the New Look. A female population starved of fashion for six years fell on it hungrily. Hemlines dropped from knee almost to ankle length, skirts were huge and circular, swinging in bias cut from tiny nipped in waists. Blouses had dramatic puffed sleeves, or ruffled collars. Everything billowed in fact except at the strategic points where the female shape was indented. It was a mass expression of release after the harsh tailored outlines of wartime clothes. Fabric was used in reckless quantity – I remember how guilty I felt at carving up a whole four yards of material to make one of those swinging skirts.

That summer I had been au pairing in France, the usual fund-raising device of the hard-up student. En route back to Dublin in September I found Paris in a state of delicious anticipation of the Dior first showings; there had been hype and rumours in the magazines for weeks, but the actual clothes hadn't yet been unveiled. I conceived an outrageous ambition to be there on one of the famous little gold chairs at this moment in fashion history. It took ingenuity, neck and a couple of downright lies to achieve this. I presented myself to the Madame of the salon, a creature of awesome elegance. I represented an important woman's journal in Dublin, I said, whose readers were even now posted at every newsagent waiting for the revelations of Monsieur Dior. I provided the name of a real magazine, confident that no emissary from Dublin would be there to show me up as an impostor. I clutched my student briefcase authoritatively. Her scanty English discouraged her from enquiring too closely into my credentials. Anyway my youth and total lack of personal style (I think I was wearing my duffel coat) would not have suggested a fashion pirate. I was waved in with a mixture of hauteur and indulgence to join the élite on the little gold chairs.

The salon, quite tiny, baked under its chandeliers. No runway, there wasn't space. The models swooped and minced amongst us to a background of elegant string music. I had never imagined creatures so rarefied and beautiful, with their handspan waists and fragile ankles on three-inch heels. The makeup of the day was frankly theatrical – flawless pancaked faces, false eyelashes, scarlet slashed lipstick. Fabulous meringues of hats topped the tailored suits, nipped in or peplumed. The long pencil skirts flashed sexy seamed stocking legs through the deep slits which were necessary to let the model move. The extravaganza ballroom dresses had minimal glittering tops, like Barbie dolls, and skirts so voluminous that the girls had to scoop them in their arms as they swayed through us and then release them in one magnificent pirouette just before they disappeared offstage.

When the last model, in a puff-ball wedding gown, had released her frothy skirts and thrown her flowers into the audience there was a polite stampede on the portly Christian Dior, now bowing and embracing a couple of his most stunning girls and looking very complacent, as well he might. The fashion writers and the rich customers cooed and shrieked and kissed the air around each other's faces. I did not wait for the free champagne and canapés, I thought I had pushed my luck sufficiently for one day.

VENUS ON THE BEACH
Sheila Gorman

In Botticelli's famous painting, the *Birth of Venus*, the goddess of love stands in the centre of the picture, looking back at her admirers. She stands modestly, almost bashfully, beautiful. Already confident and self-possessed. Powerful. There she is, arising out of the waves, her hair blowing in the light breeze as the salt water laps around her bare feet. Emerging out of an opening fluted shell. Venus, the goddess of love, is as fresh and young as a white sandy beach cleansed by a soft spring tide. Her pale russet hair resting and curling against her white shoulders and down her flank. To her right, her companion, wearing a finely printed muslin dress, waits beside her with an embroidered cloak of cinnabar red for her shoulders. Two cherubs hover at her left shoulder.

Another artist, a woman, wanted to celebrate the spirit of Venus and of women a couple of years ago. This generous and energetic painter and teacher, committed both to the continuing education of women and to the realisation of their creative potential, was with her students on a field trip in Kerry.

At first they had thought her idea mad. Make an image on the sand? Why? What would be the point? How could they do it? Anyway, they didn't have the skill. The tide would destroy it. It was too cold and miserable on the beach. Undaunted, and full of ebullient enthusiasm, the woman went to the local library and hunted for an image of Botticelli's *Birth of Venus*. What better way to mark the occasion than a celebration of Venus, a beautiful, confident and loving woman.

The artist talked to her students and showed them the image of the painting of Venus. It aroused their enthusiasm. To make an impact on the seven mile beach though, their image would have to be big. The decision was taken to make a line drawing 100 feet long, parallel to the water. The lines would be created by placing stones end to end on the surface of the sand. The next task was to collect enough stones of approximately the same size.

They began the drawing in early morning as the tide was going out. They all worked on the wet sand for over five hours to create the figure. The more they worked the more the energy grew. Energy to help one another, energy to collect yet more stones. Energy to laugh. The energy and gradual realisation that they would complete the task engendered confidence.

Eventually the image was complete. Each line in place. There she was, Venus, the goddess of love, on the beach at Glenbeigh.

I wish I had been there to join the artists as they performed a confident ritual of satisfaction and pleasure in the completion of the task. In celebration of the Botticelli painting, of Venus, of love and beauty, of women and their strengths.

The artists assembled at the head of Venus and, slowly at first, walked around the image. Over her shoulder. Down her arm, elbow and hip, down her leg and turned to go back at her bare feet and at the shell out of which she had been born. The slow walk turned into a trot and then a joyful run. They joined hands and completed the circuit in a line, running on around her head and far shoulder, making a crown for Venus.

By dusk, a small crowd had gathered to see the one hundred foot long stone drawing of Venus on the pale sand. A russet pinkness from the setting sun transformed and seemed to warm and animate her.

It was dark, and the students and their tutor had left the beach, when the first water of the incoming tide lapped at Venus' elbow.

When the students returned to the beach the following morning, there was no sign of Venus. The round stones had been overturned, tumbled and relocated by the strength of the moon-pulled tide. The water pushed and dragged the stones inwards and outwards. It eddied and swirled around each stone, undermining the sand beneath it. Thrish, tumble, strash. Thrish, tumble, schrash. The tide went up the beach slowly, erasing every mark and footstep, and eventually took the final stone line. The tide turned back again, completing the task. The sand was smooth again. Venus had gone back to the sea.

CAPE CLEAR CHALICE
Chuck Kruger

During spring of 1998, for the first time in 356 years, the Timoleague chalice overlooked Cape Clear's South Harbour. There, like a miniature pillar stone, it seemed not so much placed as grown, not so much ship-wrecked refugee as denizen. On the seawall in front of the priest's house, the gleaming chalice stood.

When the chalice first arrived on Cape in 1642, seven years before Cromwell landed in Ireland, the Timoleague Friary had just been torched by Lord Forbes and his English army. With a box full of vestments and the chalice, two friars escaped in a small boat. By the time they were found drifting on the high seas by Cape fishermen, only one friar remained alive.

The men brought the boat ashore. Islanders nursed the friar back to health, gave burial to his companion. When well enough to depart, the friar thanked his carers and instructed them that the mysterious box, which he was leaving on Cape for safekeeping, was strictly not to be opened until he himself returned and Catholics could again freely worship in Ireland.

Some two hundred years later, in 1851, when the parish priest of Rath and The Islands, Father Leader of Clonakilty, visited Cape to conduct stations in the townland of North Ballyieragh, he asked what was in the box in the alcove up over the fireplace and learned that no one knew more than that it had rested there by priestly bidding since penal times.

Father Leader ordered that the box be opened. Someone told him, 'You're not the right man to give that order', and added that another priest had promised to come back, but Father Leader prevailed. The vestments, on being lifted from the box, crumbled. But underneath them, a chalice was found as hail and hearty as on the day of its escape from conflagration. On its base, beside a crucifixion scene, is inscribed 'de Thimolaggi'.

Father Leader consequently returned the chalice to the parish of Timoleague, where it now lives – except when a priest such as Father Donal Cadogan, a relation of the island family known as 'The Cadogans of the Chalice', gains permission to bring the Timoleague treasure to Cape, as when he celebrated an open-air mass inside St. Ciarán's Cemetery in 1996, fifty years after his ordination, and in 1998 when he was the special celebrant at the youth hostel's stations.

Father Donal gave the seaside stations a special seal of approval not only by drinking wine from the historical Chalice. He also brought with him a delicate altar cloth which he draped affectionately over the table. The lacework, created by his mother Kate, depicted The Fastnet Lighthouse and a sailing ship captained by his Cape forebears. And on the wall of the room where we gathered he hung an oil painting showing one of the island's old ships under full press of sail, the Fastnet in the background.

In this atmosphere, during Mass, we sang the 'Cape Clear Hymn', which includes the lines: 'We, Your loved children, sing out our praises, From this jewel in the ocean, to your throne on high.'

When Mass was finished, I, a lapsed Presbyterian, felt as though centuries of sacrament and island tradition had been woven together and condensed into an event as simple and pure and suddenly accessible as the chalice itself.

SUNSET WITH SMUDGES
Nuala Hayes

It's a good photograph, even if I say so myself.

It captures one of those classic sunsets of the 'wish you were here' variety that you regularly see on the holiday postcards stands.

The intensity of the hot red light in its waning moments silhouettes a series of bridges. The nearest bridge is clearly recognisable.

It's the Pont De Vecchi, with its tiny buildings still intact since the middle ages. The Pont De Vecchi is the only bridge in Florence to have survived the bombs of the Second World War. It still has the look of a fairytale, a bridge drawn in the imagination. But look closely at the photograph and you notice the smudges in the foreground. The smudges will disqualify any fantasy I might have about capturing the perfect prize-winning 'sunset with bridges'.

You see the smudges were on the window through which the photograph was taken.

Yes, it was my good fortune to have been there in Florence. I was staying in a convent (but that's another story) and yes, the photograph was taken from an upper window in the Gallery d'Uffizi one night last summer.

One night? I hear you ask. What were you doing in a National Gallery at night in a city like Florence? Well to tell you the truth, I didn't know myself. I decided to go out on my first evening there, to check out the city for myself. To do a recce, as they say in the film business. I didn't want to waste any time getting lost when it came to the serious business of sight-seeing. Florence, I was warned, is a confusing nightmare of heat, tourists and queues and not for the faint-hearted.

So there I was walking along the banks of the Arno, when I came across the famous gallery with huge effigies of the great masters. They are all there, Dante, Michelangelo, Benvenuto Cellini and the rest, like stone sentinels outside the entrance.

And the door was wide open. Beckoning me in. Where was the queue? Where were the people standing patiently for hours, waiting for a glimpse of the priceless works inside? In I went and when I attempted to pay for a ticket, I was waved on, in the rather supercilious manner that Italians who deal with tourists specialise in.

I asked no questions and carried on up the stairs and around the many rooms in this massive building. I saw them all, the Rembrandts, the Raphaels, the Carravagios, geniuses all, the pride of the renaissance. All storytellers in paint, telling so many different versions of the one long story.

I wasn't alone. Others had also discovered the open door and we all moved around, meeting each other in different rooms and smiling like fellow conspirators.

If they knew why they were there, I certainly didn't. My eyes constantly strayed from the paintings on the walls, to the ever-changing picture from beyond the windows as evening fell on the beautiful city.

It was then I captured the smudged sunset forever, with my very ordinary camera.

Outside in the Piazza Del Signora, a concert was in full swing. One hundred and fifty musicians, with many varieties of wind instruments, played music by Brahms in the warm night air. It was wonderful. I felt blessed.

Next day, I discovered the reason for my unexpected good fortune on that one night in Florence. It was May 26th. The fourth anniversary of a horrific Mafia car bomb outside the Uffizi. The building had been seriously damaged and seven people had been killed, including a family with two small children.

In memory of that family and the others who died, and to take a stand against those who carried out the evil deed, the City Council had declared that the main art galleries of Florence should remain open and free to everybody that night, and that music should celebrate the hope of the people of the city. That good will triumph over evil. That creativity will triumph over darkness.

SWIMMING IN THE DARK
Peter Jankowsy

One sultry summer night many years ago, a young woman and a young man who found it difficult to be with each other and impossible to be without, cycled down to the bay. It was around midnight, and the beach was deserted. Silently the woman undressed and stepped into the tepid water, purposefully striding forwards until it was deep enough to swim. The man followed. They had not talked about this. There was no choice. The lukewarm water was phosphorescent, each wavelet, each movement of their hands stirred up a shower of twinkling sparks. They swam, mantled in light. As the woman swam ahead with calm, even strokes, he saw her head trailing a wake of shimmering light, instead of the blond hair of the day. That he followed.

The bay opened out into the estuary of a very big river. The woman swam straight ahead towards the open sea. Did she know what she was doing? Did she care? Was this an act of despair, or one of quiet communion with the elements, with water and night? He had no idea, but he followed her, making his own observations.

There was an electric storm raging above the land on the other side of the river. Lightning shone in great convulsions, but in total silence, because of the distance. And on their own side another storm was building up, with blinding discharges, but again there was as yet no sound. They were swimming between two dark curtains torn by silently erupting flashes, but directly above them the sky was clear and flooded with stars. And their every movement caused an outbreak of countless tiny lights that echoed the immense splendour up there. Wordlessly they swam, the woman led, the man following doggedly. They were by now far out, soon one would have to be reasonable and think about returning.

Slowly a fear was beginning to spread in his mind and body. Was she suicidal, had she lost her senses? Was she fleeing, or was she luring him? Was this a test, a trial, a challenge? To him, to herself, to them both? For a mad, self-forgotten moment he thought that he didn't care, that he would follow until death would take them both – but at that moment something firm and smooth touched him, a body was slowly gliding down along his own. The first idea in this uncanny environment was of course that he had bumped into a drowned person, he was clutched by fear. But then there was another one, and another one, and he realised that they must be jelly-fish. But the first shock was lingering on, they were not alone anymore in the wide, benevolent sea, there were other, sinister presences lurking. He tried to sound calm and rational: 'I think that's enough now!'

She did not react, maybe she did not listen. She swam on and on. After some frighteningly endless minutes, she suddenly stopped, turned around, passed him without speaking or looking, and swam back. This time they swam side by side, if at a distance, and stepped together out of the sea.

And stayed together for a good many years, for many good years. But they never talked to each other about their nocturnal swim. And you could say that all through those years they never truly left that light-encircled, haunted bay.

SEEING BRUJOS
Anne Kennedy

The Spanish word *brujo* means a medicine man or a sorcerer with extraordinary powers for good and evil. Most of the time a *brujo* looks like an ordinary person like you and me, but who has the power to appear and disappear suddenly. Seeing a *brujo* can be a warning or a lesson but it is never an accident.

Last summer in Ballard, a nondescript suburb of Seattle, in the space of three days I saw three *brujos*. It all began one warm afternoon when my daughter and I went into a charity shop run by elderly Episcopalian ladies where on a previous visit I had bought a remarkable string of tin and bone tribal beads. In place of the gentle ladies, a lean young man dressed all in white nervously prowled the shop. He had high cheekbones, sallow skin and slightly wolfish eyes. As he followed us around, making minute adjustments to everything we touched, we grew increasingly uncomfortable.

'Where are the ladies from the church?' I asked.

'They have me in the shop most of the time now,' he answered, 'because they're afraid of being robbed. The neighbourhood is not as safe as it used to be.'

As he spoke, I noticed that he never blinked. It was as though he had gobbled up the old ladies and taken their place.

'That was eerie,' we said to each other as we left.

The next night, as we were driving across the Ballard Bridge, coming against us in the half light, we saw a tall, thin man dressed in a white mini skirt teetering on stilettos and swinging a bag on a chain. We started to laugh, but it immediately became too poignant, seeing his peroxide beehive bobbing against the bridge's rusted girders. Our back seat passengers didn't see him at all.

The following afternoon when we went for a swim, we met an old friend who had just had a painful talk with her ex-husband, Ken. She told us he seemed strange, very changed from the man she had loved and that she regretted agreeing to meet him.

As we sped back to Ballard in the freeway, I suddenly saw my friend's ex, bare to the waist, standing beside a white Buick and wearing a striking white Steston.

'What's with all these apparitions?' I asked my daughter.

'He's another one of our *brujos*,' she answered, 'third time lucky.'

When we looked in the rear view mirror, of course there was no one there – no Buick, no Stetson, no *brujo*. All we saw was the multi-coloured stream of traffic flashing past.

Brujos can assume different shapes, and it was my daughter who decided that the man in the shop, the man on the bridge, and Ken were all one manifestation.

'But how can you tell when you've seen a *brujo*?' I asked her.

'It's very easy,' she assured me, 'you always know later that you've seen someone from the spirit world.'

When I returned to Ireland a few weeks later, I found I had a health crisis. While in hospital, I received a letter from Ken saying he had taken his tribal name, Ned Nightowl, and was practising as a healer. He sensed something was amiss and asked for a photo of me to work with.

'By the time of your next check-up,' he wrote, 'you will be cured.'

Cheerful news indeed, and to this moment, true.

MR SHARK
Chuck Kruger

Out behind the back shed, as my wife prepared to feed Mildred and Wilbur and their first farrow, an incongruous movement caught my eye. A frisky tail. Not a corkscrew flag flipping lackadaisically up and down but a swishing, swath-making tail powering side to side. Not a happy tail in our lower pasture but an inexorable tail below in the harbour. Its massive owner didn't feed on Sow and Bonham Meal, apple peelings and the occasional banana skin – but on plankton.

I ran for the binoculars.

For the next three hours I watched the twenty-five-foot basking shark quarter Cape Clear Island's South Harbour. To and fro he prowled, turning in circles before the priest's house and the Adventure Centre, cutting diagonally across the inner harbour on a sudden whim. His triangular dorsal fin reared three feet out of the water. A goodly distance behind it the tail swung steadily back and forth, back and forth. Occasionally the shark would excitedly swivel round in his wake, fins knifing through a bubbling sea.

I remembered my first experience with a basking shark, back in 1989 in the same harbour. I'd my eighty-year-old mother with me in a dinghy. A neighbour, with a ten-horse kicker on his punt's patched transom, moseyed alongside and offered to tow us across the outer harbour to view the creature. We formed a raft and motored beside the shark for half an hour. He was a whopper, some forty feet long, larger than many whales.

That Christmas friends shared a card from my mother. She wrote them about having visited Ireland – and of my having taken her out into the middle of a shoal of sharks. I called Mom to tease her about her exaggeration.

'Don't you remember?' she said. 'One was off the bow, another alongside, yet another off the stern. A shiver of sharks.'

When I explained that it was all the same shark, she made it clear she was glad I hadn't clarified matters then.

That day I hadn't fully appreciated the visitor. This day I decided I'd savour all I could of him. I donned a life jacket, snatched a paddle, descended to the pier and launched my kayak.

With respectful trepidation, I approached Mr Shark. All I could see were two fins and occasionally a mammoth nose, which created considerable disturbance. Having read that basking sharks are not only vegetarians but basically peaceful, even bovine creatures, not easily aroused, I neared the monster. I could hear the water passing either side of his slicing fins.

I was merrily keeping the bow of my kayak some forty feet from him when he turned, came at me. I didn't know if he was irritated, or just plain curious. Would he ram this interloper or merely swat me with his tail, like a cow a pesky fly.

He didn't so much surge forward as charge. His massive gill-raker head grazed the kayak's bottom. For a split second I saw black dorsal fin to my right, red plastic bow straight ahead, tail fin to my left. Rocking, holding the paddle unconsciously poised in air, I watched and listened to him pass, heard the water trailing from his swishing tail.

I began to breathe – and to absorb my foolhardiness. And Mr Shark cruised calmly on, continued to quarter the harbour. He'd discerned that the rash intruder was not only harmless but insufficiently microscopic to be on the daily menu.

Concluding I'd exceeded protocol in interviewing Mr Shark, I thanked him for his generosity, dragged the kayak up the stone steps, stowed it under the cliffs and went to check the pigs.

PICTURE
Mae Leonard

It's the kind of picture you'd love to step into and be part of the scene. A bunch of women stand in the shallows of a river – half of them, skirts hitched up, busily flaying cloth with some kind of paddle whilst the others, back a bit from the water, are wringing out lengths of dark cloth. A few more are captured walking away with buckets of water on their heads whilst a huge dark cloud up above is moving away, allowing rays of sunshine to spotlight teetering three-storey houses of old Limerick. Central to all the activity is a stone bridge with four rickety arches. And would you believe it? There is a row of houses built on the bridge itself and if you look a bit closer, in a gap between the buildings there are masts of sailing ships anchored in the harbour.

I'm looking at a W.H. Bartlett print from an engraving by E.J. Roberts entitled

'Old Baal's Bridge, Limerick'. I know it, that bridge. Well, at least I know the newer version — that little humpbacked bridge you meet as you come into Limerick City on the Dublin Road — it's where you cross the river to avoid the town if your destination is in a westerly direction.

Maps of ancient Limerick show the walled Irish and English Town linked together by this bridge which was identified, way back then, as Droichead Maol Luimneach — the Bald Bridge of Limerick — bald, some say, because it didn't have parapets.

I look at the picture and put myself in amongst the washerwomen of Limerick. I sniff the wet smell of water mingled with wood smoke coming from several tall chimneys. And fish, Moll Darby's Market is just above the river wall. It's early nineteenth century and the women are talking about a recent trial in the courthouse up the road where Daniel O'Connell defended John Scanlan, one of the landed gentry. Despite the efforts of 'the Liberator', Scanlan was found guilty and sentenced to death for the murder of sixteen-year-old Ellen Hanley, better known to us as the Colleen Bawn. The condemned man was taken from the old gaol to be executed at Gallows Green.

But was Scanlan really guilty? What do the women in my picture say? That fateful morning, they strained to get a look at the prisoner as the sound of horses' hooves clattered up Gaol Lane then came towards Baal's Bridge. Three times an attempt was made to drive the horse-drawn carriage across the bridge. Each time the horses refused. The women saw it all. There was consternation. It was a sign that he was innocent. Above the clamour one of these women shouted 'It's the hand of God — he's innocent'. I hear her telling me now, 'You should have seen him, such a handsome lad, I cried when I saw him jump from the carriage, his hands tied behind him and he walked with his head held high across that bridge there. We followed him to Gallows Green.'

John Scanlan died on the 16th of March 1820 at Gallows Green, Limerick, on the end of a rope, protesting his complete innocence of the murder of Ellen Hanley, the Colleen Bawn.

The women in my picture carry on their day's work, hands raw from wringing heavy cloth. The Abbey River flows onward to join the Shannon. A strong westerly wind blows the chimney smoke off towards Tipperary and the sun forces its way out from the big black cloud. A good day for washing and a great day for drying. Soon life will change forever for these Limerick woman when the old Baal's bridge is taken down and a new one is erected in its stead. That's the little humpbacked you meet now coming into Limerick City on the Dublin Road.

FIRST GARDEN
Brian Leyden

We called it the plot. A patch of ground in the field below our bungalow in Arigna. The plot had the calm atmosphere of a part of the earth that has been won back from the wild, and faithfully nurtured through the seasons.

There was a chain-link fence around the plot to keep out pests. The fence seemed enormously high to me when I was a child. Every time I stepped through the gate into the plot I had the sensation of entering an open space where the air on one side of the fence was different to the air on the other side, modified to create a brink beyond which the ordinary world stopped and inklings of pure mystery began.

My father was a gardener. The plot gave him his livelihood and a place of escape from the hubbub of a young family. It stood at the edge of the Arigna river and he often brought a fishing rod to work. If he saw a curl on the water, or the ripple of a trout rising in the turn-hole below the bridge, he would put down his garden tools, pick up his rod and cast a home-made fly on to the water, to play a whim, to tease a fish.

Beside the plot there was a yard with old rolling stock, left behind after the narrow-gauge railway line into the valley shut down. We made a play-house out of one of the timber-frame carriages. And it was my father who traced the source of the peculiar scratching sound we used to hear on hot days when we played inside the carriage: wasps chewing the timber sides with their mandibles to make paper for their nest.

I was enthralled by his use of words like mandible, aphid and foliage. He had an equal grasp of the antique language of garden weights and measures: the linear inch, foot, and yard; the surveyor's link, pole, perch, chain and rod; the Troy grain and pennyweight; the Avoirdupois ounce, pound and hundredweight; the liquid gill, pint, quart and gallon. A beautiful, granary-rich language that perfectly fitted parcels of turned earth, palmfuls of dry seeds and wheatgrains.

And he taught me another garden vocabulary as moist and yielding on the tongue as bruised fruit: words like tuber, tendril, succulent, legume, and loam. Soft and ripe and pleasing descriptions to encompass my growing knowledge of the world.

Visits to the plot were always special, but one visit in particular stands out in my mind. I am very young and my father has taken me by the hand to lead me through the gate into the plot. Together we walk between the raised beds and planted drills, the neat lines of plants so evidently in his care. The day is warm, the sunlight scattered through the leaves. Only the passing butterflies disturb the air. In the still air, the undersong of the garden is loud. From the mistle thrush on the highest branch of the nearest tree, to the kingfisher cheeping along the riverbank, to the clicking of the grasshoppers in the undergrowth.

My father hunkers down next to me and we start to pick garden peas. The first flush. Enough for an early dinner. Following his example, I reach into the soft, cool greenery and pluck and pop a tender pod open. I scoop the juicy peas out and eat from the palm of my hand.

My God! The sweetness. The flavour. That life could bestow such a moment of perfect delight in that first garden where my father gave me a measure and a name for every plant and creature. Where he laboured each day to transform this fallow clay into cultivated ground.

THE VICTORY HOOP
Brenner Lynch

One of the big deals of my childhood was not, as nowadays, owning your own set of wheels, but owning your own wheel. A bicycle wheel to be exact.

Back in 1957, bicycles were as numerous as cars are today. So old rusty wheels as toys were plentiful. We kids called them hoops.

Most of us in the corporation scheme at Dolphin's Barn had rusty hoops. My hoop had no spokes, no tube and no tyre. The posh kids, as we called them, from Walkinstown, could get hold of hoops with spokes and tyres. But the Rolls Royce of hoops had shiny spokes, and a tyre with an inflated tube. Be the hokey, could them yokes go! Driving power and steering were operated by a roughly cut stick about a foot long.

In our cavalry troop of rusty hoops, we had a force of fifteen soldiers. Our uniforms consisted of threadbare corduroy jackets with short trousers and the cuffs of our sleeves were damp with the product of our permanently runny noses. We wore canvas runners on our feet from which most of our toes could be seen protruding. We wore socks that refused to rise higher than our ankles and our teeth were rotten from neglect and too many sweets. The school health inspector said I would have to have most of mine out and we were all given free toothbrushes. Mine was bright yellow.

During the summer campaign of 1957, we set off up the Clogher road to the quarry land where Sundrive Park now stands. The well equipped Walkinstown cavalry came down Stannaway Road at a menacingly slow trot, their deep-treaded tyres making an almost inaudible whirring sound. The leader of the gang had a polished drumstick to propel his gleaming hoop. They advanced into the grounds in single file and lined up across the quarry pond like a tribe of Indians grouped on a ridge. Our troop lined up facing them on the opposite bank.

Shouted jeers and stones were flung back and forth, the stones falling short and landing in the water. From our waistbands hung our trusty tomahawks. These were made of empty bean tins hammered flat on to the end of short sticks. A mighty weapon that could 'put yer eye out!' as our mothers warned.

The Walkinstown warriors were easily identified by the sight of underpants beneath their khaki shorts and their pullovers were chunky and without holes.

The two armies fired each other up for about fifteen minutes then, when we had worked up enough steam, a great shout of 'ooah ooah, all the gang! Chaaarge!' went up on both sides of the quarry. With that the two armies rode around the quarry in a great cloud of dust to engage in battle.

It lasted barely ten minutes, and at the end of it all I had managed to acquire the leader's new hoop and I cantered proudly home with my trophy.

The next day the dentist pulled out all my rotten teeth except for four on top and three on the bottom, and I kept my bright yellow toothbrush and used it to clean the spokes of my beautiful new Victory Hoop.

THE GAP ON THE SHELF
Bríd McBride

The postman's parcel that Thursday morning left me in a bit of a quandary – where to put its contents?

I suppose all bookworms are confronted with the same conundrum on a regular basis, the utter impossibility of not adding to the collection. Even when we're not looking books congregate, multiply and pile up behind our backs.

The number one area of temptation has to be the myriad bookshops with their powerful, invisible magnets which pull us in and transport us to other worlds. Everyday happenings and concerns fall by the wayside as we peep into places we only ever dreamed of and people's lives which are infinitely more attractive than our own. By this stage we're beyond redemption and the little voice in the head whispers things like 'Oh go on, buy that one. You liked her last novel and here's the follow-up just waiting to keep it company. And what about the display around the corner! It was reviewed in one of the weekend supplements and sounds fascinating. Go on, you deserve a wee treat'. Before you know what's hit you, money passes hands and you've added to your collection.

Another way they pile up could be from like-minded friends. Take my own case for example. There I was practically on my way to Kennedy Airport after a stimulating holiday in New York where I had exercised Herculean-like discipline and ended up with only a half dozen extra books to squeeze into an already full suitcase when my friend started literally to throw books at me.

'I bet you haven't read that one, a new American writer you'll like.'

This went on in similar vein until I was ankle-deep in books and drastic measures were called for. Arrangements were hastily made to have them mailed home in a discarded army rucksack.

Because of this obsession with books, space is a constant problem. The floor to ceiling shelves in the hall alcove are packed as tight as a drum – likewise the fanlight shelves over all the doors. The study contains the dictionaries, reference tomes, periodicals and pieces cut out of newspapers which may or may not be useful some day – if I can find what I'm looking for, that is. Necessity being the mother of invention, the only likely place left to house the overflow was the back wall of the smallest room in the house. Shelves were fitted from the cistern to the ceiling.

But back to the tale of the postman, the parcel and the gap on the shelf on that wall. About six months ago I got a cry for help from the Big Apple, yes, the same friend who almost buried me in books. Had I a copy of John B Keane's *Sharon's Grave* and if I had, would I send it to a Mr McCormack in Canada who wanted to do the play? Yes I had and I would. Mind you it was with a heavy heart I parted with it and nothing was heard from that side of the ocean until a recent Sunday evening phone call.

'Hello, so you're a woman, wasn't sure, the name you know.'

'Yes, I am and who are you?'

'I'm Peter McCormack from Labrador in Canada. Thanks for the script, but that's not what I want to talk to you about, it's the set you see. How should a Kerry cottage look? Where would the best place be to put the outside door? What about the room door, stage right or stage left? And the fire, what should it look like? Oh and what colour should we paint the walls?'

After about a half an hour of conversation like this it was agreed that I would fax a rough sketch of a possible *Sharon's Grave* set with additional notes to this Mr McCormack in Canada who thought I was a man.

Thinking afterwards about this scenario it struck me that the playwright himself down there in Listowel might be amused by the goings on, so I dropped him a note.

And yes, you've guessed it, that's what was in the postman's parcel that Thursday morning all the way from Kerry – a pristine copy of *Sharon's Grave* and autographed by the bould man himself, John B.

Somehow it seems sacrilegious to place this precious *Sharon's Grave* back in the only gap on the shelves in my private loo library. What do you think – beside the bed maybe?

JENNY'S HAIR
Patricia O'Reilly

Jenny's hair was her crowning glory, her best feature. So the adults said. It was rippling blonde and cascaded down her back. And yes, it was gorgeous. I'd have swapped my straight brown hair for it any day… and even thrown in my white teeth for good measure.

She and I were about the same age and I'd more or less grown up with her. Her mother was my favourite aunt and, from as far back as I can remember, I spent my summer holidays with them. They'd a pub in town and a seaside cottage nearby and we'd the best of both worlds.

The year I was ten my aunt found my eldest cousin locked in a passionate embrace with the barboy. Reckoning children to be more expendable than staff, she banished the lot of us to the cottage to be minded for the whole summer by Hannah, a distant cousin many times removed.

Hannah was big and bosomy and a great one for stories and cuddles. She was reputed to have the power of healing, but she was very secretive about it, and the various people that called for consultation.

One morning there was tufts of hair on Jenny's pillow. We all thought it funny, Jenny included, but when a golden clump came away from her head in her brother's hand, we sobered up. I was glad it was white teeth that were my best feature and that they were securely in place.

Hannah looked decidedly grave as she examined Jenny's head. Then she stood us in front of her and put us on our honour. She wheeled her bike around from the shed in the back, and pedalled off in the direction of the village to phone my aunt.

She arrived in double quick time with the family doctor. He examined Jenny's head, shook his own, looked hard at my aunt and asked Hannah where he could wash his hands. She directed him towards the back kitchen, and brought him a wedge of yellow soap and a white towel that had come from America.

We were banished outside and the door closed on our curiosity. Inside the adults held a whispered conference, we heard voices gradually being raised as Hannah began arguing with the doctor. The only words we could hear were 'hospital' and 'specialist' and that's because the doctor shouted them.

Then he marched out and sat in his car. My aunt wasn't long after him, but she was crying and Hannah kept telling her that it would be all right and to trust in her.

When they'd gone, Hannah went out again and returned with a parcel of bones. After boiling them for hours, she let the range go out and when the turf had cooled she made a paste of the ash and the marrow from the bones. She smeared it over Jenny's hair and then swathed her head in strips of old sheeting.

The treatment continued for several weeks and the smell grew worse with each passing hour. The day my aunt and the doctor were to return, Hannah washed Jenny's hair. No more had fallen out and a faint chicken-like down was growing on the bald patches. We all cheered and Hannah hugged Jenny. We were too young to appreciate Hannah's powers but we did know the doctor was impressed because he drank a lot of tea and asked a lot of questions to which Hannah gave him very short answers.

THE BOTTLE
Geraldine Mitchell

When my uncle was sent home from school with suspected tuberculosis, the hush that fell on the house was unbearable. Seventy years on his sister, my aunt, still remembers it as if it was last year. There was a brief commotion while he was bustled up the stairs and into what had been the visitors' bedroom, hastily prepared while the trap was harnessed and my grandfather dispatched to the station to collect him. And then silence settled like dust.

My grandmother, a cheerful, happy person, stopped singing as she went about her work. Her brother had died of tuberculosis when he was just eighteen and the frightening memories had flooded back. My grandfather, who was a Methodist minister and a bit of a dreamer, became strained and irritable. The piano lid was locked shut. The words 'tuberculosis' or 'consumption' were never spoken but they hung over the house for those who could read.

There were three girls in the family and the news that their brother was being sent home from school was so sudden and unexpected that no-one thought of explaining anything to them. They found themselves talking in whispers without knowing why, tiptoeing up and down the stairs. He didn't look ill, the odd glimpse of him that they got through the bedroom door. But they were warned not to go near him.

My uncle was the only boy, his parents' pride and joy, and the one who was getting the education. Hadn't his Uncle Harry sent the money for it back from Africa? He was a bright boy too, and was doing well at school. Only the month before the headmaster had written to say they were going to put him up for a scholarship to the university.

And suddenly it was as if the house itself was holding its breath.

So when the postman came knocking at the door one day with a parcel, the tension burst like a balloon. It almost felt like Christmas, my aunt remembers. The packet was from Aunt Jenny, it said so on the outside, but it was addressed to their mother and she was away in town for the day. So the three girls had the whole afternoon to imagine what could be inside. They cleared the kitchen table and placed the parcel right at the centre. Then they sat around it, stifling their giggles as they played their guessing game.

It was late when my grandmother came home, tired and laden down with messages. The girls made her a pot of tea and hung up her coat and hat. They loosened her boots and fetched her slippers. Then they sat again, in silence this time, waiting, watching her, willing her to open the parcel.

She didn't seem to share the children's excitement. Her sister-in-law Jenny had an irritating way of interfering, making her feel she wasn't quite up to the mark as a mother and housekeeper.

Oh-so-slowly she opened the packet. Untying the knots, saving the twine, folding up the brown paper, opening the box inside. In a nest of wood shavings lay a flat, corked, medicine bottle. She put her hand in and half lifted it from the brown curls. The glass was clear and inside was a bright pink substance. She started reading the label: 'For successful treatment of consumption…' All colour was wiped from her face in an instant and her jaw locked in anger as she rose from her chair, the pink bottle clasped in her white-knuckled grip.

My aunt remembers so vividly how she and her sisters watched with terror as their mother, their sweet, gentle mother wrenched the back door open and, in a scattering of chickens, hurled the bottle against the back wall of the yard. They all stared as the viscous pink liquid began to drip and slide from stone to stone.

'My boy has not got TB!' my grandmother said to no one in particular. And that's when the girls knew that their brother really was ill.

SWIMMING WITH A DOLPHIN
Patricia O'Reilly

A few evenings ago a television holiday programme showed a picture of a glamorous blonde, make-up immaculate, swimming with a group of dolphins. She was a stressed career woman. And this was her way of unwinding.

But, long before dolphins became fashionable and even before I even knew the meaning of the word stress, much less experienced it, I had a swim with a dolphin.

It was the year I was fourteen. On holidays in Kerry. Smitten with Mikey, the local heart-throb and sick of being labelled a Dublin jackeen. Without hesitation, I took Mikey up on his dare to 'borrow' my uncle's kayak. In return he'd introduce me to the neighbourhood dolphin. My butterfly fears at what would happen if my uncle found out were well worth Mikey's instant attention.

As he rowed out into the bay, the pink-streaked sunset turned to gold. When he stopped, the kayak seemed to rest in a pool of cold flame. I put down my hand and stroked the sea's calm surface. I wasn't sure why. Perhaps for luck? Or maybe to call up the dolphin?

After a few moments of silence, a dorsal fin, curved like a gondola, broke the smooth water. In the early twilight, the dolphin arched upwards, its body burnished bronze. We watched in wonder as it romped near the boat. Bending, curving, emitting sounds of pleasure.

Mikey yanked off his shirt, kicked off his shoes, started undoing his fly. Omigod. I averted my eyes as he slithered out of his tight, black drainpipes. His togs were blue. Like my uncle's.

With a fierce rocking movement, he disappeared over the side of the kayak to be immediately joined by the dolphin.

'Come on,' he said.

I hesitated. But only for a moment. Kicking off my sandals, I jumped in as I was, my skirt umbrella-ing around me.

With a great whoosh, the dolphin was in front of me. Seeming to tread water. So close that I could have reached out and touched his snout. And his eyes were soft and gentle, his mouth curved in a smile.

He was full of playful cavortings, leaping balletically, trumpeting joy.

'This one sure likes the women,' said Mikey, looking at me with new respect.

The dolphin kneaded water in front of me, watching me through his button eyes, his mouth now wide open in a laugh. He'd little pearly teeth, just like a baby's, and I laughed back at him.

Switching mood, he gave off a series of squeaks and high pitched sounds.

'He's talking to you,' said Mikey, swimming beside me, his limbs long and pale in the water. 'Answer him.'

I talked back with incomprehensible soundings that came from I knew not where. But at the time, they made sense.

Then the magic was over. The dolphin hooted, leapt once more into the air, dove into the sea and was gone. With his passing, I was bereft. The journey back was shiveringly miserable. But nothing compared to the reception I got from my uncle. Yet swimming with the dolphin was an experience I wouldn't have missed for the world.

GUESTS OF THE KINGDOM
David Sowby

In 1948 my father, then Warden of St. Columba's College, Rathfarnham, took a distinguished visitor, the Bishop of Chicago, to call upon President Seán T. O'Kelly. After welcoming the Bishop, and hearing that he was on his way to the Lambeth Conference in England, the President smiled. He said he'd found the English very nice people, once you got to know them, and then he spoke of his own visit to England in 1917. He related how, after he'd been arrested in Ireland, along with nineteen other leading nationalists, they were told that they'd be sent to England. This was because of the number of escapes there'd been from Irish prisons. Within reason, they'd be allowed to choose the city of their imprisonment. So they consulted among themselves and asked for Oxford, where they'd have friends to visit them and a good selection of books to read.

They were put on parole, and allowed to travel on the train as free men, accompanied only by a young British Army captain. They reached Oxford after dark and went to a hotel. The next morning they set off for the gaol, where they were received warmly by the governor who said, 'We can't accommodate political prisoners here; you'd better try the military gaol – they have far better quarters and could make you much more comfortable.'

So they went along to the military gaol, where the officer in charge said that the prison was completely full, and in any case that it wasn't the place for them. He took the captain aside and advised him to call Sir Somebody Something at the Home Office and ask for his advice.

The official who answered the telephone said, 'I say, I'm terribly sorry, but Sir Somebody has just left for holiday in Switzerland.'

He suggested that they'd better stay in lodgings in Oxford until Sir Somebody returned in ten days time.

By this time the prisoners were on the best of terms with the captain, who gave them permission to call on friends in Oxford. They dined in college halls and explored the town. After ten days, the captain called the Home Office, only to find that Sir Somebody had broken his leg. The captain was advised to keep the prisoners in the lodgings until Sir Somebody returned.

A few days later, some of the Irish Nationalist Members of Parliament came to Oxford and told the prisoners there was to be a debate on Ireland in the House of Commons the following week.

'You must come to London; we'll get you in without anyone knowing who you are.' The captain gave them permission to go. The debate was a lively one; several Irish members misbehaved and were suspended or expelled from the House. Finally the Home Secretary rose and made a long speech defending Britain's role in Ireland. In his speech he announced that the House would be glad to know that twenty of the worst Irish terrorists had been arrested the previous month and were now safely under lock and key in England. He read out their names – but the twenty Irishmen in the gallery didn't answer 'Anseo'.

THE ART OF CHOOSING
Susan Zelouf

As I waited for eleven-year-old Rachael to fill a cellophane bag with a poundsworth of sweets at a pick-n-mix kiosk in a Galway shopping centre, I remembered how I learned about wealth, and the art of choosing. At first Rachael browsed, studying the nametags on each plexiglass cube: toasted teacakes, Spanish lemons, chocolate bananas, white mice, foam shrimp, baby dolphins, giant spiders, sugar-free worms, milk teeth, bloody fingers, golf balls, aniseed balls, giant yellow gobstoppers, monster jawbreakers, pink and whites, sugared almonds, mint humbugs, fizzy dummies, liquorice torpedoes, chocolate peppermint creams… it was a dazzling display, the Tiffany's of retail candy.

Maybe it was the glitter of sugar crystals on the fruit slices that brought me back to the *pasticceria* in Rome, or the air thick with disaccharides, the sweet powder clinging to my nostrils and coating my tongue – a double whammy. It was December, 1986, my first date with a rich Italian businessman. He was taking me to lunch *in famiglia*, a colleague's family, not his own – that would come much later, after I was deemed marriage material. I thought it would be a nice gesture to bring the dessert, and asked him to stop at a bakery. He approved of my thoughtfulness, if not my shoes. That morning I'd agonized over what pair to choose. Footwear is crucial in that boot-shaped Mediterranean peninsula. In my time in Manhattan, I've been looked up and down by construction workers… in Rome, they look you down and up.

I looked over the baked goods: meringue, *marrons glacé, pasticini misti, biscotti, torte di frutte, tiramisu, confezioni di gelati, cioccolatini* … I was particularly taken by a towering cake called *montebianco*, after Mont Blanc – a mound of cream puffs topped with tangled strands of chestnut-paste and an avalanche of whipped cream. Not exactly cheap, even with the favourable exchange rate, but I knew what I wanted. I pointed at it, and took out my wallet.

Giancarlo waggled his finger at me, clicked his tongue and shook his head in the way all Italians do to express shock horror or gentle disapproval. He took out a wad of *lire*, as thick as a *cannoli*, and paid for the cake. I didn't know whether to be insulted or honored.

Giancarlo presented me with the beautifully packaged sweet as if it was the Palio I'd just won, the blue ribbon.

'E facile comprare,' he said, looking into my eyes. *'E un' arte scegliare.'*

'Paying's easy. The art is in the choosing.'

A Sense of Place

FROM MY BEDROOM WINDOW
Mick Doyle

'What I see from my bedroom window.'

So went the title of the composition our first year English teacher announced to the class moments before the bell rang out and released us into the blissful freedom of the weekend.

'Describe in detail,' he told us, 'everything you see when you look out your bedroom window. I'll read the best four and the winner will be given a prize.'

The compositions were to be written over the weekend and turned in to him on Monday. The weekend flew by, like they all did in those days, and Monday afternoon found us watching as the teacher stood up to read, his hands clasping either side of his high desk, the four copies he'd chosen stacked one atop the other in front of him. With a smile on his face he told us he intended to read them in ascending order, like they do on Top of the Pops, he said.

Everybody but the three runners-up and the winner had had their copies handed back earlier. Mine was safely tucked away in my school bag. The room was hot. The smell of chalk dust hung on the air. The class gave the teacher the benefit of its tired attention.

I was sitting next to Martin McCreash, and what caught my interest was that Martin actually seemed to be listening. It was then that I realised his copy had not been returned. We all knew that Martin was more than capable of writing, or of doing anything else he set his mind to, but he didn't seem to care about school at all. His was what would now be termed a 'dysfunctional' family and he came from one of the toughest estates in the town. But on that lazy September afternoon, he was all ears.

The teacher opened the first copy. He began each composition by reading out the title and the author's name. They were pretty much what you'd expect from thirteen-year-olds, full of green fields and songbirds and trees, but were mercifully not more than two or three pages long. Whenever he finished a composition its author would collect the work to a half-hearted round of applause.

One after the other the teacher went through them and still Martin's copy hadn't been returned. I was all ears by this time myself.

As the teacher neared the bottom of the stack Martin seemed to become more and more uncomfortable. He'd gone a little red in the face and he shifted around on the seat of the bench we both shared.

When the teacher opened the last copy Martin stiffened visibly, and I could have sworn I heard him mutter, 'At least I wrote the truth.'

'What I see from my bedroom window, By Martin McCreash.'

The whole class fell still.

The teacher paused before reading on, 'I see houses, all just like mine'.

THE CORTINA
Michael Harding

When I lived in Glangevlin, I had a green Cortina Mark 2. It cost me three hundred and ten pounds in 1974. The lights were put on by connecting two wires underneath the steering wheel. The steering wheel wobbled when the car went faster than a bicycle. But there was a tape deck. An invaluable item in any car of the time in West Cavan. Tapes by Philomena Begley and Ray Lynam could be purchased in Mullan Mart, an outdoor Sunday morning event on the border between Cavan and Fermanagh.

The windows of my Cortina didn't wind down. The doors rattled. The exhaust pipe had holes in it that made the machine sound like a Kalashnikov AK 47, and caused British Soldiers at the checkpoints near Swanlinbar no end of anxiety. But if you put four girls in the back seat, and three more in the front passenger seat, and put the Philomena Begley tape up to maximum volume, then the Cortina became a dream machine. Heavier on the road, it glided along, freewheeled down the hills silently. Not a rattle could be heard above the steel guitar of Daniel O'Hara.

Glangevlin at the time was like an extended family. People belonged to each other. The girls took a lift from me on weekend nights to the Mayflower Ballroom in Drumshanbo, or the Ballroom of Romance in Glenfarne. At the end of the night they all gathered with their men along the long bench by the wall of the tearoom, drinking mugs of tea.

Men... pronounced 'min'.

Min were often lads in platform shoes with tractors in the car park. Sometimes you might see a smiling guard in his off-duty jumper, moving around like a pike among the perch. Some min were troublesome. I knew a girl who always took a knitting needle with her in her handbag, and dealt with any idle hands on the dance hall floor with a firm poke of her pointed weapon into the offender's belly.

More often than not the girls chatted in the tearoom and shared cigarette butts for an hour and then came looking for my Cortina. On the way home they would laugh their heads off discussing the merits and otherwise of their dance partners. Sometimes we returned to one of their houses.

There was more tea. The record player went on. They danced quicksteps round the kitchen to Hank Williams and other American Country artists until four or five, and always put a few sods of turf in the range before retiring, so that the fire would be 'in' and the kitchen warm for their parents in the morning.

But life moves on. I left. They all left. I once drove a carload to the airport. Their mother skited holy water on the bonnet of the Cortina and ran straight back into the house. She had her door closed as the car moved off.

I sometimes think of that kitchen. And the old parents that remained. The range unlit. The porridge cold. The terrible silence of the long winters.

And recently I drove past an old car cemetery behind a filling station and I stopped to stare at an upturned green Cortina Mark 2 that lay on its side by the ditch. I got out and walked around it. No glass in the windows. No wheels at all. And even the back seat was gone. But, as I said to the boy on the petrol pumps, other than that, she's in good nick.

He filled my Nissan with Unleaded and stared at me as if I wasn't right in the head.

A DREAM OF MANDARIN DUCK
Norrie Egan

I wasn't expecting a lot from our visit to Wuhan – capital of the Hubei Province in China. We had arrived there late the previous evening after a cruise on the Yangtze that took us through some of the most awe-inspiring scenery in the world. We had negotiated the rapids in the beautiful Three Small Gorges, and at Yichang had visited the construction site of the controversial dam which will displace over a million people and destroy this premier scenic area. After all that Wuhan seemed very small beer. Surely a chance for a much needed snooze on the bus.

I had reckoned without our new guide Wei! She was tiny and frail with greying hair, but her voice compelled our attention. In perfect English she welcomed us to her city, one of the most beautiful in China and Mao Tse Tung's favourite. It was en fête for the Fiftieth Anniversary of the Founding of the Republic and the streets were decorated with flowers and lanterns and lights.

The museum she was bringing us to was new – specially built to house the treasures recovered from the tomb of the Marquis Lui, who had ruled the area over two thousand years before. The most significant find was a set of chimes, sixty-six in all, ranging from enormous bass bells to small treble ones. Each bell, when struck with a hammer, produces two notes, a tone apart, depending on whether it is struck in the centre or at the side. The chimes, now restored to their original magnificence and re-hung as they once had been on a three-tiered wooden frame, are on display in a huge glass room that forms the centre of the museum. I was fascinated. My snooze would have to wait.

In the museum Wei showed us a mock-up of the tomb. It consisted of four chambers. In one were chariots, weapons and armour. In another enormous amphorae and food containers, cooking utensils and a primitive barbecue! In the third were the chimes and other musical instruments. And in the fourth and largest, the remains of the Marquis himself in a gigantic double sarcophagus. This was displayed nearby, the colours on the outer casket still amazingly fresh.

In this chamber were also found twenty-three small coffins. Each contained the body of a young girl. All had been poisoned. Wei paused and her voice became dreamlike.

'Who were these maidens?' she wondered. 'Concubines? Servants? Or were they musicians needed in the after life to make the chimes sing again?'

In one coffin a mandarin duck was found.

'These are very special in China,' Wei continued. 'They mate for life and so replicas are traditionally given to young girls on marriage as a good luck charm. Who was this girl's husband? Had he placed the duck beside her in death, or had she died alone in agony clutching it for comfort?'

I was hanging on every word.

Wei sighed. 'I like to dream,' she said softly.

Later in the basement theatre, eight musicians in period costume gave a recital on a replica set of bells and other instruments like stone chimes, zithers, mouth organs and two-stringed fiddles.

In the shop on the way out I bought a wooden hand-painted mandarin duck. It will always remind me of Wei, who turned just another visit to another museum into an unforgettable experience. At the appropriate time I will give it to my daughter, and hope that its magic will work for her – even if it failed that little Chinese girl two thousand years ago.

YANK
Ivy Bannister

I first arrived in Ireland on a bright October morning in 1970. As I stepped off the airplane, an unusual language fast and furiously assaulted my ears. It was a language at once familiar, yet bizarre. It sounded like English, only not proper English – by which I meant, of course, American English. Instead, it seemed to be some extraordinary tongue of its own, full of strange expressions, weird pronunciations and new words.

And the most salient of those new words to assault my ears was 'Yank'.

'Oh, you're a Yank,' everyone said, the minute I opened my mouth and sometimes before.

The word 'Yank' required no explanation, not like 'Holy hour', 'flahoolock' or 'How's me oul' segotia.' I understood at once that Yank meant me, and I didn't much like it.

There seemed to me to be some nastiness hidden inside Yank, an undertone that was vaguely pejorative. Yank was, after all, a four-letter word, and it simply didn't sound very nice. Yank was full of mixed messages. When applied to me, I could hear both admiration and grudge; admiration, at the glamour and city-lights of me (I was, after all, from New York City), but grudge for the very same reason. Just so, I could hear fascination – and revulsion – for my presumed wealth and New World sophistication (both of which were not, in fact, represented as well in my nineteen-year-old self as I would have liked them to be).

But most of all, I disliked the word 'Yank' because it highlighted my difference, and after a few weeks wandering the enchanted streets of Dublin, I wanted nothing more than to be taken for a true-born Irishwoman. And so – for a while – I struggled womanfully to develop some sort of an Irish accent, cantering in one breath from Finglas to Counties Cork and Cavan. Meeting someone new, I would babble cheerfully in this colourful mode, until inevitably my new friend would look at me pityingly and inquire, 'And what part of America are you from, then?'

I was too innocent to realise that it wasn't only the way I sounded that made me stick out like a sore thumb. It was the way I looked. Almost every detail of my appearance proclaimed my Yankdom to an Irish audience that – thirty years ago – was remarkably homogenous. My colouring was too sallow to be Irish. My teeth gleamed too whitely from the attentions of an American orthodontist. And my clothes – from my shoes, plaid skirt and red tights, to my jaunty beret – all advertised my origins as unmistakably as if I'd been waving the Stars and Stripes.

Oddly enough, looking back, it is the times that now seem innocent. For if the girl I was suddenly reappeared on the streets of Dublin, nobody would look at her twice. The days have long passed since the presence of a solitary American caused comment. Now the streets have become a sea of heterogeneous faces, speaking languages that would make De Valera revolve in his grave, wearing labels you'd see in New York, or anywhere else for that matter. And the word Yank has been shouldered out by infinitely more ominous terms of racial abuse, unequivocal words, unsweetened by any mix in the message they convey.

A MORNING WITH AN ORACLE IN LADAKH
Marguerite MacCurtin

In the Himalayan Kingdom of Ladakh, the April full moon cast an icy glow over the ancient town of Leh. Its buildings, glazed with frost and icicles, shimmered in the shadows of surrounding glaciers.

In the dining room of a local hotel, I joined a diverse collection of people gathered around large pots of bubbling hot food arranged along a rectangular table. The atmosphere was warm and chatty until a bearded man, who had been speaking in hushed tones, leapt suddenly from his chair and proceeded to dance wildly around the centre of the room. He touched his chin with his knees in the course of a frenetic limb-throwing performance. A fellow traveller informed me that he had been miraculously cured by an oracle who was said to be possessed by the spirit of a god. Three weeks ago, according to my friend, the dancing man could not even walk.

Next morning I entered the crowded, smoke-filled kitchen of the oracle's house in the village of Saboo. A tiny woman with deeply lined skin and dark hair was raised on a stack of cushions in the corner of the kitchen. She was dressed in a red and turquoise silk cape lined with shocking pink and embroidered with Chinese cloud motifs. On her head she wore a narrow brimmed top hat which was strewn with layers of white gauze prayer scarves. Her mouth was covered with a red triangular piece of cloth.

She clutched a bell and shook it violently and then she began to chant feverishly as she went into the rituals of her trance. Her face became contorted, her eyeballs flicked up, her body writhed and shivered, her voice shrieked.

She screamed for pilgrims. The crowd pushed a reluctant woman forward. She staggered half upright from her kneeling position to place an offering of a white gauze prayer scarf on the oracle's hat. Then she fell to her knees to outline the details of her problem. The oracle emitted some high-pitched rasping and hissing sounds, removed her mask and buried her face in the exposed flesh of the woman's abdomen. She raised her face and spat a black looking bile that she had apparently sucked from the women's stomach without wounding her, into a bowl of hot ashes which was placed beside her. Pilgrim followed pilgrim. The oracle's responses grew more frantic. Her healing methods varied only to include the use of a bamboo tube for releasing the black bile of evil from pilgrims' necks, tongues, cheeks and abdomens. A mother with a very sick baby knelt before her. The oracle's daughter handed her a knife which had been reddened in the fire. She placed the burning blade on her own tongue until it sizzled. Then she gently blew over the head and body of the baby. Finally she prayed over some barley and handed it to those nearest to her. She also blessed the people who knelt before her by touching them on the shoulders, head and back with the dagger and *dorje* or thunderbolt symbol which are the sacred ritual instruments of Buddhism. She came out her trance as noisily as she had entered it and slumped in an exhausted frail-looking bundle amongst the cushions.

The pilgrims filed from the room. I sat in silence with some local women on the smooth mud floor. The oracle's daughter seized a bellows and fanned the yak dung fire in the great black stove. She offered large mugs of hot sweet tea to everyone in the room. We watched as the oracle folded her ceremonial clothes and placed them neatly in a box. She then turned towards us and dissolved the tension which had gripped the gathering with a wide smile.

She spoke to me through a Ladakhi friend who acted as an interpreter. We chatted about the hazards of mountain travel and I told her about the injuries that I had sustained in a recent car accident on a treacherous road nearby. Before I left she handed me some barley and a chain of coloured threads to protect me on dangerous trails and to keep bad luck at bay. In a land where paralysed men get up and dance, the westerner soon learns to adopt the native's ways.

WORLDS AWAY
Matthew Byrne

It was a sultry day in Greystones. August 6, 1945. Woolly clouds ambled across a summer sky. Even the sea was lazy, no more than shingle-whispering on the long beach. Up at the house a group of people, on a well-mown lawn, idled at a game of croquet.

It was a lazy day. And yet, for all its dreamy listlessness, there was an uneasy feeling to the day. As though there were something hidden in the quietness.

The newspapers in the next week gave substance to the shadowy feelings.

They had dropped the bomb on Hiroshima.

In the next few weeks, John Hersey's report... column after column in the Irish Times... put names and human faces on the brutality.

But, for all the reading, Hiroshima was still no more than a name I filled in for myself on my school atlas. An island of sorrow that was worlds away. A lament whose throbs soon lost their melancholy in the bedlam of a teenager's summer.

The summer passed.

And the years.

Now it was 1954. I was an Army Chaplain on leave from Korea.

And I was in Hiroshima. Standing at the spot just above which the bomb had burst on that fateful day a few years earlier.

Noise and city sounds drifted towards me. Out beyond, the darkening river. And the bridge, thronged with bustling people putting shape on their day.

But here, where I stood, was desolation. Devastation, tidied after the shadow of the mushroom-cloud had gone.

A shanty-town landmark on the road of history.

In the huddle of sacks, stretched tins and bits of wood, I found the building that stored the artist's impressions of the inhuman night.

Burnt yellows, blacks and gory reds painted scenes that seared your eyes. Faces screamed. Great buildings buckled. Bodies, bleeding, burning, raw on their desolated homesteads. Women and children, men mangled in the debris. Or running frantic through the streets where raging fires burnt out a pathway for them.

Outside this gallery of torment, the stalls where they sold the weird paraphernalia salvaged after the explosion. In aid of 'Atomic Bomb Casualties'. A roof-tile charred by the bomb flash. A bottle melted by the heat and re-formed into a cruel shape. A piece of soap turned to stone as an old man washed his hands at the time the bomb burst.

Dominating this dereliction was the Peace Building. In its former glory it was the Industrial Promotion hall. But now... jagged against the sky, twisted, raw, a ruin browsing in tatters enclosed by a wire fence.

Along the road, a little lad squatted at his mother's feet. His intent face followed every movement of his hand across the drawing-block resting on his knees. Every now and then he'd look up, scanning the scene before him. And then he'd dig his pencil, carving, as it were, into the paper the cruel outlines of the Peace Building.

From where he sat he could clearly see the great, modern plinth set up outside the fence. But he couldn't read the message it bore in Japanese and English.

In fact, it said 'Once a stately building serving as the nerve centre for the development of industries in Hiroshima Prefecture, it was turned into ruins by the first atomic bomb that exploded 570 meters above it on August 6, 1945. Of the thousands of buildings that met the same fate, this alone, marking the centre of the explosion, is now being preserved to symbolise our wish that there be no more Hiroshimas'.

Above the panels, in concrete letters, the word PEACE.

TORTOISE TEARS
Madeleine Going

I looked into the eyes of the tortoise – shiny, opaque eyes, like chocolate drops, then at his wrinkled face, receding chin and scaly neck. Tears began to roll down his leathery cheeks.

Sympathy? Crocodile tears? Tortoise tears, perhaps – but that was fantasy, for they flowed down well-worn channels. Secretions from ancient and almost certainly dim eyes. We had been told that he was well over two hundred years old.

And no ordinary tortoise. Upright on short, sturdy legs, he reached my waist. About as broad as he was long, he was one of the several dozen that roamed the tiny island, off Zanzibar. The contrast between his vast bulk and his gentle expression was very moving.

We were spending a week on Zanzibar. Warm, spicy scents – clove, nutmeg, vanilla – intoxicated us. In the small harbour, *dhows* (Arab sailing ships from the Persian gulf) dipped and swayed at their moorings like ballet dancers practising at the barre.

'You must visit Tortoise Island,' friends had said.

I hesitated. I remembered once, driving around Kenya's Tsavo National Park, coming upon a tortoise asleep in the middle of the track. I jumped out and picked him up. He rewarded me with a copious stream of urine splashing over my legs and into my shoes. I was so startled, I just stood there, making no effort to avoid the cascade. But these Zanzibari tortoises were giants – quite different from their Kenyan cousins.

The visit to Tortoise Island sounded fun, so we made up a small party and hired a boat. After about two hours at sea, we were deposited just before noon in a narrow rocky cove. We told the boatman, in stumbling Swahili, to return at six o'clock – *saa sita*, the sixth hour, we said firmly.

It was a day of a lifetime. Spice-laden breezes fanned palms and baobabs fringing the coral strand. The sea ebbed and flowed, rattling the shells on the beach. The water was crystal clear and sun-warmed. After a long swim, we found the deep shade of a mango tree, picnicked and snoozed.

As the sun set in a blaze of red, gold and turquoise, we walked around the island – catching glimpses of these amiable creatures who went about their business with such stately dignity. It was hard to believe that some of them were born when America was just getting her independence.

Darkness swept over the sky and night fell. We scanned the crumpled sea again and again, but no boat arrived. We were benighted. Nevertheless we were soon settled around a makeshift campfire, with a few boiled sweets and a battered banana. We tried to open a couple of coconuts but they defeated us. We were pretty incompetent Robinson Crusoes.

But it was wonderful. Attracted by the fire, the tortoises gathered, settling motionless, just beyond the ring of firelight, watching and waiting, the flames burnishing their enormous shells or glinting in their tiny eyes.

Towards midnight rescue arrived. We'd been missed and an ancient motor boat had been sent to pick us up. Later we were told what had happened. In East Africa, the first hour – *saa moja* – is daybreak (our 6 am). The last hour, the twelfth, is nightfall (our 6 pm). By this reckoning *saa sita* – the sixth hour – is midday for the boatman, that would have been the following day. But – no regrets – it had been an unforgettable experience.

Before the boat left, I ran back to the fire to thank the tortoises for letting us get to know them a little. Several were weeping and I promised that I'd go back. But I never did.

MARRAKECH
Mary O'Donnell

In 1939, George Orwell wrote an essay on Marrakech, a place in which his attempts to feed bread to a gazelle were intercepted by a hungry navvy, where anti-semitism was rife, women like beasts of burden, and children numerous as flies. Some years later, Elias Canetti's lyrical and haunting work *Voices of Marrakech* also responded to the complex mélange of life in central Morocco.

The fact is, it's simply impossible to see Marrakech and remain untouched, because even a short stay assaults the senses with a battery of impressions as thrilling as they are sometimes unsettling.

Last year, I finally succumbed to the dark magic of 'the pink city', as it is known. We followed the tourist trail with a small bus load of Germans, over the High Atlas mountains, our guide Habib regaling his captive audience with preparatory details of the intricate relationship that exists between Berber and Arab populations throughout Morocco. We were warned not to deviate from the walking tour he was to bring us on in Marrakech, but to follow him at all times. Because this is a holy Moslem city, Habib had to change on arrival into the long white garment which all men are obliged to wear within its walls.

A few hours later, the labyrinthine markets, or *souks*, unfolded at an almost too brisk pace. We walked by metalworks, local artisans and craftsmen, wood-turners making bowls, beds, cupboards, spindles, good luck charms; the dye *souk* was a spectral hell of steaming cauldrons, with vibrant dyes in flame orange, iridescent green, reds, blacks and yellows.

The cacophony of Place El Djemaa Fna rises over the city, even before you reach this open-air emporium of human drama and squalor. This is the huge square in the old part of town without which, according to the writer Paul Bowles, Marrakech would be just another Moroccan city. The snake charmers who rightly cover the reptiles with a drum if the tourists attempt to photograph them without paying a few *dirims*, beckoned to us to 'come over, come over'. Which we did. For the second time in my life I had to hold a snake for the sake of photographic bravado. There was misery and magnitude about this place; people of unbelievable raggedness and destitution: here, fire eaters, there, tooth pullers, with the pulled teeth on display, further on, hermaphrodite water vendors dressed in red and gold fringed costumes, their brass bowls clanging like bells.

The next morning, we were led through the rambling nineteenth century Palais de la Bahia, residence of the Grand Vizier of Sultan Moulay al-Hussan I, where today the Imam's chamber is open to public view. An adjacent chamber was retained for the preparation of concubines. In the walls were doors, and behind them delicate oils, scents and cosmetics were once recessed. A glance at the ornate walls, the high, painted cedarwood ceilings, confirms the sensitive aesthetics of the era. That chamber led to a shaded courtyard in which twenty-four concubines could sit and chat. I still have a photograph of my straw-hatted daughter in that deserted courtyard, by the empty fountain, encircled by the turquoise-topped verandah, with scalloped lattice-work and white pillars.

Back on the narrow streets, women hawked various items, from jewellery to henna, and they were formidable, dark-eyed and fierce. We, the tourists, were the fools, and we knew it. In Marrakech, there is filth, child labour, and many things startling enough to cause the average European nostril to quiver slightly. It is a challenge to every correct notion in existence, and that's what I enjoyed.

That, and the kaleidoscopic patterns of beauty, those cinnamon-drop walls, the cramped Jewish quarter, and perhaps most of all, the spacious sheltered square where the Imam's women could chat at evening, above them, the wheeling swifts of the Moroccan sky.

HEADHUNTING IN FERMANAGH
Nuala Hayes

County Fermanagh is famous for heads… ancient carved stone heads. We were on tour in Enniskillen, the town that tells the story of the conflicts of our history. It was early summer, a beautiful and peaceful time to be there. The air of grim despondency that had struck me other times I'd been to this town had lifted. We were playing in *Dancing at Lughnasa* at the Ardhowen Theatre, the theatre with the best views in Ireland, overlooking the lake.

I thought it appropriate that the five Mundy sisters (the characters in the play) should go headhunting for the day, since one of the themes of the play is that fine line between ancient pagan rituals and Irish life. I was finding it difficult I suppose, to separate from my schoolteacher role as Kate, the eldest sister, and the bossiest.

I only managed to organise three sisters and we set off from our digs at the Railway Hotel to find White Island, our first stop on Lough Erne. We were delivered by boat to a small pier on a deserted island, with a promise of a lift back in half an hour's time. 'That should be long enough for ye,' the boatman told us.

You couldn't miss the carved figures, six stone statues and a head, set in concrete in the wall of a small ruined church facing the pier. Surrounded now by grass and chomping cows, the figures had been found on different parts of the monastic island and were lined up as if for inspection. Christ was represented in four different guises, with a face far removed from the familiar suffering one. Here he looked more like a benign contented monk, a man that would enjoy the pleasures of bee-keeping and mead drinking. David was there with his hand to his mouth, a reference to the divine Word perhaps, and a grotesque female figure with bulging cheeks and crossed legs. Her wide lascivious grin suggests that her function might have served as a warning to the monks of the sins of the flesh.

Interesting and masterful carving but not pagan enough for us, so we abandoned the cold stone statues for the bluebells and primroses that grew beneath the trees on the shore of the lake. Then on to the boat and to Boa Island to find the Janus head, a remnant of a past we can only imagine. Boa, though an island, can be reached by a causeway. We turned off the road at the sign for Caldragh graveyard, walked past a slurry pit and the farmyard, opened the gate, and in an old cemetery, surrounded by ferns and a backdrop of blossomy sloe bushes, there it stood.

Nothing, no number of John Hinde postcards of the image, or brochures from the Northern Ireland tourist board can prepare you for the shock of seeing this ancient twin-headed God in the flesh, or in the stone, I should say. In pagan belief, the head of a god was thought to contain its divinity. The impression was of strength and an energy that drew us in to wonder at the power contained in the stone.

The colour is brownish, not grey as I'd imagined, and the two faces are back to back, almost a mirror image of each other. Triangular shaped, with large staring eyes, upwardly curling moustache, and in one of the open mouths, just a hint of a tongue. Though the head dominates, there are arms or crossed legs, like a Buddha figure, and a phallus, clearly etched, in case there was any doubt about its masculinity.

Seamus Heaney, in the poem 'January God', has described it as:

'God-eyed, sex-mouthed, its brain
A watery wound.'

The day we were there, its brain, that is the hollow between the two faces, was a trough of silver coins. Punts, pounds, Deutschmarks and US cents had been tossed into the space by visitors, echoing the response the world over, when people are touched by a moment or a mystery, to leave something behind. Is it superstition? Wish fulfilment? An offering? Here the mystery is the presence of a pagan form in a Christian graveyard. It fits this spot better than any museum, and long may it stand, tucked away on this island in Fermanagh.

THE FIRST DAY OF SPRING
Judith Hoad

More of the tiny, sweet-scented, waxy-ivory flowers of the date palms were bursting from their pods each day and drooping among the fronded leaves. The oasis orchards and the gardens of this Tunisian town were busy with men who climbed each female tree with the flowers from the male tree to fertilise them. Pink peach flowers, snowy apricot blossoms, pearly lemon blooms all brightened and perfumed the shadowy places beneath the palms. Spring had come to the desert.

I met my neighbour, Tebia, every day when I took our foodscraps for her goat.

'Come with us tomorrow,' she said one day, 'we're going to the desert for a picnic, it's the first day of spring.'

March 1st. Another day of clear blue skies and gentle breezes. We met at Tebia's house. All our women neighbours were there – and all their children. We shared the bags between us, Tebia checking the contents to make sure we had all we needed. At the pace of the smallest child, we ambled out of Tebebsa, our district, onto the main road. Drivers passing hooted and waved. There was another group ahead of us. We walked little more than a mile, but it took us almost an hour. The place we'd reached was not so much the desert as a large clearing of sandy ground in the oasis palmery. As the women's black robes slipped or were discarded, revealing coloured skirts or tracksuits, we looked like a cloud of migratory butterflies. We settled under an overgrown palm whose neglected side shoots provided lots of shade. Tebia and Moona selected a place for the fire. We found stones to surround it and to support the teapot. The charcoal was unpacked. Zohra had a lighter. The children scattered, playing and exploring in all directions.

We learned that every year it was the turn of a different woman to bring the meat. This duty brought the reward of a wish. It was Tebia's turn this year and as she unpacked it, she held it up and closed her eyes.

'May I see my eldest son in his military uniform, tall and strong,' she murmured, tears sneaking out from under her lids.

As we nibbled dates and bread, the coals of the fire grew hotter until they were deemed to be hot enough to cook the meat. Greasy membrane and unidentifiable gobbets of organs from a goat killed that morning were draped over the charcoal creating pungent smoke. This was no ordinary picnic. Something ancient was happening. These women were responding to a seasonal habit far older than the customs of Islam that circumscribed their daily lives for the rest of the year. Moona took the first pieces of cooked meat from the fire and began a slow dance, counter-sunwise around the seated group of women. At every third or fourth step she tossed a scrap of meat away into the sandy distance.

'For the spirits of the Spring,' she said as she passed me. We ate the tasty pieces of meat, then, from tiny glasses we drank mint tea with pine-nuts in it – more was brewing in the embers of the fire. This time we sipped it with halva in it – then minute cups of strong, sweet black coffee, glasses of fizzy orange and Coca-Cola. Last of all a sprinkle of incense in the ashes of the fire. The sun was lower now and sending fingers of light into our shade to touch the tendrils of fragrant smoke. The incense all consumed, the fire was quenched and the place where it had burned was brushed clean with palm fronds.

Homeward bound – if anything we were slower than the outward journey.

Babies found pickabacks, heavy baskets were shared. The sun was almost touching the horizon as we entered our street. An old lady hobbled up to Tebia and muttered something to her. Tebia broke into a trot, dropping the bag she was carrying. We could hear the joyful ululations of the women before we got to the gate of the courtyard. We saw her release her tall, handsome, eldest son, in his military uniform from her long embrace and, with tears streaming down her smiling face, she opened her arms and told us, 'He's here for the whole weekend!'

CUBA: TRANSPORTS OF DELIGHT
John Horgan

The recent visit by the Pope to Cuba introduced the inhabitants of that famous Caribbean island to that most extraordinary vehicle, the Popemobile. A cross between a Range Rover and a gigantic travelling showcase out of Madame Tussaud's waxworks, it enables the Pope to see and be seen on his many pilgrimages. Those who accompanied John Paul II on this visit, however, will have marvelled at the many other forms of wheeled transport which the Cuban people have preserved, maintained, and developed in the four decades or so since the American blockade began.

When Cuba and the United States fell out all those years ago, one of the most noticeable results of the blockade was the total absence of modern cars. It meant that the cars on the island at the time are, in many respects, the cars they still have today. The hot dry Caribbean air has helped to preserve them: but their owners have also had to develop a whole range of skills, of ingenuity, of making-do, that puts our comfortable world to shame. Here, when something goes wrong with the car, we take it to the garage to be fixed. In Cuba, you melt down scrap metal in your oven at home to forge a bit to replace the bit that broke. The roads in Cuba – when they have any traffic at all – feature antique Dodges, Cadillacs, and Oldsmobiles so old that they are hardly mobile any longer.

It was in one of these – a 1946 Dodge, if I remember correctly – that I found myself, one afternoon in 1969, being driven up to the palace of the Bishop of Santiago, at the eastern end of the island. The bishop was, by all accounts, a most unusual member of the hierarchy. It was early days in the Cuban revolution; most Cuban bishops were at best deeply suspicious of their new regime, and many actively hostile to it. This man was an exception: every summer, when all the able-bodied citizens in his diocese were dragooned by the government into the cane fields for the sugar harvest, he would join them, stripped to the waist, sharing their privations and their fatigue in every respect.

He was plainly someone worth talking to, even in fractured French which was the only language we shared.

Earlier that day, my guides – somewhat bored bureaucrats of the revolution – had taken me to see a school in the city. As I entered each classroom of eleven- and twelve-year-olds, the children stood up smartly and chanted an enthusiastic verse about their socialist commitment and about their readiness to die on the battle field, like Che. Curious about this, during the interview I asked the bishop if he was worried about Communist indoctrination in the schools.

'Not at all,' he replied.

Reasoning that it was probably quite some time since he or other members of the clergy had been allowed inside the doors of any school, I described the scene I had encountered in some detail, and repeated my question. The answer was the same. But why, I asked, was he not concerned?

'I think,' he said slowly, after a pause, 'I think... that they are making the same mistake that we made.'

A PLACE FOR EVERYTHING
Maureen Keane

My mother was a good cook and an excellent housekeeper, and one of those stay-at-home wives at a time when a woman working outside the house was frowned upon. My mother always insisted that she had learned her skills from a book she had studied at school. This was *How Mary Fitzgerald Learned Housekeeping* by a woman with the lovely name of Charlotte O'Connor Eccles.

I came across the book lately and instantly recognised my mother's favourite maxims. 'A place for everything and everything in its place' was one, and the other, more imperative, was 'Clean and clear as you go'. All the good advice that my mother profited by is contained in the form of a simple story. The Fitzgeralds are a poor but hardworking family who live in a country cottage. The father is a farm labourer but he has enough time and energy to cultivate a garden full of vegetables, fruit and herbs. Mrs Fitzgerald uses all these in cooking and points out that for the price of a few packets of seeds she can feed her family cheaply and well.

Not only is Mrs Fitzgerald a good cook, she is also a dab hand at cleaning, polishing, sewing and interior decoration. She has transformed what was once a dirty, drab cottage into a bright, cheerful and comfortable home, using nothing but distemper, whitewash and elbow grease. The time has now come for her little daughter Mary to acquire her mother's skills so Mrs Fitzgerald starts training her. It's tough going for a little while – Mary is less than keen to learn – but eventually she learns all that a young girl needs to know about running a home.

As I say, a simple story, more of a tract really, aimed at the women who would be expected to stay at home. However, it is written with freshness and charm. It is also amusing, for in contrast to the good Fitzgeralds, are the bad O'Briens. The father likes the odd drink, the mother is a lazy slattern, the children are rough and unruly. No garden there, but a stinking dunghill outside the door. The house is filthy, the children in rags, and meals are late and badly cooked. Mrs O'Brien refuses to learn from Mrs Fitzgerald's good examples, and suspects that the family's comfort is the result of a secret legacy rather than thrift and hard work. The contrast between the two households is most painful when each family acquires a basket of cooking apples. Mrs Fitzgerald makes an apple pie and her family sleeps soundly that night, but Mrs O'Brien can't be bothered to cook. Her children eat the apples raw and spend the night roaring with pain. You'll be glad to hear that the O'Brien's are eventually converted to cleanliness and order. Mr O'Brien envies the lifestyle of his neighbours and orders his elder daughters to learn from Mrs Fitzgerald. Mrs O'Brien is such a hopeless case that the author sends her on an extended visit to her sister in Dublin so that the girls can take over. A bit of a cop-out really, but killing her off would have been too drastic.

So, all ends happily, and in real life little country girls at school in early twentieth century Ireland learned how to make the best of their expected lot. They would grow up to marry farm labourers and run homes on very little money in small cottages. It turned out like that for many of them, but not all. Others like my mother, went on to further education, moved to the big city and ran modern homes with somewhat more money. However they found, as did my mother, that the lessons they had learned along with Mary Fitzgerald, were of practical use in any household, and that there was indeed a place for everything and that everything would be in its place.

A NIGHT IN THE HIMALAYAS
Bill Kelly

I sometimes think about him and wonder whatever did become of him. He was tall and blond, looked like an athlete. We met at the Taj Mahal in India. A strange place to meet a fellow Irishman. I had a few things in a bag, including drinks and salt tablets to take care of the 110 degrees of heat. I left it down while taking a photograph and with the speed of a camera shutter it was gone. Indian thieves can do three card tricks even when the cards are in your hand. I turned around and released a few expletives.

'Hello, that sounds like an Irish accent.'

It was him. It must be a chance in a million, two Irishmen at the Taj Mahal, brought together through a stolen bag and a little foul language. There was a second coincidence. The following week I was going to Kashmir and so was he. We agreed to meet in the capital, Srinagar. From there we would take a bus to Gulmarg. He wanted to visit a monastery and I just wanted to see the place.

At six thousand feet and in the foothills of the Himalayas, Srinagar was green and cool. A far cry from the sweltering heat of the Indian plains. Now if you have never experienced a bus journey in India, it is hard to imagine. There is seating for forty but there's at least eighty souls on board. A third of them are on the roof. The odd low branch sweeps off two or three, but no one minds. It's a kind of a blessing, it makes it easier for the rest to hold on. The windows are glassless and passengers enter and leave by them more often than by the doors. Thus it was as we climbed ever higher into the Himalayas. The air was getting colder and colder and the snow and glaciers were all around. He had been here before, he knew the place. There was an old house we could stay in. It was owned by an Irishman. He was an alcoholic and he was away in Ireland drying out – again.

A pot bellied stove stood in the middle of the living room and with difficulty we got it to light. Outside the snow towered above the building and the temperature that night dropped to twenty-five below zero.

My new friend was a Christian Brother and this was another of his many dark nights of the soul. He was unsure of his vocation. He had just returned after a year's sabbatical and a relationship that left him in turmoil. Going back to India looked like the solution. But he hadn't reckoned with the fact that a man's problems tend to travel with him. And on this bitter cold night I fell in for the role of counsellor, confessor and guru. And I had neither the knowledge nor the wisdom to attempt any of them. The man might as well have been searching for darkness using a torch.

You can't buy decent booze in those parts, perhaps part of the reason why the house owner was away in Ireland with a clapped-out liver. But anyhow my friend went outside and from some contact or other he came back with a bottle of something that had been distilled locally. It was like paint stripper, but these were desperate hours.

I think he knew he wouldn't get any solutions from me but the fire that raged inside him could be temporarily cooled by telling me his story. Sitting around that stove we were like trees leaning into each other in a storm, a degree of mutual dependence keeping us on our feet. That night it seemed that the answers to both our problems lay far away from that Himalayan hill. But then far away hills are always green.

From the beds we got heavy grey blankets, all weight and no warmth. We wrapped them around us and leaned in over the stove. The paint stripper began to taste better, while more and more of the man's story unfolded. But the bottom line was always, 'What the hell do you think I should do?' but when you are thirty-five years old and it's twenty-five below in the Himalayas and your mind is fogged by paint stripper, you too have a question. 'What the hell am I doing here?'

I didn't sleep much that night, it was too cold. The next day I went back down the mountain, leaving my friend to the cold and his thoughts. That's the last I ever saw of him and as I said I sometimes wonder about him. Did he marry that girl and has he a grown-up family now, or is he perhaps the abbot of a monastery somewhere or other? The only certainty is I didn't contribute much to whatever decision he made.

A WHISTLING WIND
Martin Malone

The wind sighs deeply through the valley, carrying in it a bite of ice from the snow-encrusted mountains. The Kurdish town of Sulaymaniyah in Northern Iraq sleeps in the pre-dawn darkness as our patrol vehicles lumber past its centre.

1988 and a fragile ceasefire between Iraq and Iran was being closely monitored by UN personnel along the border between both countries. UN Observers patrolled on foot, and by mule, landcruiser, and helicopter. From the marshes of Basra in the south, to the pastel coloured desert in the midlands, and high mountain ranges in the north.

Violations of the cease fire were reported by both sides and the truth of these was probed by the UN. This morning, the skies overhead streaked with blue, grey and slivers of amber, we were to find out what we could about reported sightings of mujahidin crossing to Iraq. The patrol would last five hours and take us through Halabjah to an Iraqi mountain position.

Our first stop is at Division Headquarters of the Iraqi brigade whose territory we're in. We sip *shi*, a local tea, and eat freshly baked pita bread.

This area before the foothills of the mountains is flat scrubland. Burnt out tanks litter battlefields. Anti-tank mines like giant buttons lie precariously close to the dirt roads we travel. We drive through miles of trenches where shells, used and unused, and helmets are strewn about. The mud squelches under the tyres. The silence is eerie. It's too easy to imagine the shells raining down, the rattle of heavy machine-gun fire and tanks rolling over the towering earth embankments. You could sense the fear in these trenches, so real is its presence many months after the position had been overrun by Iraqi forces.

A kilometre from the shadows of the trenches an eagle spreads its wings across the scrubland, flying low and effortlessly. I'm amazed at the length of his wingspan and the noble manner in which it glides: its aura of presence. Then the vehicles slow as we pass a rocky outcrop on our left and begin to drive into Halabjah.

We meet some bullet-peppered buildings and some scorch-marked trees. Remarkably, the town is still standing, given that the Iraqi policy has been to level villages within a 25 kilometre radius of the border. But already there are signs of dismantlement. Kurdish militia in the employ of the Iraqis are starting to strip buildings of reusable materials prior to bulldozing.

The narrow streets are deserted. Opened doors of dwellings reveal mattresses, plastic buckets and basins, a child's doll… the bric-à-brac that one would associate with any vibrant community. Human touches. The wind whistles down these empty streets with its tattered posters of Middle Eastern popstars. Whistles after us as we pass the mass graves on the outskirts of the town.

The graves face a railed-off cemetery overgrown with weeds, now that there is no one left to tend to it and to light the mint leaves as is the custom in other Middle eastern cemeteries.

The road climbing the mountain above Halabjah twists and turns. We meet with ice and snow and progress is halted. We won't reach our destination… it will remain so for most of the winter. The tyres on the escort trucks are treadless, making for a hazardous descent. The soldiers in the back are poised to jump should the truck begin to slide towards the ravine. There's a collective sigh when the vehicles roll onto asphalt and we begin our journey back to our HQ at the Abu Sana Hotel in Sulaymaniyah.

We hadn't come across our mujahidin. We never did. What that patrol imprinted on my mind was empty streets and mass graves and trenches of death. And a whistling wind that was raw and unreal. Begging the question that every act of murderous violence leaves unanswered – why?

AN OUTSIDER
Molly O'Duffy

I had been living in Nicaragua over four years when I learnt that my friend Felipa, who lived in wretched poverty in the mountains, was dying of liver cancer. After a period of hospitalisation, the diagnosis was finally made and she was sent home to her tiny overcrowded one-room hut to die. She needed a mattress, medicines and fresh fruit and vegetables, all of which were beyond her means. I took to making the long journey to visit her once or twice a month, bringing with me anything I could to make her more comfortable. I also brought my little instamatic camera, in order to take some portraits of Felipa, as mementoes for her extended family after her death. I am a terrible photographer, but managed to produce some acceptable shots, with Felipa's grinning face belying her swollen belly and emaciated features.

One day, when I arrived home from my work in the capital, I found a message that Felipa had died. This was the first close Nicaraguan friend of mine to die, and the first funeral I would attend. I hurried into my bedroom to pack my case for the overnight trip, and dashed off to the station to catch the last bus to the mountains. Next day I arrived at Felipa's village, and when I entered the house, saw her body laid out in an open coffin wearing a white shroud, and her weeping family and neighbours squeezed into the remaining space in the tiny room. There was an air of expectancy, as if they were waiting for someone or something. Wordlessly they turned to look at me, and I realised that it was me they had been waiting for. But why? The only explanation I could come up with was that they wanted me to pay the gravediggers.

Finally Felipa's mother spoke to me.

'The camera,' she said softly, pointing at the little backpack where I usually carried it.

'The camera?' I repeated stupidly.

'We're waiting for you to take a photo of Felipa,' she said.

My mind started to race, as I replayed the moment I had decided not to pack the camera, and willed myself to have made a different decision. My head filled up with images I had seen so many times in Nicaraguan newspapers, of the dead laid out in their coffins, and I realised, with a surge of panic, 'Of course, if those photos exist, it means someone came to the funeral with a camera. That's what was expected of me, and I've fluffed it.'

I wanted to go through the floor. And still they were waiting politely for me to put my hand in my bag. When I finally regained my voice, I spluttered, 'I'm sorry, I haven't got it. In my culture we don't take photos of the dead, it never occurred to me to bring it. I took photos of Felipa when she was alive instead…'

It was no use. Nothing could make it all right. After more than four years of living in the country I hadn't picked up a basic fact about life and death in Nicaragua. The memento the family wanted was not the one I was offering them.

No one reproached me, but I couldn't forgive myself. In a desperate attempt to make it up to them, I suggested they send for the schoolteacher in the next village, who I knew doubled up as a photographer in his spare time. The funeral was held up for another hour as two young boys were despatched to look for him, but he wasn't at home. Finally, with no photo taken, the coffin was closed and loaded onto the truck which took Felipa to the little cemetery.

At the graveside, I felt like what I was, an outsider, and the next day I returned to the capital chastened by the knowledge that it takes a lifetime to understand the culture and customs of a people, and experience is, as always, the best teacher.

GROWING UP IN NO MAN'S LAND
Mary O'Donnell

As a child in the 1960s, I was a true-blue fan of most things British, seduced by glimmers of Carnaby Street, by names like David Hockney, Mary Quant and The Kinks. If the choice was British music versus Irish showband, between *Fab 208* or *Spotlight* magazine, there was, simply, no choice. *Spotlight* was scanned for its liberal problem page but little else. The Republic of Ireland, *Spotlight* magazine, the showband scene and indeed the infant RTÉ television, were essentially pale and ineffective imitators of things which our former colonist was simply better at.

I grew up quite happily in our no man's land on the southern edge of the border, never certain of who the border people were or what we were supposed to be. Aware of being pulled hither and thither by rarely articulated passions and forces outside myself. County Monaghan straddled two opposite cultural traditions. Ulster people we certainly were, yet sometimes it seemed we were a forgotten sidekick of the *real* Ulster. We had our own writer, of course – Patrick Kavanagh, who by virtue of his banned novel *Tarry Flynn* had obviously done something right – but *real* Ulster seemed to mean the Six Counties, where things seemed brighter, more efficient and, in an unspoken sense, better.

As well as having the M1 motorway, the shopping experience in the North, for housewives from south of the border, offered greater variety; hence the convoys which regularly crossed the border on a Thursday afternoon, Monaghan's half-day, to buy provisions and clothing. These would be smuggled smoothly through the customs post on the return trip, though this too depended on the mood and outlook of the Customs official on duty on any particular day. For children, Armagh, Middletown and Aughnacloy were like ships, regularly plundered for their cargo of Mars Bars, Milky Ways and Maltesers.

Other things too worked to subtly alter our world and parish view. South of the border, when most of the Republic had to put up with RTÉ television and radio, we could choose to listen to the BBC and UTV, as well as BBC Radio 1 and 2. England was bursting at the seams with new music, with maddening themes of freedom and new fashion that pulsed its way excitingly down the airwaves.

Living as many of us did under a false sense of cultural inferiority, something quite different occurred on family holidays at my father's home in Kilkenny. Once south of Dublin I'd watch out for familiar landmarks, the Wicklow glens with their oak and beech groves, deep-banked rivers that contrasted with the slim sparkling line of our local river, the Blackwater. Finally, the sight of the Blackstairs Mountains, which meant the journey was almost at an end, for on the other side of that great sun- and cloud-swept immensity, lay Ballyneale, with its limestone pillars, the house with its unique, paraffin oil odour, and outside again, a rushing stream, deep, bosomy pastures. For me, this was *the* bucolic idyll. Once I heard my grandparents' rich southern voices, or caught the thread of local sayings and expressions in and around Ballyneale, I felt as if I had come home. I was bewitched, partly because I sensed unconditional acceptance in that house, but for another reason too: the place, the people, these voices, these ways of living, conveyed themselves to me – unpretentiously and naturally – as *really* Irish. On an unformed level I picked up the automatic ease of the cultural habitat in which my southern grandparents and aunt lived. There were, quite simply, no influences, there was no pull towards foreignness, otherness and the different ways which distinguished us in Monaghan from communities in both North and South. That independence charmed me. I have never forgotten it.

SARLAT
Ann McCabe

In Sarlat, a medieval town in the château-bejewelled Dordogne area of south-western France, lies a square, large enough to hold the once-weekly market of local produce: cheese, wine, honey, *charcuterie*. Except on market day, the square is quiet, peaceful, always shaded on one side or the other by quiet sandstone sleepy buildings. A cappuccino, frothy, deliciously chocolately, sipped slowly over an hour or so, or a Coupe Sarlat, an enormous helping of ice-cream lusciously adorned with cream, chocolate sauce and nuts, can be enjoyed quietly to the gentle background music of birds, French voices hailing greetings to each other, and quiet conversations.

The evening changes the square so dramatically that when adorned with its lights, sounds and activity it would hardly recognise its former, sleepier self. First, at sundown, come the swallows in their hundreds, shrilly calling to each other as they swoop, swing and dart about the evening sky. Next, the cafés and restaurants which line all four sides of the square one by one turn on their lights – soft green, pale blue, a red in the corner. Candles flicker in empty wine bottles on the tables, casting cheerful shadows. The chatter becomes louder, more animated, and more international as the evening progresses. French mingles with German, English, Italian and a plethora of holiday accents.

Ant then, at exactly ten each evening, comes Pierre. We don't know his real name but we are sure he must be a Pierre. He looks like a Pierre. Grey-haired, beret-clad, his dark navy trousers held up by navy braces, his collarless shirt slightly open at the neck, he sits in the right-hand corner of the square, beside the café with the soft green light, and brings to life a small nondescript-looking accordion. He begins with a few tentative squeezes, a few breathy puffs, in and out, a ripple of fingers on the buttons and suddenly you could hear a pin drop in the square. For Pierre is making magic, not music. As his squeeze box is pushed in and out, as the fingers push and prod the ebony knobs on the side, magic flows out. The music has the power to lift, cheer, make pensive, soothe, and calm. The first piece, a plaintive melody with a repeating refrain of haunting melancholy, makes diners stop with glasses half-raised to their lips, and causes lovers to clutch each other's hands over the red and white checked tablecloths. A few seconds' silence to let the mood settle and then Pierre takes off in a flight of jigs, jumps and can-cans that makes fingers tap on the glass stems, feet tap on the heavy cobble-stones and smiles break out on faces.

From ten until eleven each evening the square is suffused with magic. Conversations lace through it, entwine around it, are started or stopped according to the rhythm and tone of the music. When Pierre folds up his little music box, puts on his jacket and unassumingly slips out of the square, a hushed silence falls over the diners. To speak too loudly now would be a sacrilege. Voices whisper to the backdrop of a few tardy swallows. By midnight all is quiet and the yellow sandstone buildings settle down deeper on their foundation. Sarlat is now asleep.

THE SWINGING SIXTIES VISIT CLOGHER ROAD
Kevin McDermott

My pal, Gerard Williams, had the first telly on our road. I'd go after school to watch it. Gerard's Da had things neatly arranged. His armchair was strategically placed so that he could watch the racing on UTV and then, during the ads, throw a few darts at the board, which hung on the door to the coalhole. Years later, when the board was gone, the door looked like it had been infested by mystic woodworm, who wove intricate patterns around a magical circle.

'Fix them ears, Gerard,' his Da would say when the screen got cloudy, as if a better reception might improve his nag's chance of winning. It rarely did.

You can't imagine the excitement when we got a telly of our own. And then to add to our amazement, someone from our road became a star.

This was around the time I made my Communion, and everyone's ma seemed to dress the same – big roomy, shapeless, grey, calf-length overcoat, headscarf, flat shoes and a leatherette shopping bag. Some of these women were young, but they too dressed in the uniform, as if Crumlin was an outpost of Stalinist Russia. When our new neighbours Vera and Sean moved in, it was like the Iron Curtain had parted. Vera was a Doris Day look-alike and Sean was tall and handsome. And Vera didn't wear the regulation issue.

But it was when Olive White started to appear on the telly that the Swingin' Sixties came to Crumlin. Big time.

Olive was beautiful, in fact she was crowned Miss Ireland. In fact, she was fourth in the Miss World Contest. So there. Better still, she got a job in Radio Telefís Éireann, working with Gay Byrne on *Jackpot*. Every time she appeared on the screen, I'd recite, 'That's Olive White – her sister is best friends with my brother's girl friend.'

It was my personal mantra.

And then Olive went away and married Daphne du Maurier's son. I hadn't a clue who Daphne du Maurier was, but I knew, from the way my brother's girlfriend said it, that she was rich, glamorous and famous, like Grace Kelly who was all these things, and a Catholic.

And then Olive came home to visit her ma, driving this trendy little Austin Mini, wearing knee-length, white boots and a fitted coat that flared out above her knees, and, you know, the world was never the same again.

Now, all of this had a profound effect on our psyche. If God had been good enough to single out Clogher Road, Crumlin, as a special place, then my brother was ready to answer the call. With the savings from his summer job, he bought drainpipe trousers and a shiny jacket with a velvet collar. What with Doris Day as a neighbour, Olive White a celebrity, and my brother a teddy boy, my head was in a spin.

But it was too good to last, and it all came crashing down in the Savoy cinema on a Thursday afternoon.

My brother, the teddy boy, invited me, as a special birthday treat, to the pictures in town.

'What's on?' I said, sick with excitement.

'A surprise.'

Too true. My brother, my hero, had used me to get himself into the Savoy to keep a date with a young one. And while they oodled and canoodled, my eight-year-old self sat transfixed and terrified by a film called *Séance on a Wet Afternoon*.

Well after that, the Swinging Sixties lost some of its glamour and I reverted to football and ordinary pleasures, like robbing orchards or making carts.

Still though, Olive White was gorgeous in her knee-length boots, and she was on the telly and she was from our road.

A TALE OF INISHMURRAY
Joe McGowan

Inishmurray, once home to a thriving community, is now an uninhabited, storm-tossed island off the coast of Sligo. A diminishing population and deteriorating economic circumstances brought about the final migration to the mainland in 1948.

When fires burned there in welcoming hearths, neighbours gathered in on winter nights to pass the time. Accounts of mysterious happenings, ghost stories or enchanted islands were passed on to young and old; anything was possible in the mellow light and dancing flames.

One such story concerned the mysterious island of *Banc Ghráinne* a mile or so south of Inishmurray that, like the magical Hy Brasil, appeared once every seven years on the surface of the water. Dominick Harte, a native of the island, often recalled a bright morning early in June when he and some other men were hauling lobster pots at this unusual place.

'There were four of us in the boat haulin' up the pots,' Dominick recalled. 'It was the same as within a garden of roses. It was like we were within five acres of roses – all set within one inch of each other – and every man got the scent.'

A Teelin, County Donegal boat had a more frightening experience here when they came on the mysterious island while on a voyage to Sligo Town. As they approached, the skipper sensing something unusual, detoured around it. He spotted an old woman knitting on the shore and he was so close to the land he spoke across to her.

'I think,' he says to her, 'I'll put this piece of iron ashore on the island.'

'Well,' says the old lady, 'if you fire in that iron, I'll fire out this clew and I'll drown you.'

At that the island started slowly to disappear under the water. Puzzled, the crew continued into Sligo harbour to deliver their goods. At the end of the day, their business completed, the crew prepared to leave for the return trip to Teelin. As they were pulling away from the harbour they were hailed by a man carrying on his shoulder a large, three legged iron pot such as was used long ago to boil spuds or Indian meal. Approaching the skipper the man addressed him.

'Would you mind takin' me and this pot across the water with you?' he said.

The skipper agreed, so the crew and the stranger set off from Sligo pier for home.

A strong breeze of south wind, and sails set full, sent the Greencastle yawl at a cracking pace across the water. When they came within a mile of Inishmurray the stranger, without a word, dropped the pot over the side of the boat and jumped in after it. The skipper, swearing at such a foolhardy act, put his boat about immediately to search for the man. But it was in vain, for he could find no trace of the stranger. Night was falling and giving up the search he reluctantly headed his craft for the Donegal shore.

Some time later, on their next trip, their business finished, they were on the point of leaving Sligo pier when who should they see coming down the harbour again but the same man that jumped off their boat near Inishmurray.

'I thought,' said the skipper, 'that you were down with me the last time I was here and when we came to a certain spot you threw the pot out first and jumped in after it.'

'I did,' says the man. 'What eye do you see me with?'

'I see you with the right eye,' the skipper replied, wondering at such a question.

The man walked over and jabbed his thumb into the skipper's right eye upon which the stranger disappeared from view.

And so the story ends. Men still go in their boats to fish on *Banc Ghráinne* to this day. If you ask them whether strange things still happen there, or if they have ever seen this island, or smelled the roses there, they will only look at you with a smile and reply that there are certain things on this earth that are better left alone.

WALKING ON WATER
Barbara McKeon

The little Peruvian girl sat between my legs happily slapping my thighs to the beat of a tune she was humming. The whiteness of my limbs contrasted with her cinnamon coloured hands rhythmically keeping time to her music. She spoke only Aymara; Quechua and Aymara being the languages of the Andean Indians, so we could not communicate with words. The gentle slapping and her singing were the only sounds that pervaded the silence as the reed boat bearing us drifted like a green cloud over the sky-mirrored lake. Her father eased the boat over the glass surface of Lake Titikaka, so high in the Andes at twelve and a half thousand feet that we seemed to be floating above the world. He smiled at his daughter as he silently punted the reed boat, as his Inca ancestors had done since time immemorial.

He and the girl lived on an island on the lake, no ordinary island but one of the Floating Islands of Uros. For hundreds of years Aymaran Indians have inhabited these artificial islands constructed entirely of reeds, or *totoras*, which are interwoven to a depth of several metres. Over countless years they have formed a solid mass floating on the calm lake waters. As the underneath rots away, the top layer is added to and so the reed islands survive intact, supporting whole communities of Indians. People live in sturdy reed huts, fish the lake from reed boats, have even built a tower of reeds to house the solar equipment that harnesses energy from the sun's rays. Legend tells us that the divine offspring of Inti, the Inca god of the Sun, emerged from the deep waters of Lake Titikaka to found the Inca empire.

When I stepped on to the island I had the incredible sensation of walking on water for the reeds seemed an integral part of the lake itself. Women in bowler hats, flared skirts and brightly coloured shawls went about their business, tending their homes and animals, men chewing cocoa leaves fished the lake and from somewhere unseen came the sound of the pan pipes, a sound so unmistakably evocative of the Andes.

A cluster of children rapidly surrounded me, smiles on their grubby faces, outstretched upturned hands thrust towards me. They had so quickly learned to tap the false generosity of tourists. I distributed some pencils I'd brought with me for the purpose and they were delighted. Then I moved on to admire the handcrafts produced by the women, multi-coloured shawls made of llama wool and vivid wallhangings depicting daily life of the islanders, one of which now hangs in my home in Dublin. The men made souvenir reed boats which they sold for a few pesetas so they could buy jeans and tee-shirts. I wondered how long the unique way of life on the Floating Islands of Uros could remain uncontaminated as more tourists came to visit them.

As we glided over the tranquil waters unable to communicate except by smiles and gestures, the boatman's daughter sat on my lap slapping my thighs to the rhythm of her humming. Then she began to sing a song I recognised. The words were in Aymaran but the tune was unmistakably *Frère Jacques*. Holding her in my arms I joined in, singing my childhood French version. She gazed up at me in delight and sang the song over and over, her childish joy uncontained. For that short, precious time, we shared a togetherness that could not be reached by any other means. And Inti, the Inca sun god, smiled down on us.

A SMALL TOWN IN WYOMING
Leo McGowan

We wouldn't have stopped at Green River in the ordinary course of events. But it was too far to drive back to Salt Lake City in one day and Green River looked like one of the few places we could stay in a state that is still largely prairie.

We spent the night in an unremarkable motel. The following morning, Annabel was feeling upset.

'I didn't sleep well,' she said, 'there are bad vibes in this place, like someone was murdered here. Or maybe several people.'

I shrugged. 'It could be, I suppose. This was part of the Wild West.'

From past experience I knew better than to dismiss her feelings out of hand.

'Let's not hang around,' she said, 'we can stop somewhere on the road and get breakfast.'

But on taking the cases out to the car we discovered a flat tyre. No quick exit now. The spare wheel turned out to be one of those modern skinny things that looked as if it came off a scooter. I fitted it anyway and gingerly drove to the nearest garage to ask the young man there could he fix a puncture.

He looked at me strangely.

'Oh, you mean a flat?' he asked eventually.

'Yeah, one like this,' I answered, pointing to the punctured wheel to make sure we had achieved a meeting of minds.

Sure, he replies slowly, he can fix a flat but not until later, why don't we folks have breakfast while we're waiting? It is the kind of question to which there is only one answer, so still in our three and half wheeled car we drove down the main street in search of breakfast.

The waitress had emigrated from Liverpool many years before and was glad to chat to people from close to the country she dimly remembered. But Annabel was still feeling the dark vibes of the town. On impulse she asked:

'Was there ever a mass killing in this town?'

'Oh yes,' came the reply, 'the massacre of the Chinamen.'

'When was that?'

The waitress was unsure. 'Sometime in the last century, I think.'

Breakfast over, we made our way back to the garage where the young man replaced the wheel, tightening the nuts pneumatically with a lot less effort than it had taken me to get them off. We were ready to roll again but somehow couldn't leave without finding out more about this massacre which still seemed to hang in the atmosphere. In the town's history museum we found the sad story.

Green River's nineteenth century economy revolved around the local mine. The miners were of many nationalities, including a group of Chinese, who always worked together and kept to themselves. It wasn't clear why the management decided to allocate this group a different section of the mine but the other workers felt it would enable the Chinese to obtain greater output and so earn more money. The perceived injustice, linked to xenophobia, flared into racial hatred. A couple of Chinese were shot. Instead of bringing people to their senses it triggered a killing rage that swept through the town. The homes of all the Chinese were invaded and the inhabitants killed, about 30 in number, it's reckoned. A small scale crime by the standards of world genocidal atrocities. But enough to leave a tragic wound in the air a century and a half later.

Although we aren't particularly religious in the conventional sense, we nonetheless felt moved to say a prayer for some kind of release for the town. Sombrely we got back into our rented car and headed out across the prairie.

VISITING DACHAU
Thaddeus O'Regan

As a child, I knew little about the reality of war. I read *Victor* and *Hotspur* where military combat was often portrayed as an extension of the sportsfield. The hero would yell 'Share that among you' or 'this one's for Chalky' as he successfully stormed a machine-gun nest, thus paving the way for the entire Allied advance. I built up a sizeable collection of toy soldiers, planes and tanks and we replicated such comic book heroes in our boyhood games.

When I was eleven, my father asked me to help him prepare an attic for conversion. The premises had once been a lending library. I was still small enough to crawl out towards the eaves and retrieve memorabilia from the cobwebs and the mists of time. It was there, in a damp, mildewed box, that I encountered pictorial histories of the First and Second World Wars. I started to turn the pages, staring intently at the graphic images. Time and space blurred and with a childish addiction to know ever more, I continued until I came upon the liberation of the concentration camps, late in World War Two. I still vividly recall the contrast between the liberated and those who came to free them. Robust, burly Americans grinned or forced a smile for the cameras, while alongside them, the shadowy, skeletal remains of European humanity seemed frozen in a rictus of incomprehension. They gazed out at a world that had finally found them but for many, perhaps too late.

In time, I read more about the Holocaust and while my intellect absorbed the material, my heart still found it hard to understand how it could happen. Then, one beautiful, autumn afternoon, I visited Dachau. The sky was a strong, cloudless blue. The trees in the vicinity had lost few of their varicoloured leaves. The sun was warm as I walked through the gates and along a pathway beside the former administrative buildings, now a museum. I rounded a corner and found myself on the edge of the Appelplatz, a grey, open, gravelled rectangle where the prisoners mustered twice daily. The boundaries of this huge space are formed by the museum, the camp walls, complete with watch towers and two long, wooden huts. Originally, thirty-two such huts housed the prisoners. Their concrete foundations still exist and occupy the remainder of the huge rectangle that forms the overall camp. I strolled down the long space between these foundations to the far end. Small birds flew across the silence. The concrete seemed as fresh as if it had been poured the previous day. The administrative block did not look unduly harsh. It had many graceful features, typical of Bavarian architecture. Try as I might to visualise the countless prisoners, I could not. The blue sky and distant, golden foliage defeated me. Then I entered the museum.

Huge black and white photographs dominate the rooms. They depict every aspect of camp life. Like the boy in the attic, I was drawn inexorably from image to image. But this was different, I could now recognise the walls, the huts, the building I was in and went back out into the sunshine with new eyes and ears. Now, in my mind's eye, uniformed figures strutted about, orders rang out, prisoners assembled. I could see what had happened in this very place at another time. I began to understand, to grasp the wisdom of maintaining the camp as it is. Standing in lovely, leafy suburbs outside Munich, the Dachau Camp Museum embodies the worst excesses of perverted humanity. The deep, deceptive silence that pervades it is like the surface of a placid sea. For those who look beneath this calm, the lessons and the wreckage of the past are clearly visible.

ST. JOHN'S WELL
Tadhg Ó Dúshláine

Tipperary, the most famous of all placenames, is only one of the numerous names containing 'tiobraid' or 'tobar', corresponding to the English 'well' and referring to that most fundamental for life – water. Charles Plummer, in his celebrated study of the Irish saints, estimated that there were more than 33,000 holy wells in Ireland, with every parish having its own pattern day between late spring and early autumn, when the waters were believed to have special medicinal powers.

The belief was originally part of the midsummer day festivities and throughout Europe people went out and bathed at night in streams and rivers to cure their diseases and strengthen their legs and gain protection for their animals. In the old Irish account of the epic battle between the Tuatha De Danann and the Fomorians, Dian Cécht, the legendary physician, treated the wounded in the magic well like the pool of Siloam where Jesus told the blind man to wash his eyes, or the pool of Bethesda, where the invalids waited their turn to step into the 'troubled' waters and where Jesus empowered a man who had been a cripple for thirty-eight years to take up his bed and walk.

Because of its pattern day on the 24th of June, St. John's Well in Warrenstown demesne is the most important of all the holy wells of Meath. The story goes that St. Patrick used this water to baptise converts and that on St. John's Eve the water boils up and has great curative powers. In 1708 the Irish House of Commons passed a vote to prohibit pilgrimages to this well because of 'the great hazard and danger to the public peace and safety of the kingdom, and the fear of violence following such large and riotous assemblies'.

I stumbled upon this well quite by accident during my dark night of the soul, during those troublesome transitional years of the early seventies. I had just left a bewildered Maynooth, where the certainty of religious vocation that had been refined over a period of two hundred years, was all swept away in the fervour of renewal that followed Vatican II, when all the old devotions and pattern days were regarded as out-dated piseogs.

The neglected state of St. John's Well symbolised my own spiritual aridity at the time. The entrance gate was rusted solid and knotted with overgrowth. The wooden frame rotten at one end and tilting into the earth. The drinking cup for the traveller in smithereens on the stone slab, now covered in moss, where once pilgrims knelt on the naked stones.

And still the clear spring water jutted from a chink in the earthen bank. I cupped the palms of my hands and drank three draughts; sat for a minute on the decayed form and mumbled my three prayers, less in belief, than in anger that the institution in which we had put our faith and trust for centuries had in recent years been exposed as less than perfect.

Then my anger passed as though it was a gust of wind and I was at peace. I don't know what happened but it worked. Now I saw the daisies and buttercups and the majestic candelabras of the flowering chestnut and I knew this awareness of the beauty of creation would sustain me in the winter of my discontent, refresh my thirsting soul, revive my drooping spirit. And as I made my way from this timeless well towards the N3 to Dunshaughlin and Dublin, I remembered the mischievous little verse, written by an Irish Franciscan in the seventeenth century, and realised that the history of our native spirituality reminds us that we've been down this road before:

> Golden priests and chalices of wood,
>
> In Patrick's Ireland, that was good.
>
> But wooden priests and chalices of gold,
>
> In our own time we all behold.

PRAGUE, AUGUST 1968
Hugh Oram

I was in Prague in August, 1968, just a few days before the Soviet tanks rolled in. The atmosphere in the city was absolutely electric with the excitement of the reforms of the Prague Spring, but you could sense that everyone was deeply fearful of the inevitable Soviet invasion.

One evening I went to a jazz club just off the main Wenceslas Square. Someone had tuned in a big old radio to a French station on longwave. Through all the crackles and fading, I could just make out the newsreader. The forces of the Soviet Union and the other eastern bloc countries were on the move. The tanks were massing, but no one knew just when they would roll.

At the time, I was working for a business magazine in Dublin and it was decided to do a supplement on business links between the two countries. Although I was the youngest member of staff, I was delegated to go to Prague to put everything together.

The taxi driver in from the airport told me in good English that many people like himself, driving taxis in Prague, were academics or media people who had fallen out with the authorities. Later, I met a journalist on a business newspaper who told me he had been judged politically incorrect in the early 1950s for something he had written.

As a result, he had spent several years working in a coal mine to atone for his sins.

I stayed in a bed and breakfast place right on the main street of Prague. The room was vast, scarcely changed since the 1920s, with old fashioned furniture and a big white tiled bathroom, all very east European. The landlady and I didn't have a word in common, but we got on fine with sign language and smiles.

In between all my work, visiting Government departments to put together all the material for the supplement – there were no private firms then – I saw plenty of the city, including the great castle and cathedral on the hill overlooking Prague. I saw the church with the Child of Prague, a fat little statue, once the cause of avid devotion in so many Irish households.

I remember the colourful folk dancers with their rousing music. In restaurants, you could wait for hours for service and it was the same in banks. A Kafkaesque bureaucracy was everywhere. At every turn in the city centre, I was accosted by illegal moneychangers, who gave such good value for dollars that, if you accepted, a stay in Prague would cost practically nothing. At one corner, the money changer turned out to be an unemployed juggler, who kept half a dozen black balls in the air with remarkable dexterity.

On my last night in Prague, I went to the National Theatre, just across the street from where I was staying. They were staging a Janáček opera.

The raw emotion simply poured off the stage and the whole performance was like a metaphor for the flooding out of people's hopes.

Next morning, my plane lumbered into the grey, rain-laden skies, bound for Brussels.

A couple of days later, the world was filled with TV images and photographs of the people of Prague beating their fists on the Russian tanks in Wenceslas Square, where I had been walking along, perfectly peacefully, just a short while previously.

It's impossible to forget those events of thirty years ago, when the curtain fell in Prague. Despite everything, the business supplement was published a couple of months later, just as planned. It was almost as if the events of August 1968 had never happened. I went back to Prague once more, the following year, but the city's atmosphere was dead. Young Soviet soldiers with their great fur hats were everywhere. Prague had been closed down for the next twenty years in a conspiracy of silence.

MAKING CONNECTIONS
Michael Reeves

I have yet to visit Butte, Montana. I wonder if I ever will. In truth, I had never heard of Butte until I met an old friend who had just returned from an eventful tour of America. He spoke of Heuston, Texas; Los Angeles, California and Denver, Colorado, among other places. Like the Ancient Mariner, he went on, determined to mesmerize me with yet another adventure. He caught me by the arm.

'Wait 'til I tell you about the time I was in Butte, Montana,' he insisted.

It wasn't easy to keep pace with all the dramatic detail.

He had led the St. Patrick's Day Parade in one of the towns, he said. I was sceptical. You see, he was in a café one morning and he had read about the Mayor's distress at the loss of her beloved dog. That day he was befriended by a stray dog. The companionable mutt turned out to be none other than the Mayor's. The dog was duly returned, and you guessed it, the reunion was so joyous that the Mayor invited Liam to lead the St. Patrick's Day Parade with her and, of course, her dog. I could just imagine Liam's presidential waves to the good people of the town.

Liam must have dined out on that story, and others, for the next six months. Every time I heard him ask another friend, 'Did I ever tell you about the time I was in Butte, Montana?' I stopped listening. There was no point in telling him about the time I was in Limerick, Limerick, or Ennis, Clare.

Years later I was sitting on a bench in Central Park, New York, chatting to my son. We were some distance behind a statue. My son thought it was of Christopher Columbus. I thought it might be Thomas Jefferson. A friendly voice from a nearby bench said it was neither of them. Carved in stone was none other than the great bard himself, William Shakespeare. The friendly stranger quoted liberally from the sonnets and then he introduced himself.

He was a New Yorker, born and bred, man and boy. With a Leitrim mother and a Kilkenny father, his knowledge of both Irish counties was encyclopaedic.

He named townlands of which I had never heard, and for good measure, out of the blue, he sang a couple of verses of *An Bunnán Buí.*

'Ever heard of place called Butte, Montana?' he asked casually.

Ever heard of it, I thought. Wasn't there a time when I was fed up hearing about it. Many of his Leitrim relatives had settled in Butte. They worked in mining.

'Sure earned their corn,' he said proudly.

'Yes I know about Butte,' I said.

'You do?' he asked, greatly surprised.

'Oh yes,' I repeated, as if the whole world had heard about Butte.

'Been there?' he asked.

'No,' I said, 'but I know a man who has.'

I told him about Liam, the dog and the Mayor. He was impressed.

'You gotta visit Butte now,' he insisted.

'When did you last visit Ireland?' my son enquired.

'Ireland? I have never been to Ireland.'

'Never?'

We were astonished. He had spoken as if he knew it like the back of his hand.

'My father always said, an' he meant it. *Read my lips* he said, *we're not going back.* And we never did go back.'

We parted on a handshake. I couldn't help but think of his vivid images of Ireland. Of all the people he felt he knew but had never met. Ireland is a place which lives in his imagination. Butte, Montana lives in my mind's eye.

'Will you ever go to Butte?' my son asked.

'I wonder,' I said. 'Perhaps… perhaps not.'

We looked at our map trying to plot the quickest way to Brooklyn.

THE FLEET STREET SHUFFLE
Peter Woods

Old Speedy had an answer for everything. He was from Wexford. He'd been in more accidents than any man I ever met.

'Keep away from me,' he'd say, 'it's been a while now, something's about to fall on me.'

I met him on Fleet Street in London. That was back in the days before an Australian Press Baron, the British Prime Minister and what was termed 'new technology' conspired to make Fleet Street an irrelevance. But, in those days, if you worked in the building industry and were out of work, Fleet Street – or the art-deco offices of the Daily Express – was the place to go. That was where the London Evening Standard first saw the light of day, paradoxically at about eleven o' clock in the morning. The Standard contained all the advertisements for building work.

'It's easy to get work when there's work to be got,' was what Speedy used to say. Every time I was ever in Fleet Street, Speedy was there. It got so I began to think he wasn't after a job at all. He was just there to observe the rest of us trampling over each other when things got bad.

It paid to know your way around Fleet Street, particularly when work was tight. You needed to know where the telephone boxes were and what ones were out of order. There would be a stampede to get to the nearest one. There were no second chances on Fleet Street.

I remember the crowds after the bad winter of '85/'86. There were men that hadn't worked for a couple of months, men willing to take anything they got. The first morning I went down there I was about to go home until I met this young lad from Clare. We agreed we'd help each other. There was no conflict between us – he was after a driving job. He leapt in among the swinging boots and fists and emerged clutching two papers.

I had a bicycle. That was like a kind of secret weapon. An employer would ask you to show up on site. He'd want to look you over, like a man buying cattle. If you looked right he might start you. He might start the one or two men he needed and another couple, for the next morning, in case the first two didn't show up. That way it paid to be early for work – the first day at least.

That winter of 85/86, I wound up on a site on Waterloo Road. There were two men there before me, asking where the brickie foreman was. I got the job because I climbed the outside of the scaffolding as they were walking up the stairs. That and being early the next morning, because of the bike, of course.

It was never the same after the papers moved to Wapping, though I used to smile when I read journalists bemoaning the demise of Fleet Street. When I was there I had never had much time to admire the architectural wonder of the Express building – the Black Lubyanka, they called it. What the journalists missed was the sense of community they had, that and their watering holes. But for all they eulogised, not one of them wrote a column inch about what was happening under their noses – about the invisible economy. About what my friend Speedy called, the Fleet Street Shuffle.

AN ENCOUNTER IN IRAN
John Heuston

My initial impression of Urumiah was of a totally Islamic city. Dozens of mosques dominated the skyline and any women I saw on the streets of the city wore the obligatory *chador* – the all-enveloping black garment which conceals every part of the body except the eyes.

But appearances can be deceptive in Iran, as in any other place, and I was soon to learn that Urumiah and the surrounding region is home to a long-established and sizeable Christian community. Known as Nestorians, after the fifth-century bishop who broke with mainstream Christianity in a now long-forgotten theological dispute, the Nestorian Christians of north-western Iran have lived for over a thousand years in a society dominated by Islam.

I learned this interesting aspect of Iranian life when, by chance, I found myself speaking to one of these Nestorian Christians as I queued patiently in the local equivalent of the GPO; waiting for a phone call to Ireland. He was a pleasant young man in his mid-twenties, a farmer who had several acres of apple orchards outside the city. We had a long and interesting conversation about the position of the small Christian minority in Iran and, after helping me to make my telephone call, he invited me to see his church, which, he assured me, was not too far from the post office.

I accepted his kind invitation but, as he led me down some very narrow back streets, I was beginning to have a few misgivings about this unscheduled part of my visit to Urumiah.

At last we arrived at a large compound surrounded by a high wall. As we entered by a narrow gateway, I saw hundreds of men, women and children walking about the compound or squatting by the walls – and I soon discovered that they were Kurdish refugees who, just a few days before, had fled in terror from the helicopter gunships and chemical weapons of Saddam Hussein.

My guide introduced me to the elders of the community and I spent several pleasant hours as their guest, answering many questions about Ireland and discussing the likely outcome of the refugee crisis which was growing more acute by the hour.

When it was time for me to leave, the leader of the community beckoned me to follow him to a large, carved wooden door in a nearby wall. Unlocking the door with an enormous key, he led me down several flights of steps until I found myself in a small chapel with a vaulted ceiling supported by high, white-washed walls. He explained that the chapel was built in the second century after Christ and as such, was believed to be the oldest place of Christian worship in the world. He told me that it was built on the site of a building in which one of the Magi – one of the Three Wise Men of the Christmas story – lived and died almost two thousand years ago.

He explained that the Magi who brought gifts of gold, frankincense and myrrh to the stable at Bethlehem are believed to have been followers of Zoroastrism – a religion centred on the study of the stars which was dominant in that part of the world at the time of the birth of Jesus.

And almost as an aside, he remarked that Marco Polo had prayed in the same chapel of St Mary of Urumiah as he made his way to China in the fourteenth century.

The atmosphere was cool and refreshing. But to me, the most striking aspect of all was the silence in that ancient building. And yet there was something else which I will always remember. The little chapel was filled with sleeping bags, clothes, shoes and other items intended for the refugees.

It was explained that the chapel was only used for worship on very special occasions – such as Christmas and other important feastdays – but that outside of those, it was put to good use as a secure place in which to store the supplies so desperately needed by the refugees.

By the time we made our way back up a flight of steps worn by the footsteps of almost two thousand years, it was getting dark and the stars were beginning to twinkle over the city. Then the leader of the Christian community at Urumiah bade me goodbye and as he wished me a safe journey back to Ireland, he handed me a small container filled with a whitish substance that looked like coarse-grained sugar.

'What's this?' I asked.

'Frankincense,' he replied with a smile.

A Sense of Humour

MILKING THE VICEREGAL COW
Gregory Allen

For a period in my Garda service thirty years ago, I was in charge of the headquarters Central Registry, a dusty domain crammed with the files of half-a-century of history. In my next reincarnation as Organisation and Methods Officer I recommended the creation of an archive. My proposal for preservation of historical papers resulted in my appointment as Archivist – a consequence I hadn't foreseen.

Reading myself into my new job, I called at the old State Paper Office in Dublin Castle. I was brought on a tour of the Record Tower. Up the winding stone steps, on each level, the papers of the British Government in Ireland in the nineteenth century were stacked to the ceilings in identical green document boxes. Selecting one of the brass-handled boxes at random, among the perfectly preserved papers I turned up a complaint of unbecoming conduct against a constable of the Dublin Metropolitan Police, stationed at Cabra barracks – then located at the back gate to the Viceregal Lodge in Phoenix Park.

The background was this. Early one morning, a military gentleman attached to the Lord Lieutenant's entourage, taking the air in the grounds, had found a police constable milking one of the Viceregal cows. Over the breakfast table the equerry reported what he had seen. A request for an explanation was sent in the first instance to the Chief Secretary for Ireland, who in turn passed the Viceroy's note to the Under Secretary, head of the civil service in the Dublin Castle administration.

The Under Secretary passed the note to the Commissioner of Police, who directed an investigation. In time-honoured tradition, the Dublin Metropolitan Police closed ranks against a common enemy. The culprit's Section Sergeant extolled his efficiency and dedication to duty. The Station Sergeant respectfully described the burdens for a constable of having to provide for a family of ten children on a wage of one pound a week. The Inspector pleaded that the extra milk was a lifeline for the children's mother who wasn't strong. And so on back up the ranks.

In the shorthand of civil servants transmitting a file when there's no more to be said, the Commissioner marked the file to the Under Secretary with the words: 'To see'.

When the Under Secretary had seen it, he sent it on to the Chief Secretary, again marking it: 'To see'. The Chief Secretary, in turn, handed it on to His Excellency the Lord Lieutenant with the same laconic message: 'To see'.

After a reasonable delay for consideration of the case, His Excellency, with good-humoured tolerance, wrote on the file: 'I see'.

GANGS OF THEM DIGGING
Ken Armstrong

When I arrived in London in 1984, it was to work in the soft business of architecture and, for a long while, that's just how it was. But it happened that the tide quickly turned. That work all dried up and, if you wanted me in March 1991, I was to be found in a back garden in Queensgate Place, labouring; digging my very first hole.

I had my pick, my spade and my steel-toed boots. I had a big plastic bottle of lemonade and a Mars bar for sustenance. I had my shirt off and the beginnings of a muscle. By noon I was no longer at surface level but chest deep in the planet... if I crouched.

You might imagine that when an excavation caves in, it would give some prior warning. Not so. Mine fell in on me without so much as a polite cough. One minute I was in it, the next it was on me.

I decided it was time for a break. I pulled my tee-shirt over my rippling bicep and quit the garden site. Once outside, I realised I had left the front door key inside. I was unfazed.

'I will get back in,' I told myself, 'by ingenuity, guile and analytical examination of my situation.'

Here's what I worked out.

My worksite backed onto a mews house of the kind lately inhabited by unassuming billionaires. If I counted the houses up my street and then counted the mews houses down the next street, I should arrive at the one that backed onto my site. There was a kitchen window which had overlooked my digging, I could use it to climb through.

I counted them out and counted them back and arrived at a royal blue door through which television sounds were seeping. I knocked.

An Arabian gentleman in full Kuwaiti clothing opened the door and gazed evenly at me. I smiled winningly, his moustache twitched.

'I wonder would you mind... ,' my little speech was eloquent but obviously in the wrong language. Using an inept charade I managed to gain access to his small but elegant kitchen. There, above the sink, was his rear window and through it, just as I remembered, sat my collapsed dig.

The sink was stacked with unwashed dishes. Despairing of any understandable explanation, I proceeded straight away to empty them onto the draining board. The Arabian gentleman stood back and took this re-arrangement of his domestic affairs silently in his stride.

At last the dishes were emptied. Now I could show him what I was all about. I climbed into his sink, opened his little window and threw myself out of it. I was back inside my own garden!

It took me a moment to get my balance. I turned to smile my thanks at this most tolerant of men and there he was, looking more bemused than ever, standing at his open kitchen door.

Had I taken more time, I might have noticed there was a kitchen door as well as a kitchen window but, to my lasting regret, I had not.

I dug my hole, and it didn't fall in on me again. And as I packed my things that evening, I could still see the shadowy figure standing quietly in his kitchen recess. No doubt wondering what the hell I had been playing at in his sink.

SELLING THE PLASMA
Peter Woods

It was the day of my twenty-second birthday, the day we got lost in the Black Forest – Donnegan wanting to go right and me left and the sun blanked out the trees so we couldn't even tell east from west. It was pure luck we emerged from there at all out onto a road and got the lift from the woman that left us at the bottom of the steps that led to the town of Leonberg and its famous Porsche factory. The week before this we'd arrived back in Germany from a winter in the Negev desert – sunburnt and wearing summer clothes – to face into a snowstorm and freezing cold weather.

And those seven days chastened us. There was none of our friends to be found in Germany. Phones were disconnected and, in the bars where they'd drunk, their presences were only memories. The Germans said they'd all gone home or to London and that there was no more work for us anymore.

And then we met the Limerickmen and, although we didn't think it at the time, meeting them was a lucky break. We knew them vaguely from the year before. They were as badly off as we were and we were broke and starving. They told us about selling the plasma and we went up to the hospital, were registered and graded and had blood extracted and the plasma taken from that. We got two hundred Deutschmarks each. 'Ye might as well go home now,' the Limerickmen told us. The only work they knew of was rumoured. Building a big, long wall somewhere down the south near the Swiss border, though no one was sure exactly where. There was supposedly months of work in it.

Germany was like that – there'd be rumours about rumours.

Then they said they'd met a Scotchman called Freddie the Frog who said he knew me. He was a waster, they said, and he disappeared overnight. Maybe he got a job somewhere – that's what it was like now, men weren't telling each other about work, they just disappeared, they weren't pulling together anymore.

When they left I told Donnegan about Freddie – how I'd met him in Cologne and how sound he was and always in the know about work. Freddie was half-German and his brother had a bar near the Austrian border. That's it, Donnegan said, phone the brother. So I did and Freddie was there and had a start for a job in Karlsruhe. He'd meet us at the train station there in two days, he said. Though when we got there – and how we got there was another story entirely – there was no Freddie and we were back where we started, penniless again and without the money to make a phonecall.

So Leonberg and the shortcut through the Black Forest seemed like our last chance the day of my twenty second birthday. Donnegan thought vaguely that maybe a cousin of his was working in the Porsche factory there for the winter. All he could remember was the name of a bar, the 'Eisenes Kruz' he said.

We were weak and dizzy with the hunger by the time we arrived at the bottom of the steps leading up the hill to that town. Every so often we'd have to stop for breath – leaning on one another. 'Eisenes Kruz', Donnegan kept repeating like a mantra and, in the years since then, the number of those steps has grown in my mind until they seem now as many as the islands in Clew Bay.

When we arrived panting in the bar, Donnegan's cousin sat at the counter, a copy of the *Donegal Democrat* before him.

'Jaysus lads,' he said, 'it was a fierce bad winter at home.'

MAKING A FIERY IMPRESSION
Mary Arrigan

When my son's girlfriend and her parents were due to visit, we were warned to behave ourselves.

'Don't do anything weird,' we were told, 'I want for us all to make a really good impression.'

My husband promised to wear a tie and I promised not to wear any of my Oxfam stuff in case Girlfriend's mum might have been the donor.

They were due at six for dinner at seven. They arrived at four, before the impression-making leg of lamb was fully thawed and before the sitting room fire was lit. Cups of tea in the kitchen would have to fill the gap while my husband slipped away to light the fire. As I shovelled a spoonful of Earl Grey into yet another pot to give the teabags a touch of class, I noticed the heavy mist outside the front window.

'Bit of a fog,' I said.

'Different weather out the other window,' commented Girlfriend's father. Sure enough, the side window showed winter sunshine.

'I think actually that's smoke,' said Girlfriend helpfully. Billows of smoke wafted into the kitchen. But, as we'd been warned against weirdness, we tried to keep a half-decent conversation going while husband and son ran back and forth with wet sacks and shovels. The bewildered visitors pretended not to notice the smuts that settled on their hair and faces and continued to sip cold tea from pale-grey cups.

Finally my son stuck his blackened face around the door.

'No good,' he said. 'You'll have to call the fire brigade.'

The phone was on a shelf beside Girlfriend's father's shoulder. As I dialled I noticed smuts on his white shirt and leaned forward to blow them away before they'd get ingrained into the fabric. He turned suddenly, catching me with puckered lips close to his neck. Before I could explain, I got through to the fire brigade. The emergency service was answered by a woman who I knew had been in hospital recently. I thought it fitting that I should enquire after her health, as one does. It's good manners.

'By the way,' I said when we'd got all the pleasantries out of the way, 'my house is on fire. Do you think you could organise the brigade lads to come out?'

The tea got colder and the cups and the visitors got blacker. Still, nobody mentioned the raging chimney in the next room. Finally my son, responding to a quiet threat from me, asked the visitors if they'd like to see the Hiberno-Romanesque arch in the ruined church across the field from our house. I hadn't known they were so passionately interested in Hiberno-Romanesque arches. Their enthusiasm brought tears to my eyes as they fought their way out the back door. It was simply grand when seven large firemen with confidence-inspiring helmets and gear finally made it into our yard.

Across the field we could see our guests at the ruined church. Funnily enough they weren't looking at the Hiberno-Romanesque arch at all.

When the last spark had been stamped out, we gratefully invited the seven firemen into the kitchen for tea. By now the visitors had arrived back and were wedged between the beefy brigade men. I caught my son's eye and wondered how we were rating on the making-an-impression scale. Then again, maybe I didn't want to know. It was only then I discovered that my electric kettle was banjaxed. That meant a boiling saucepan of water on a gas ring.

'Anyone got a match?' I asked.

Seven firemen, three esteemed guests and sundry neighbours all shook their heads. In a house recently visited by fire, we hadn't the means to light a gas ring. At this stage Girlfriend's parents, in the best tabloid tradition, made an excuse and left. Pity really. They missed the fine roast lamb dinner we had just after midnight. They'd have been really impressed.

HIGHLY STRUNG
Richard Beirne

You had to hand it to her, she knew her own mind. She drove my father wild, as she'd always do the wrong thing.

'How is it that you'll always do the wrong thing, hah?' he'd shout at her as she sped off down the fields. I tried hard not to laugh at the sight of my father emerging from the yard gripping a torn and bloodied shin, a big red face on him as he gave vent to his rage and frustration. I knew that I'd be dispatched to go after her, seeing as he was out of it for the moment at any rate. So I grabbed a length of black plastic piping. That made for the best type of stick.

I quite liked this part, going off after the straying black. At least it meant I was allowed off on my own without the intimidating presence of my father around. I knew exactly where she would go, she always headed for the same spot, the spot where she had calved a month ago. The problem wasn't finding her, but rather getting her back to the house without running and racing all over the countryside after her.

'Highly strung, that's what she is,' according to my father.

I thought she was a great one. Mad as a hatter, sure, but she was determined to find her calf. I felt sorry for her sometimes. I knew she was bewildered and didn't understand why he had taken the calf off her. I didn't really understand it myself, it had something to do with a Charolais calf sale in town.

She was driving us all mad, roaming and roaring after her lost calf. It was quite unnerving as it had gone on for several weeks now. She was hoarse from all the crying. She would take a big deep rattled breath and there would be a second's silence and the next thing, this massive roar would issue forth, only to break off harshly into a hoarse crack. This would go on all night and the neighbours were driven mad. My father had had enough. He decided to get rid of her, she wasn't worth it apparently.

I could see her now, nosing and smelling the ground and lifting her long neck suddenly now and then to let a roar out of her. I was sure she was crying for her calf and imagined I could see tears around her eyes. I tried to reassure her that everything was going to be all right. She stopped moving about and looked at me, her head cocked in a nervous angle. She watched me warily as I approached, all the while murmuring what I thought were reassuring noises. Surprisingly enough she didn't bolt. I had resigned myself to a couple of hours running through the countryside after her, but not this time, she came quite easily. Her udder was still quite full and it was probably very painful, not having it milked out. It amazed me how she could run so fast with the pendulous weight of her udder beneath her swinging to the left and to the right.

We were nearing home and I was quite proud of the fact that I had got her back so quickly. I knew father would be surprised. He was coming out to meet us and I could tell by the impatient blustering strides that he was in bad humour. I began to get nervous and so did the black as I called her. He had reached us now and was starting into his usual tirade about wasting time and so on, when all of a sudden she took off right back in the direction I had just brought her from. I didn't say anything as father started roaring and cursing her. I looked after her, her head was strained up high, there was no stopping her now. Father was raging and I thought he'd burst with the annoyance and I couldn't help thinking that he was a bit highly strung himself and that they were well matched, the pair of them.

WHAT WE DID ON OUR HOLIDAYS
Pat Boran

I was about ten years old when I first saw an adult feeling shame. Of course I didn't understand it then, but maybe that's what memory's for after all: to store things away until you're old enough to understand them.

There were seven of us in all, five kids, our ma and our da. Ma was wearing sunglasses; Da, wherever he'd vanished to, was in a short-sleeved shirt. We'd swept the house, unplugged all the plugs, locked and bolted the front door, and now had piled into our battered old Ford Consul. We held our breaths and waited for him to come. There was always something about that last cup of tea before the road he could never resist.

And then he came. And it was summer, perfect summer, and finally we were heading off on holiday to the fabulous, the mythical seaside town of Tramore. Triggy Mucky More, my father called it disparagingly, but even he could not conceal his affection.

It was in the middle of Kilkenny City that it happened, which seems ironic now, Kilkenny being my father's native place. I think I was singing *Ten Little*

Ducks to my mother's delight and my own growing embarrassment, when, without warning, like a piano from a cartoon sky, the right-hand back door of the car simply fell off into the street, my brother almost certainly following it had it not been for my sister's quick hands.

Da applied the brake – which meant he kicked down, hard, on the middle pedal. The car stopped. And then we sat there in silence, a whole street, a whole city in silence around us, as the door of our sky blue Ford Consul shuddered to a standstill in our wake.

I'll always remember my father's terrible expression as he opened his own door, climbed out of the driver's seat, and walked slowly back up the street to retrieve it, that renegade door. Infants peered at him from prams, blackbirds stared down from roof tops.

But the story doesn't end there. In order to secure the door for the rest of the trip – so all his children wouldn't be lost en route – my father dug a length of heavy rope from the boot and, with the door propped back in place, wound it a few times around the D-shaped inside handle. Then he played it out across the back seat to the opposite door where it was similarly wound a couple of times, pulled taut as a mooring rope and firmly knotted. To gain entry to the back seat now, we had to clamber in from the front.

So, along with that look in my father's eyes, that first glimpse of a weakness I might call shame, I remember the sheer delight of my brother, my sister and myself as, on arrival at our rented accommodation, we made straight for the bathroom, stripped to the waist before the mirror, and spent whole wonderful minutes admiring the fading rope burns on our skin.

BEES AND ONIONS
Brendan Jennings

My mother really knew her onions. Quite literally, for in her time she grew just about every member of the onion family that is worth growing: leeks, garlic and chives, pickling onions and spring onions, Welsh onions and Japanese onions. Every year she planted onion sets and produced truly enormous maincrop onions for which she became famous both at home and abroad.

But she didn't purchase her onion sets just anywhere. Only the best would do. The best came from a firm in England – Bees of Chester. A read through Bees' seed catalogue was a much cherished-pleasure. Plump peas popped from their pods; crisp carrots cried out to be crunched. You could almost feel the flawless vegetable marrows, smell the ripe tomatoes, taste the luscious water melons.

Bees' catalogue made gardening seem a pleasure. And easy too. When I was old enough to handle a spade, I asked for, and was given, my own small garden. My father fenced it in. He even broke up the soil to make my work less heavy.

I planned my garden down to the last detail. Even had a little map. A drill of carrots here, two drills of potatoes there, and so on.

I immediately saw that my small plot had money-making potential. My fresh vegetables would surely fetch top money from the local shopkeepers. By the end of my first year's work I would have more money than I had ever dreamed of. My plans moved from gardening, to spending the profits of gardening.

Alas, Bees' catalogue showed the joys of gardening but none of the sorrows. No mention there of the hard work involved – weeding and sowing, digging and hoeing, watering, thinning, pruning, trimming. Nor of the dedication needed – all that work used up precious time which could be better spent playing games or reading comics.

No warning was given of the pests that would descend on my little plot – greenflies and blackflies, wireworms and cutworms, centipedes and millipedes, dogs and cats, slugs and snails and a million creepy-crawlies, all determined to live at my expense. Worst of all were the diseases – rust and scab, gall and gangrene, brown rot and crown rot, foot rot and root rot.

You couldn't see any of these in Bees' catalogue. In my garden you couldn't see anything else. Eventually disillusionment set in. Many times I deserted my garden for the rock pools at Port Cairn, the sun warm on my face, cool water trickling over my toes, a million miles away from the trials and tribulations of the horticultural world.

Meanwhile my mother was growing champion onions with an ease that made my attempts at gardening look rough and ham-fisted. She claimed no credit for herself, however, putting her success all down to Bees' wonderful onion sets.

My mother and Bees of Chester entered their declining years around the same time. One day she and I were in the gardening department of a large Belfast shop when she spotted a display of onion sets. She called the shop assistant over and pointed to the bulbs.

'Are those Bees'?' my mother asked.

The shop assistant, obviously unaware of the existence of a company called Bees, was completely nonplussed by this apparently ludicrous question.

'Are they *what*?' she said.

'Are those Bees'?' my mother asked again.

The assistant looked at me with understanding and sympathy. Then she turned to my mother and said gently and kindly, 'Oh, no dear. Them's onions.'

QUESTION NUMBER FIVE
Tony Brehony

Travelling in Eastern Europe is no longer the adventure it used to be. There's no dark mystery any more, no lurking suspicions, no hostile scrutiny of documents. It's not like the bad old days when every Western traveller was suspected of being a spy.

I once had a revolver held to my head by a female border guard at the checkpoint between Vienna and Brno. What aroused her suspicions was the fact that my travel documents stated I would enter Czechoslovakia directly from London to Prague. Why then was I coming in from Vienna? It took two hours of questioning and some telephone calls to her superiors before she reluctantly accepted that British Airways, due to overbooking, had rearranged my travel schedule. The fact that the guard was about 23 years old, ash blonde and very beautiful didn't make the experience any less frightening.

Fortunately, travelling behind the Iron Curtain, which I did regularly as a journalist, wasn't always full of fear and uncertainty – it sometimes had its moments of fun and black comedy.

Once, I remember, I had flown into Prague from Brno and a guide who introduced himself as Emile met me at the airport. He was, he told me, 82 years old and his full-time job was escorting visiting foreigners to their hotels. When we were settled into the waiting taxi he produced a clip-board and biro.

'If you don't mind,' he said, 'there are some questions I must ask.'

I told him to fire away.

His first question was to establish that he had my name right. When I confirmed that it was so, he ticked off the question with a flourish.

'You come from Dublin, Ireland?'

I nodded and he ticked again.

'You wish to stay in Prague for three days?'

I nodded; he ticked.

'You wish to stay at the Intercontinental Hotel?'

Another nod, another tick. Then:

'Do you wish for a horizontal companion?'

I thought about that for a puzzled moment or two before the penny dropped.

'Emile,' I said in disbelief, 'are you asking me if I want a woman?'

He shrugged his shoulders.

'Or a man or a boy, which ever is your preference.'

His biro was poised waiting over the clipboard.

'Lookit here,' I said, 'I'll have you know that I'm a happily married man. I've been married for thirty-five years…'

He cut me off with a wave of the biro.

'Please, please, not to be annoyed,' he said, his voice patient. 'You understand I am obliged to ask these questions and that was just question number five.'

That was all of ten years ago. The Iron Curtain is gone, the Berlin Wall has been demolished and with them went the dark brooding mystery, the fear and the uncertainty. Unfortunately, with them too went those fragile touches of black comedy which helped light up what was then a very dark scene.

GOD'S POCKETS
Rita Curran Darbey

I had just turned six and wanted to know where babies came from. And my Aunt Kate, who raised me, said they came out of Holy God's pocket. That satisfied me. But on reaching the age of reason I began to wonder. After all, God would want huge pockets to hold all them babies. So I approached Aunt Kate again while she was hanging out the washing.

'Ah what ails ye at all,' she said, 'sure didn't I tell ye He had two pockets – one for the boys and one for the girls.'

I still wasn't convinced.

'Well then, why can't you get one?' I whinged. She let the washing pole drop.

'Will ye ge long ou' o' dat with ye,' she said. 'You're givin' me a splitting headache.'

Well, I thought, that's the end of that, and decided I'd ask my cousin, the one who gave me the low-down on Santy. It was while we were on our way to the Bayno that I asked her about it. She boasted about knowing everything about babies but said she wasn't telling me because I was a tell-tale-tattler. My lip dropped while I tried to convince her I'd never tell again, but she wouldn't give in.

When we got to the Bayno, the first thing we had to do was to sit round in a circle while the woman told us all about the Iveagh and Guinness Trust which was set up in 1903 for the people of Dublin. It included the Iveagh Baths,

Iveagh Market, Iveagh Hostel and lots more but best of all was the Bayno, a recreational centre for the children of Dublin. When she was finished we all clapped, then queued up for our bun and cocoa. And then it was time for games and songs. I loved singing and doing the actions. The only song I dreaded was 'Harvest Moon', ever since that time when I was with all the big kids, sitting on the Liffey wall singing 'Shine on' up at Mr Dawson who was baldy-headed. And when Mrs Dawson ran into my Aunt Kate, giving out, didn't Aunt Kate tell her she'd be better off chastising her own young fella who was forever scutting. But when she got me on my own, Aunt Kate said I'd be very lucky if Mr Dawson, baldy an' all as he was, didn't come in and box my poor father. I said a fervent three Hail Mary's that night.

On our way home from the Bayno we swapped shoes and I told my cousin she could stay with me that night if she told me all about how you get babies. Then I remembered the last time she stayed with me, the time when she said the Sacred Heart was winking at me from His picture on the wall, and when I screamed and Aunt Kate came running in, didn't she deny it and told Aunt Kate I was only dreaming. So this time I made her say 'honest to God' and cross her throat with a spit, that she wouldn't do it again. When we were washed for bed and Aunt Kate had given us bread with sugar on it along with fair warning about trick-acting, we got into bed. We made a few tumbles then tried to see who could stand on their head the longest, and when we both fell down with the laughing, didn't Aunt Kate shout in at us to go asleep. Eventually we settled down and when our whispered chat finally came round to babies didn't I learn the real truth once and for all, and it had nothing to do with Holy God's pocket.

'Ye see,' said my cousin, 'when your mammy wants a new baby she has to take a little white tablet and when she wants twins, well then she has to take two.'

I fell asleep plotting ways and means of getting Aunt Kate to take a right good handful of them little white tablets.

FAIRWAY TO HEAVEN
Tony Flannery

In my line of clerical work house calls are becoming increasingly difficult. People spend less time in their homes, and they are generally less welcoming of unscheduled visitors; whatever their purpose. One fine summer's day I was visiting in a new, middle-class estate on the edge of the town. By mid-afternoon I was tired of talking, and the lure of the golf course was too much to resist. So I hopped into the car, quickly changed my clothes in the house where I was staying, and was safely on the first tee well ahead of the after-work golfers. Having taken a few practice swings, I was ready to hit off, delighted to have the place to myself.

'Hello! Are you on your own?'

The interruption wasn't exactly welcome. He had just got out of his car, a man in his mid-thirties, and obviously friendly.

'I am. Just out for a few holes.'

That is what golfers say when they don't really want to commit themselves. But it didn't put him off at all.

'Do you mind if I join you?'

As he made his way on to the tee we shook hands. Introductions were of first names only. Our handicaps were similar, so he suggested that we play a match, and put a fiver on it. Never one to resist a challenge, I accepted, and only then realised that in my haste to change my clothes and get out to the course, I had left my wallet behind me. So now I needed to win, to avoid an embarrassing situation.

We hit off. He was straight down the fairway; me, shorter and slightly hooked, but not in trouble. As we walked towards our second shots, we fell into conversation.

'You are not a regular around here?' he asked.

'No,' I said. 'I am just visiting for a week or two.'

'I shouldn't be out here at all today,' he continued. 'I have more than enough to do. But, you see, there is a mission coming up in the parish. And the bloody missioner was visiting my estate. I was working at home and my daughter told me he was getting near our house. The last thing I wanted to do was to meet him. I gave up on all that religion lark a long time ago, and I don't need someone trying to brainwash me back to it. So I left it to the wife to entertain him.'

'Good on you,' I said, and we addressed our second shots.

He was a good golfer, and I struggled to stay with him. On the eighteenth tee he was one up, so the fiver was beginning to look vulnerable. His drive was, as usual, long and straight. This time I matched him, but a half would be no good to me. I had to win the hole. To be beaten by a stranger in a game of golf, and then to have to confess to not having any money, it would seem like the ultimate meanness. Driven by desperation, my second shot was good, a six iron into the heart of the green, about ten feet from the flag. But his was even better, ending some two feet inside me. I got the putt for the birdie, but I still needed him to miss. He hadn't missed anything all afternoon. I was desperate.

I decided that a certain amount of gamesmanship was called for. As he lined up his putt I said,

'I have something to tell you.'

He looked up absentmindedly, his attention totally on the job at hand.

'What?'

'I'm the missioner!'

For the first time that day his smooth swing was replaced by an ungainly jab and the ball sailed well past, not even threatening the hole. Even though he was still left with a three-foot effort, I felt it incumbent on myself, in the interests of not further alienating him from the Church to concede the putt. The match ended all square with our dignity intact.

A SEASON FOR CROQUET
Tadhg Ó Dúshláine

'There is a season for everything, a time for every occupation under heaven...'

But the good book of Ecclesiastes doesn't mention the game of croquet, which was an essential part of clerical training in Maynooth in the lull season between the end of class and dispersal for summer, from soon after the foundation of the College in 1795, until it began to lose its clerical shape and uniformity in the early 1970s. Each of the 26 dioceses had its own croquet lawn and its own distinctly coloured chest, containing a set of balls and hoops and mallets. Of course it was only right and fitting and proper that croquet would have been encouraged in such a venerable institution founded by the British Government for the education of gentlemen of the Popish persuasion and organised according to the motto of the Jesuits: *mens sana in corpore sano; healthy mind, healthy body.* So the game of croquet, with its emphasis on decorum, intelligence, discipline and skill, became an essential part of the seminary curriculum.

The basics of the game are simple enough – four coloured balls, blue, black, red and yellow, driven by mallets through a series of hoops. In fact, croquet is not unlike snooker, or its more sophisticated cousin, billiards. A turn consists initially of one stroke but can be extended by scoring a hoop or roqueting off one of the other three balls on the court. So, like snooker or billiards, a player could make a continuous break and finish the game, much to the frustration of his opponent. One marvelled at fellas from Matt the Thrasher or Longford Slasher country now transformed into sophisticated, gentlemen croquet players.

But the vision, the discipline and the skill weren't acquired overnight and when a mere novice of a first year was matched with a seasoned shark in his final year of formation, it led to ungentlemanly conduct on the croquet lawn where the rules of engagement resembled more that of a faction fight than that of the after dinner propriety of the billiards room. When the games got out of hand, shouts of 'Boulavogue', 'Fág an Bealach' and 'Crom Abú' echoed around the walls of Maynooth.

My immediate in first year, that is, the student designated to sit next to me, in the oratory, in the refectory, in class and at all assemblies, was a simple soul of a saint by the name of Bruadar, from Ballydehob. But the saint at prayer was a savage at play, where all his frustrations, animosities and prejudices were sublimated in the mock battle of the game, be it football or croquet. Under adverse conditions, a croquet ball became a cannon ball in Bruadar's hands, and a croquet mallet a Viking two-headed axe.

Bruadar had the misfortune to be drawn against Corbally, the reigning champ, in his first year, first round game. Corbally hit off and hooped his way around the court, using all his fancy stickwork. This was exhibition stuff; he played a pass roll, aligning his own ball with the next hoop and banishing Bruadar's to the far corner. Bruadar became despondent. Corbally played a split shot, leaving Bruadar's ball where it was in no man's land and shot the next hoop. Bruadar became frustrated. Then Corbally tried a pass roll and fouled the shot but denied it. Bruadar freaked and leapt out of his soutane, his face a bowl of anger. He sucked one eye back into his head, while the other bulged out along his cheek; his mouth became distorted, spewing flakes of foam; his hair stood on end. So fierce was his fury, as he brandished his mallet over his head, that he resembled an army helicopter as he lunged across the lawn, mouthing a litany of obscenities. It took four deacons to finally restrain him.

As an apprentice priest Bruadar had failed the anger test and though not expelled was given an honourable discharge from Maynooth and sent to Rome to study theology. When 10 years later he returned to the staff of Maynooth as a distinguished Scripture scholar, he is reputed to have remarked to the then President, who as Dean at the time of the croquet battle had advised he should leave, the immortal words, 'the stone which the builders rejected has become the corner stone'.

IT'S NOT THE WINNING THAT COUNTS
John Fleetwood

Any gathering of sports fans will be sure to produce stories of fantastic scores, wonderful saves, record-breaking performances and occasionally of incredible flops. Goal keepers in any game tend to feature in these last tales of failure but Isadore Trandir of Brazil, who was never likely to feature in that country's World Cup team, must get first prize for letting in the fastest goal ever. A deeply religious man he knelt down for a brief prayer to the patron saint of goal keepers, whoever that may be, before every match. So intent was he on his devotions that on one occasion he missed the referee's starting whistle. Three seconds later the ball whizzed past him for the first goal of the match.

I don't know what the final score was but it could scarcely have been worse than the twenty-one-nil defeat inflicted on a Wolverhampton amateur club from England whose secretary had written to the wrong address. He had written to Maintz, then one of the top German teams. Their secretary in turn got things wrong for he thought he was arranging a friendly with Wolverhampton Wanderers, then one of the leading English First Division teams.

If a boxer fails to come back fighting within ten seconds of being floored he is counted out. The record for attaining this state was achieved by Ralph Walton in 1946. As he was still adjusting his gum shield, his opponent Al Couture bounded across the ring to give him one mighty wallop half a second after the bout, if one can call it that, had started and flattened him for the necessary ten seconds. On this side of the Atlantic some sort of similar record was recorded by Harvey Garthy and Denis Outlette. After forty-seven seconds of the first round, during which neither ever looked like landing a blow at all, Harvey let fly with a haymaker which missed Outlette by a good twelve inches but had so much power behind it that its would-be deliverer spun round so many times that he became dizzy, fell on the canvas, was unable to get to his feet for well over ten seconds and was counted out.

Racing may be the sport of kings but for at least one aristocrat, the Duke of Albuquerque, the annual visit to Aintree for the National usually included a side trip to the local hospital for running repairs. Seven times he started the race but came off at an early fence. Bookies were offering sixty-six-to-one that he would not finish the course and in 1974 you could have made a nice profit if you had put a few pounds on this unlikely event, for two days before the race started he had broken a leg and a collar bone. Still, he climbed aboard, plaster and all, to complete the course for the only time in his life. Interviewed afterwards he said in heavily accented English, 'I sit like potato sack and not help thee 'orse'. Maybe that's how he managed to finish. Horses can do great things if you just let them get on with it.

One doesn't have to be in the international class to break records and lots of other things as well. At a small sports meeting at Cumberland in 1952 the hammer thrower worked up such a momentum that when his unguided missile landed, it caused £150 worth of damage to his own car, bounced off that and through a window where it flattened one of the organising committee. This athlete was a one-man disaster for in previous throws he had hit a police car, a petrol pump and a portaloo, the occupant of which dashed out minus his trousers believing that his tigeen had been struck by lightning.

Still the Olympics can always be relied on to produce records of all sorts like that of Eddie the Eagle who carried the idea of competing rather than winning to extremes. He became world famous in 1988 during the Winter Olympics in Calgary when he finished last in the ninety metre ski jump which wasn't surprising for his only previous experience had been on the artificial ski run in Cheltenham.

But the prize for the biggest para-athletic clanger of all time must surely go to Mayor Jean Drapeau of Montreal, the city which hosted the 1976 Olympics. He nailed his colours to the mast and declared 'the Olympic Games can no more have a deficit than a man can have a baby'. Three weeks later Montreal was three billion dollars in debt and twenty years later is still in the red. How wrong can you be?

PUNTING
Bryan Gallagher

The summer before I went to Queen's University Belfast, we started building a new house. Times were hard and to save money we ourselves made the concrete blocks for the house. With shovels we mixed the gravel and cement (three times dry, twice wet) and, in a contraption called a blocker, pounded the wet concrete into rectangular blocks six inches thick. These had to be carried on wooden pallets and left in rows in a field to dry. You had to hold them out in front of you dead weight and the strain it put on your arms was colossal.

I wasn't helped by the fact that working with me was a labouring man who knew every trick in the book. I was the one who had to do the mixing, the carrying, while he did things like fetching the water or opening the bags of cement. He called me 'College boy', told me I was a softie and laughed at my blisters and my fatigue.

And always after work he would challenge me to arm-wrestle. He could beat me easily. He would distract my attention and slam my arm down, or he would hold steady against my frantic efforts and when I had tired myself out, he would contemptuously down me.

The work went on for weeks and the only break was on Sunday when a couple of other lads and myself would take a boat out on to the lough and row for miles and swim and fish.

But as the summer wore on, my body toughened, until one evening he broke off in the middle of a bout of arm-wrestling and said, 'Ah sure it's all a cod' and I knew I had passed my finals.

But I had no time to gloat because I was off to university. As first years we were invited to join various societies and I put my name down for the Rowing club and ticked 'Yes' in the section where it said 'Previous experience'. The next day there was a note asking me to report to the captain and I did. Two large chaps in blazers with crossed oars on the crest were seated at the table.

'Ah, Gallagher,' the captain said, 'Previous experience I see. Where were you at school?'

'Enniskillen,' I replied.

'Ah yes,' he said, 'Portora', mentioning the famous school where Oscar Wilde had been a pupil.

'No,' I said, 'I went to St Michael's.'

'Saint Michael's, I didn't know they had a rowing club there.'

'They don't,' I said.

'But where exactly did you row?' he asked.

'Oh, on Upper Lough Erne,' I said.

There was a puzzled silence and then a look of absolute horror crossed his face.

'Good Gad,' he said, turning to his companion, 'chap's talking about *punting*!'

And they both laughed loud and long at the idiocy and a couple of other big lads in blazers came in, and they were told, and they looked at me as if I was a sub-species of the human race.

And then a few nods and winks passed between them and I could see that they were planning a further humiliation.

The biggest and broadest of them came over to table and said, 'You have to pass a test of physical strength, you know, before you can be allowed to enter this club. Have you ever heard of arm-wrestling?'

'No,' I lied.

And he explained the rules as if he was talking to a backward child. Then he took off his blazer. He was big, all right, but when I looked at his forearms I thought that they would never be able to carry a six-inch block of wet concrete over a soggy field in Fermanagh.

He tried catching me unawares but my labourer friend had taught me well. I held my ground and when I felt him weaken, I slammed him to the table with a lot more force than was necessary.

'Good heavens,' said the captain, 'How did you get arms as strong as that?'

'Punting,' I said, 'Punting on Upper Lough Erne.'

RAW SARDINES
Padraig McGinn

People under the age of fifty don't realise how much life in rural Ireland has changed in the past fifty years, particularly our eating habits. We have jumped from open-hearth cooking to Chinese and Indian take-aways in one generation. This was brought home to me in my local supermarket recently when I heard a middle-aged lady discussing what she liked to cook with one of her friends. Words and phrases like 'eggs Benedict', 'couscous', 'stir-fry prawns with chilli and mango', 'kebabs', and 'beef Stroganoff' tripped off her tongue with an easy familiarity. I listened with some amusement because, as the begrudgers say, 'twas far from eggs Benedict she was reared. I happen to know this, for, when she was two or three and I was eighteen, I lodged in her house, in a backward part of County Meath, for three months. We were bringing electricity to rural Ireland and the parish priest persuaded her mother to take in Jack Ryan and myself as lodgers. The house was an old-fashioned farmhouse with an open-hearth fire in the kitchen, a flagstone floor, a big deal table, where we ate our meals, hens picking the scraps off the floor and an old-fashioned dresser along the wall.

Dinner every week-day consisted of fried rashers, boiled turnips and potatoes, except on Fridays, when Catholics were not allowed to eat any kind of meat.

'I don't know what I'll give you on Friday. Y'don't ate eggs?' Our landlady said to me.

'What d'ye usually ate on Fridays?'

'Fish,' I said, aware that I was upsetting the household.

'Fish!' she spat out as if it was a dirty word. 'I never ate fish in my life. I often seen them in the town but the smell of them would turn your stomach.'

'Maybe they'd have tinned fish in the shop at the crossroads,' I ventured.

'Y'd ate tinned fish?' she asked in amazement.

And so it was settled. Ryan said he too would prefer tinned fish to eggs and so every Friday after that we got a grey-black waxy mess with a fishy smell on our plates along with the usual turnips and potatoes. We covered up the stuff with mashed potatoes and hoped from week to week that we might get a herring or a mackerel instead of the grey waxy mess. But the punishment continued and when she said one day she was glad we liked tinned fish, it was time to do something about it. We went home early for dinner on Friday and watched as she opened three tins of sardines in olive oil, poured the sardines and the oil into the frying pan, added a lump of dripping from the Sunday roast as big as your fist and fried the lot for twenty minutes, stirring occasionally. We decided she had to be told not to cook the fish. How to do so without giving offence was the problem.

I lost the toss and on Friday morning Ryan lost no time, kicking me under the table to remind me of my duty. His enjoyment at my discomfort was already audible. I stood up, cleared my throat to get her attention and blurted out.

'Mrs M, if , if it's s… s… s… sardines for dinner today will you p… p… p… please not fry them.'

There, I had it said without laughing. She could see something was amiss but assumed Ryan's snorts and giggles were at my queer eating habits.

'Ye don't want them fried? And what way d'ye want them cooked? D'ye want them boiled or something?'

I could hear Ryan squealing and cups and saucers dancing on the table but I kept a straight face and managed to say, 'No. Just give them to me straight out of the tin.'

'Raw!' she gasped. 'Y'd ate them raw?'

Ryan screeched and I couldn't keep a straight face any longer. I just nodded helplessly and laughed until my stomach got sore. She thought Ryan was laughing at the Monaghan man that ate raw fish so she sat down, tears of laughter rolling down her full-moon face and the three of us sat there laughing until eventually we got up and went to work.

When we came in for dinner I saw she had left only two tins of sardines opened in the middle of the table. I took one but as Ryan reached out to take the other, she rushed over from the fire with the pan in her hand and screeched, 'Oh, good God, no, Mr Ryan. I have yours here, cooked as usual.'

Yes, things have changed a great deal in the last fifty years.

WORKING AT THE RITZ
Marian Gormley

As an impressionable ten-year-old I considered our family privileged to have Lizzie help run our home. For not only had Lizzie worked in the Ritz but she had also been in service in a big house where the brother of the lady of the house was actually a Lord! Better still the lord's wife had once been a lady-in-waiting at Buckingham Palace.

Famous names tripped lightly off Lizzie's tongue and her stories about the royal family were, as she said herself, straight from the horse's mouth.

When my mother and father had people in for bridge, Lizzie, dressed in black with white starched cap and apron, would hold them spellbound while serving supper.

'Winston Churchill was having his dinner in the Ritz one day, during the height of the rationing, and he says to me, "Lizzie what sort of soup is this?" And I says to him,"It's the same as yesterday's only a different colour."'

While her audience marvelled at her cheek she would launch into an account of her meeting with Field Marshal Montgomery.

Enquiring how an Irishwoman came to be working in the hotel during the blitz, Lizzie replied, 'For the same reason an Irishman is head bottlewasher of the English army. We have the brains, that's why!'

Years later when Lizzie had retired and was living on the outskirts of town, I was home on holidays and took my children to visit her. She was still an authority on the British royal family and on the inner workings of the Ritz. Only then did I ask her, like Monty had all those years ago, how she came to be there. She told me that the house she was working in, in London, had been bombed. Her employer (brother-in-law of the lord) his wife, daughter and herself had moved into the Ritz until their house in Kent was ready to live in.

'And of course I could not sit still doing nothing,' she informed me, 'so I asked if I could help and they were delighted. I worked in the kitchens and in the dining-room, I even made beds.'

I was suitably impressed, it sounded like Lizzie ran the place single-handed.

'And how long were you there?' I enquired innocently.

'Well now let me see,' said Lizzie. 'It was nearly a week, six days to be exact although it seemed much longer.'

And those were the truest words she ever said.

A FLY FOR THE SALMON
Bill Hammond

It's that time of the year again, the time when the salmon season is in. The days are brighter. The fall of night seems to be getting further away. Once more the fishermen will be checking their gear, looking at the colourful scatter of flies on the table and giving the trusty old rod a few reassuring swishes as they get ready for the trip to the river bank.

It is also a time for sociability, when you meet friends and discuss your chance of getting the big one. Time also for a quiet drink in a bar, close to the babbling water, where anglers come to sip a welcome pint and talk of times past.

Usually the tales go on into the night and along the Blackwater there is bound to be mention of the famed gillies who worked their craft along the stretch. Men who helped with record catches will be spoken of and there will be comments that the really big salmon are gone forever.

Someone in the party is bound to repeat the great saying of the famed Billy Flynn of Careysville, 'the fish are gettin' smaller by the year... like the people, I suppose'.

This sentence is sure to trigger more tales about the great gilly and some will remember the story he told about his father, Sean Rua, fishing with Edward, Prince of Wales, who was later to become King Edward VII of England.

The story goes that the Prince was on a visit to the area back in the last years of the eighteen hundreds, and it was felt he might like the thrill of visiting the famed stretch at Careysville, now owned by the Duke of Devonshire. Billy told the story.

'My father fished with Montgomery up to the time he let the waters to the Earl of Warwick, and it was then that all the great nobility came to Careysville.

'One of the first my father fished with was the Prince of Wales. A very pleasant gentleman, indeed he was, and he took an instant liking to Sean Rua. I suppose the friendship began the day my father hooked the King. They used to call him King, even though he was still a Prince. It all happened when they were standing on the bank near the spot where the Lechinaan runs to the Flats.

'My father had one of them heavy rods with a Mallock reel, which they used in those days. Well, after giving it a few swishes to impress the Prince, he started to demonstrate his skill.

"Watch now, yer majesty and I'll show ye how to make a good cast."

'My father swung the rod back and as it started forward, the line caught around the handle of the reel and it swung sideways, hooking the Prince in a very delicate part of his trousers.

'Well I won't say where it hooked him, but me father, who was always a great man for a crack, said "Well, bedad yer majesty, we're really fly-fishin now."

'The Prince took it in great spirits, and he handed a knife with a spike in it to me brother Tom, who was dallying on the bank watching the exhibition, to cut the hook.

The Prince later gave the knife to me father and remarked, "Sean Rua, be sure to take this with you the next time you go fly fishing."

'And you know,' Billy Flynn concluded, 'we still have the knife in the family.'

A SUBLIME MOMENT
Michael Judge

Now and again there comes a sublime moment which makes everything seem worthwhile.

We were holidaying in the little port of Puerto Rico in Grand Canaria. It was a package holiday, the cheapest we could get, and our apartment was halfway up the side of a mountain.

We lived in little holes in the whiteness of the apartment block, like kittiwakes on a cliff face. And we were happy enough. The apartment, though small, was comfortable. There was a large swimming pool, with sun beds around the edge. The sun shone every day, God was in his heaven and everything was more or less right with the world.

Then came the yacht... like the serpent dropping into the Garden of Eden for a chat.

One morning there it was, anchored about half a mile off the port, gleaming and resplendent in the brilliant sunshine.

Now, I'm no expert on such matters, and I couldn't even attempt to give an estimate of its tonnage. But it was big. Brass fittings glinted and glittered, the snowy whiteness of the paintwork reflected the sunlight blindingly back at us.

And then we noticed two astounding facts. The yacht was carrying a helicopter... *and* an aeroplane with its wings folded back.

This was serious wealth, we told ourselves. It was as if the King of all the Islands had come to visit us.

For two days the yacht stood off the harbour. Now and again the helicopter rose in the sunshine and disappeared on mysterious errands to important places, before returning and squatting down on the immaculate deck again.

As we stared at the boat from our hole in the cliff-face, a gradual change came over us. Our apartment no longer seemed comfortable. It got smaller, the beds got harder, the sparse furniture became increasingly Spartan. The swimming pool shrank into a sordid soup of sun-tan oil. Even the ubiquitous sun seemed to lose some of its warmth. Our conversations became dark discussions on the inequalities of life, the vulgarity of wealth, and the psychological damage which must inevitably be suffered by the rich of this world.

Then, on the third day, the yacht came into the harbour. Various other boats already moored there had been cleared out of the way to leave space for this most important visitor. We troglodytes rose in our sweaty hundreds and descended the sloping streets to the water's edge. The air was heavy with sun tan oil, sweat, after-shave and envy. At the harbour we sat on the wall and waited, a resentful, muttering multitude.

The splendid yacht arrived at her mooring. Men in white uniforms bustled about the deck. A ramp was dropped. Two jeeps thundered up from the depths and stood panting on the quay. Whistles were blown. A personalised gangway with a white awning over it was lowered. More whistles were blown.

Then he came. A small fat man, in immaculate white ducks. A white cap with gold braid stood jauntily on his head, gold epaulettes framed his portly chest. He saluted, skipped onto the gangway… and fell into the water.

A huge sigh of satisfaction washed over the assembled troglodytes. We rose and made our way back up to our caves, without waiting to see the captain being fished out of the sea.

God was safely back in his heaven.

BONES AND ALL
Cyril Kelly

Dryden was of the opinion that madness and genius were 'near allied', so, as O'Keeffe was at least half crazy, his musical ability could be described as borderline genius. Needless to mention, mechanical objects were anathema to him. His car, for instance, that Triumph Herald… it had a soft hood and a perverse heart. O'Keeffe christened it Maria Callas because its dodgy temperament reminded him of his favourite diva!

But as the saying goes, the biggest problem with cars is the nut behind the wheel. If Callas did not fire after one turn of the key, O'Keeffe's febrile disposition went into overdrive, full choke, pedal to the metal. By the time I was summoned to the scene, Callas would be in the consumptive throes of a flooded carburettor, her starter motor emitting valiant but despairing whines that would have done justice to Mimi's demise at the end of La Bohème.

However, I do believe that there was some sort of symbiotic relationship between Maria Callas and O'Keeffe. Invariably whenever he was embarking on a journey that he would rather have avoided, that would be the very morning when Maria Callas, as if divining his deepest misgivings, would refuse to cooperate. And certainly that famous morning when O'Keeffe rang me, the last place he wanted to be was in Mother Consolata's school examining the Leaving Cert girls in the Music practicals. According to O'Keeffe, Mother Consolata was an enormous woman and he was petrified by her visceral, all-embracing nature. So by the time I got Maria Callas started that morning, O'Keeffe was even more edgy than when I arrived. Too stressed to drive, he beseeched me to oblige. I had the day off so what else could I do? A friend in need is a blooming nuisance.

On the way O'Keeffe gave me yet another reprise of every crotchet and quaver from his visit to Mother Consolata's school the previous year and then, grasping his briefcase, he got out commanding me to collect him at 4pm. Sharp. At intervals throughout the day snippets of O'Keeffe's tribulations came to mind; yet another student in a navy gymslip blinking nervously as she nominated her choice of songs: *She Moved Through the Fair*, in the key of D-flat, once more with feeling and Mother Consolata at the baby grand, pudgy hands plopping on the ivories, a florid crescendo of chords before soft pedalling the intro. And then, after that student… ditto, and ditto again till lunch.

O'Keeffe was waiting outside the school for me that afternoon. He sagged into the car, a pale film of perspiration on his brow. Clasping his arms around his briefcase he groaned, 'Oh *my* God!' As was her wont Mother Consolata had escorted him to the parlour for lunch. There this finicky eater was seated at the polished oak table beneath the gimlet eye of Archbishop McQuaid on one wall and the benign, rustic smile of Pope John XXXIII greeting him from the other. Mother Consolata herself served him, placing The Irish Press at his elbow just beside the linen napkin. Depositing a heaped and steaming plate before him, she admonished him for barely nibbling the free-range turkey she had given him twelve months before and then she left him to enjoy his meal.

As I drove O'Keeffe back to his flat, he flicked the clasps of the briefcase and carefully withdrew a crumpled copy of The Irish Press. When he spread the broadsheet on his lap I glanced at its contents; half a colander of moss green curly kale, dollops of mashed turnip, floury spuds and two pork chops that should have been calibrated not by weight but by area.

The moment O'Keeffe had surveyed these victuals on his plate, the old peptic ulcer had stabbed him in the solar plexus.

'No way,' he thought. '*No way!*' Panic stricken, he turned his back to John Charles McQuaid and swept the entire repast onto the newspaper. Stuffing the lot into his briefcase, he snapped it shut. When Mother Consolata returned, her ruddy face beaming from her wimple, she bustled towards the table.

'You poor man,' she commiserated. 'You must have been starved.'

She removed O'Keeffe's plate and placed it on her tray.

'Starved entirely. Devoured every scrap, so you did ... bones and all!'

DA'S WAR
Gerard Lee

My Father has been at war for fifty years. Of course I've tried talking to him about the futility of it all, but to no avail. He's like one of Siegfried Sassoon's red-faced generals in 'Base Details', studying the latest range of weaponry available, planning new manoeuvres; victory always just one more battle away.

Now on the 50th anniversary of this guerrilla war, it's time to name the enemy, to roll-call those who have turned my father's hair grey. In no particular order they are: the codling moth, the cabbage-white butterfly, the carrot root fly, the greenfly, the mealy bug, the leather jacket, the wireworm, the wooly aphid, the chafer grub, the cutworm, canker, blackfly, blackspot, blackleg, blight, worms, slugs, bugs – need I go on?

These pests and some of their cousins have turned the serenity of our back garden into a battle zone, a no man's land. In the midst of it all stands my father, unrelenting, his trusty spray gun by his side. If the back door is open you may hear him chant 'I love the smell of Dithane in the morning'. In calmer moments he reclines in a deck chair, but like all good soldiers he sleeps with one eye open. The sight of a dainty cabbage-white flitting over the hedge from next door sounds the alarm. Before you can say 'blood pressure', he is off down the orchard path, ducking under pigeon-netting, side-stepping rows of baby lettuces and scallions, mother's geranium cuttings flying in all directions. The cabbage-white zig-zags like Biggles in a dog-fight, but Da stays on his tail like a heat-seeking missile. It's so good we all move to the back window to watch with our cups of tea. In due course the fine mist clears, and Da emerges, red-faced but triumphant, another cabbage plant saved from the voracious jaws of another generation of caterpillars. Reload, check spray-nozzle, at ease.

I have seen poor Da despondent for days at the sight of a big candy-red apple that he had watched daily ripening, only to find a tell-tale bore-hole in the skin, a sure sign that the codling moth had visited the fruit undetected by Da's radar. There could be no doubt but that the codling larva had destroyed the apple's core, and it was only fit for the compost heap.

I try and console him on such occasions; saying something like 'you win some and you lose some, eh Da?' But it's no use. Somebody should give him a medal, you know. 'The Garden Trouble-shooter Award' for courage and commitment above and beyond the call of duty.

CEDRIC
Melosina Lenox-Conyngham

My father was a tea planter so I was brought up on an estate in Sri Lanka where we continued to celebrate our religious festivals as if we were living in Rathgar. On Easter morning, when I was about six, a large silver cardboard egg from my godfather was placed in front of me and when I carefully opened the top, out hopped a tiny, but indignant, bantam cock which we named Cedric Seebright. He eyed the assembled company malevolently and made a large mess on the linen tablecloth. I was prepared to love and nurture Cedric, and in fact I kept him under my jumper for a short time, but soon, like Macbeth, I was trying to 'cleanse the stuff'd bosom of that perilous stuff'. For such a small bird he had a very sharp beak and razor-like spurs which he used indiscriminately against friend or foe. So Cedric was banished to the backyard to consort with the other chickens.

The hen-run was much frequented by me and my brother and my sister for nothing is nicer, except finding wild mushrooms, than collecting eggs. I still think of it as one of the keenest pleasures in life and as children we eagerly volunteered for the duty. We had little bamboo baskets specially woven for the task. Most of the chickens were Rhode Island Reds, but they were supervised by a fat Australorp hen with soft iridescent black feathers who looked like a successful Parisian Madame. The rooster, a huge white Leghorn, had once been photographed for a Shell petroleum advertisement and since then spent his time practising poses on the hen-house roof.

Cedric revolutionised the hen-run – Stalin could have picked up a few tips. The white Leghorn rooster, after a single skirmish, never again strutted with his best side to the camera, but bald and bedraggled, skulked in dark corners, occasionally joined by the Australorp whose feathers drooped sadly in the mud. The Rhode Island Red hens, on the other hand, thought life was a lot more fun and squawking excitedly would run off, not very fast, whenever Cedric cast a cold eye on one of them.

For us, there were no longer any joyous little expeditions to collect eggs.

'Attack, attack', Cedric would shriek as he half ran, half flew at any man or beast who invaded what he considered to be his territory. To venture into the hen-run was now a military manoeuvre. Even when under escort and armed with cudgels, we had to accoutre ourselves in an armour of rubber boots, mackintoshes and scarves wrapped around neck and face, for Cedric went for the jugular. But as his owner I could not bring myself to sanction Cedric's execution and so it was that he lived to suffer a hero's death.

In Sri Lanka, the great fear always was of rabies. Early one morning the bull terrier belonging to my father's assistant went mad. It bit a dog and two people on the estate and then raced through the yard and in at the open back door of our bungalow to a room where, a few seconds before, my baby sister had been playing on the floor. It rushed on through the house and onto the veranda and into the garden where my father shot it. It was by great good fortune that no one was in its way and that our dog was confined with puppies. The only fatality was Cedric. The mad dog must have run into the yard and Cedric must have gone into his Red Baron mode and launched an attack. All that was left of him was a pathetic little bundle of bloodstained feathers. But for those few vital seconds, Cedric had delayed the dog and probably saved my sister's life.

WHY MY BROTHER NEVER BECAME A PROFESSIONAL FOOTBALLER
Kevin McDermott

My Dad was a man of strong conviction and like all true Dubs he confessed to certain articles of faith.

'Phoenix Park,' he'd say, 'is the biggest enclosed park in Europe.'

This was always followed by:

'And O'Connell Street is the widest street in Europe.'

And then he'd complete his trinity:

'And never forget, son, that your brother is playing in the world's greatest soccer academy, the Dublin and District Schoolboy's League.'

Now, I never considered it a matter of filial disloyalty that I gave no credence to the claims made for the Phoenix Park and O'Connell Street, but I inherited my Da's faith in the Dublin Schoolboy's League so, when I tell you that my brother was one of the finest players ever to grace that league, you'll know I am talking 'quality' with a capital 'Q'.

He was a centre-half. He could turn on a sixpence, play off either foot, strike the ball with finesse. For a tall, gawky young fellow, he was beautifully balanced and had an unflappable temperament. He could outleap opposing forwards and he delivered the ball forward with the vision of a Franz Beckenbauer.

In short, the brother was a class act. I couldn't wait till he began to play at Under Sixteen Level, for then the scouts would come knocking on our door, and he'd be off to England to play for Leeds United, alongside Johnny Giles and Billy Bremner. And how I'd bask in the reflected glory.

After each match, Eddie, the team manager would just say, 'Macer, me ole flower'. And we all knew what he meant.

But then my Ma took an unwitting hand in the proceedings, and all our might-have-beens crumbled to dust. Ma had her own guiding principle, and clung to it with a frightening tenacity. 'A mother's love expresses itself in the food you put on the table.'

And my Ma was in the *haute couture* league when it came to dressing up ordinary cuts of meat, and we ate like French Kings.

Well, summer faded into autumn and the new soccer season was upon us. Me, Da and my brother were mad with excitement. This was going to be *the* year.

'I'm off, Ma,' the brother called, on the first Sunday in September.

'Where are you going, love?'

'I've a match at two o'clock.'

'But your dinner?'

These were the fatal words, 'Your dinner.'

'You can't play on an empty stomach,' said Ma, 'and a beautiful dinner all ready for you.'

'I'll have it when I come back.'

'Don't be silly! I'll lift yours now. It'll only take a minute.'

'Ma!'

But the brother's protestations were in vain. Up came the dinner and he sat chewing like a condemned man, on his last meal. Every Sunday, the same. The brother chewing in grim silence. Da and me helpless. My Ma hovering, heaping his plate and fussin'.

I felt for him, watching from the sidelines.

'What's wrong with your brother, he's stuffed!'

'If you only knew, pal.'

Turn on a sixpence? The brother couldn't turn in the centre circle! Leap like a salmon? He couldn't get off the ground. The loss of form was as complete as it was baffling. Soon the scouts stopped coming. And after the game, when Eddie, the manager, said, 'Macer, me ole flower', his words carried the ineffable sorrow of 'what-might-have-been'.

Really, it was a situation worthy of Greek tragedy – a son's ambitions dragged to the ground by an excess of maternal love. (I wonder if Sophocles follows Bohemians? Now, that's a real case of tragedy.)

THELONIOUS
Nicola Lindsay

Living in a small apartment in Dublin meant that having a pet was impossible. Living in a spacious house with a large compound in Nigeria was a different matter. I had grown up with run of the mill dogs and cats but when we were asked to take on the handsome Thelonious by a friend who was going back to Ireland, we accepted the challenge with delight.

Thelonious was pearly grey, sleek-feathered and scarlet-tailed with white encircled, bead-black eyes that missed nothing. His wings had been clipped before he came to us, so he was unable to achieve more than low altitude, clumsy flutters around the garden.

He was a one-person parrot and I became his person. He would show his affection by perching on my shoulder and putting the end of his dangerously powerful beak into my ear and making strange throaty noises. When he was feeling particularly loving, he would thoughtfully regurgitate dribbles of groundnut, which I hurriedly caught in the palm of my hand.

He got called 'Bird' for brevity. We had originally named him after the jazz pianist Thelonious Monk because, like his namesake, this parrot was a real artist, a musician of the highest calibre, with a breathtaking ability to extemporise and embroider a musical phrase. There was a resonance in his lower octaves that was spectacular and he was the only African Grey I ever met who could colour his notes with a powerful vibrato. He would attend my practice sessions on the flute with great interest, waiting until a piece was finished before launching into a similar melody, with variations. When he was not singing he talked. His vocabulary was not large but the few sentences he knew were spoken with clarity and style and frequent repetition.

Thelonious hated two things in life. One was the small dog from next door who would try to steal the peanuts scattered on the ground under his large cage. The bird would sit motionless and the dog would be lulled into a false sense of security and start to worm his way underneath to reach the nuts.

When he was as far under as he could get, with his bottom sticking invitingly up in the air, Thelonious, never one to miss a chance to create mayhem, would creep down and give him a good nip on the vulnerable rear end. The bite wasn't very hard, just enough to make the intruder squeal and run. His retreat would be accompanied by mocking, mimicked dog yelps from the bird as he smugly sashayed back to his perch.

The other thing he detested was the gardener's rake. Perhaps because the handle was long and thin and reminded him of a snake. Whenever the poor man, who revelled in the gloriously appropriate name of Hyacinth, appeared with the implement, Thelonious would suffer a bad attack of hysteria. He would hurl himself against the bars of his cage, squawking in terror and it would take several minutes of stroking and soothing before he would calm down.

He was fussy about his food. He liked his plantains ripe and would discard unsuitable slices, deliberately dropping them with great distaste. He adored pawpaw but this was forbidden because it made him ill.

One morning I realised that something was wrong. He was huddled on his perch, looking miserable and would neither move nor talk. From the state of the droppings in his cage I guessed that he had probably had a pawpaw binge the day before and was now paying the price. I tried feeding him boiled rice and tempted him with sips of water but he just turned his head away and sat, listlessly staring into the garden beyond.

By the time nightfall came he was so weak that he hadn't the strength to remain on his perch and crouched, a miserable collection of untidy feathers, on the floor of his cage. I decided desperate situations required desperate measures and so I half filled an egg cup with good cognac, forced his beak open and tipped the lot in. Thelonious wasn't much taken with this treatment and coughed and spluttered before settling back into the corner of the cage where he regarded me with a baleful glare. I went to bed, fearing that his demise was imminent.

In the early hours of next morning, after a troubled night, I went downstairs with a sense of dread. The house seemed unnaturally still. I quietly opened the door and tiptoed out to the shadowy veranda. I was greeted by a surprised croak. Thelonious was back on his perch, a little dishevelled but vertical, observing me in a rather quizzical way, with his head tilted to one side. 'Good Morning Bird!' he said in ringing tones.

THE LAST PIECE OF TART
Enda McAteer

The plan was to celebrate Uncle Paddy by *eating*. Every surface in the kitchen had food on it, including the chairs. Cream cakes sat side by side with honey-glazed hams and cold chicken around the room. There was some order in all this cuisine chaos. As each type of food was required, it was promoted to the kitchen table, from where it was distributed among the masses. The masses in question were every uncle, aunt, cousin and other relative I had, bar one, my Great Uncle Paddy.

He had recently passed away and this occasion was the funeral aftermath. He had always been a dapper man, having a penchant for topping off his appearance with a hat. His face now stares off my own wall from an old-fashioned photograph in which he wears a dashing straw boater. By the time I met him, he was totally bald. He wore a three-piece suit in dark green tweed, and his feet were always clad in polished brown brogues. To an eight-year-old he looked like an Oatfield sweet, crumpled green in the middle and shiny at both ends. Up to this, the only time I saw him was the odd Friday afternoon when he would visit. My mother would serve him tea in a china cup and a plate of steaming hot apple tart with fresh cream. I always got to carry this out to him. I had to make sure I got to him before the hot cubes of sweet apple had oozed and tumbled out from between the pastry in a slow-motion avalanche into the softening cream, the syrupy apple odour massaging my nose. I longed for a piece. But, apparently, it would spoil my appetite. I always wondered, what sort of an appetite did Uncle 'Starvo' Paddy have, that he always got such a big whack of the tart.

Although Uncle Paddy was now dead, there were still plenty of impressive appetites in the house on this particular day. Wee sausages and sausage rolls, mushroom paté, cheeses, mini pizzas, the list was endless, as was the demand. The cakes, buns and biscuits were just as varied and desired. Everybody was recruited to help out and wait on these relatives, hand and foot, but mostly mouth. We had all been given additional duties as well. Apart from shoveling foodstuffs into the kin, we had to chain-gang the tea to them and remove the empties. My two additional duties were, one, to keep Uncle Paddy's dog out of the kitchen, and two, not to say, 'have these feckers not eaten for a week?' I failed on both counts, but I did manage to get the dog out of the apple tart, off the kitchen table and out the back door without being caught. I should point out that the dog was called Paddy as well. We had named him after Uncle Paddy due to the dog's liking for apple tart as a pup. When I passed a piece of the apple tart to another starving aunt, she remarked, 'ach, sure that was Paddy's favourite.' I was about to agree and to say he'd just eaten the other half, when I realised she was talking about Paddy the Uncle and not Paddy the dog.

'Bet you wish you could share that with Paddy,' I said as I checked to make sure I had cut the paw-prints off.

THE GENTLE CLASSICS MASTER
Sam McAughtry

For most of my life I have been mixing with men who look back on their schooldays with great fondness. As someone who hated nearly every day at school, it's a state of mind that I have always found absorbing. I once jumped at the opportunity to travel in a bus full of educated, nice, mature, erudite men, on their way to see the boys of their old alma mater play rugby, so that I could study the breed at close quarters. On the way down to Dublin from Belfast, the conversation was delightful ranging from literature through history to politics, to society and back again. It showed the benefit of a grammar school education. It's no wonder they hold such loyalty to a school that, instead of going horse racing, they'll go and watch a new generation play rugby.

In the company was the sort of figure I'd never met, but had often read about – the old, revered, classics master. White haired, serene, gazing absently out of the bus window, I couldn't take my eyes off him. What was he thinking about, I wondered. I liked to imagine the old chap linking the coming game with the odes of the Greek lyric poet Pindar, an early sports writer, I suppose you could call him, who celebrated the winners of the Olympian games in his odes. The idea of being taught by truly learned teachers is one that I have a problem in handling. I saw in the classics master a gentle Latin and Greek scholar who taught his boys to face up to life honestly and never to take the easy way out.

In all the years that I spent at St Barnabas Public Elementary school not one teacher ever tried to persuade me to face up to life honestly, or never to take the easy way out. Indeed when the bell rang to end school it was risking broken bones to get in the way of the sprinting teachers.

Although I say it myself, I was a whizbang at English; my stories sold around the class for two caramels a reading, and while the other kids in the class were sucking their pencils, labouring over the first page of a piece entitled 'The Main Places Of Note In Belfast', my essay had to be ripped from my grasp when the time was up. I didn't go for nominating places like the ropeworks, the shipyard, or the City Hall; instead I heartily recommended a visit to a dockside sawmill, where a man once lost two fingers of his right hand on a circular saw, and a week later lost the same two fingers on his left hand, showing a workmate how it had happened. After the second accident the doctor asked the man if he'd brought the severed fingers with him.

'No,' said the patient, 'I couldn't pick them up, d'ye see.'

Mr Morton, who taught the only four subjects we studied, didn't once compare my imagination to Homer or Horace, as a gentle classics master would have done. Instead he told me that I was a headcase. And as for Shakespeare? He once took me by the lapels of my jacket, flattening me against the wall and snarling: 'We'll get this correct should the two of us have to stay here till midnight. Right – to be or not to be, that is the question…'

When we arrived at the Dublin ground, the college old boys hit the bar smartly. They were probably all taught to hold their drink by the gentle classics master, I surmised, comparing it to the way I took my first mouthful. It was in the RAF and when I got back to camp I was going to fight the cook. You wouldn't have got a grammar school man doing the like of that.

The college team won, they had saved themselves from relegation, we all got into the bus, and I started up a conversation about Beckett with the gentle classics master. 'Did you see an allegory with *Endgame* in today's match?' I asked him. He completely ignored me, stood up, and with his eyes wild, pulled the shirt out of the front of his trousers, and yelled, 'Who's going to beat us?'

Next thing I knew he was leading the whole bus in singing the first verse of *O'Reilly's Daughter*, unexpurgated version.

After I got over the surprise, I saw the point. What I was watching was the gentle classics master's updating of Jason and the Argonauts, in search of the Golden Fleece. His version was actually more arresting than that of the original by Apollonius Rhodius. You talk about college education? You can't whack it.

WHITE ELEPHANTS
Padraig McGinn

Sammy and David were neighbours of mine, both were keen gardeners and both played in the local Orange band. But there the similarities ended. David was a leading figure in our local Gardening Club. He was friendly and helpful, and willingly shared his knowledge of gardening with beginners like myself. Sammy was not a member. He knew all he wanted to know about gardening, he said, and why should he allow young upstarts to pick his brains. Both were keen exhibitors at all the vegetable and flower shows for miles around, and between them they scooped most of the prizes.

I was a frequent visitor to David's garden and he always delighted to show me any new varieties of roses he was trying out, or any new tricks of growing exhibition vegetables he had picked up. Sammy on the other hand kept the gate to his garden locked and nobody ever got into it. But when I started to exhibit vegetables at the local show and won the occasional prize, he soon found excuses to inspect my garden. He would walk past my house, several times a day, until he caught sight of me over the hedge, working in the garden. Then he'd let himself in the side gate and he could be there for several minutes, taking stock of everything, before you'd be aware of him.

'I rang your doorbell and when I got no answer I knew you must be in the garden,' he'd say. Of course you knew it was a barefaced lie but you couldn't very well order him out. His eyes took in everything and if he thought something was doing particularly well he was not above asking what variety of seed it was and a hundred other questions. His excuse for calling was always the same. He had lent a gardening book or a soil testing kit to a fellow gardener and he couldn't remember if he had lent it to me or to someone else. This was another lie because he never lent anything to anybody. In fact if he could have prevented the sun from shining on your garden, he would have done so.

Every year he won the prize for the five largest potatoes at our local show. I guessed they must be Aran Banners, which were said to be very big but tasteless, but as I had never seen Aran Banners, I decided I'd ask him, for curiosity's sake. So when he won that category again, I congratulated him and asked him what variety they were.

'White Elephants,' he replied, without hesitation, and without the slightest trace of a smile. I knew I was being made a fool of but I acted the innocent and thanked him, saying that I hadn't heard of that variety before. As usual he was going around the exhibitors discussing their methods or the varieties of seeds they used. My revenge came sooner than I had hoped. Seeing that I had won a first with my parsnips, which were nearly twice as long as his, he suggested that I must have set the seed very early in the year.

'Oh, not at all,' I said, 'they're a special fast-growing variety. I got the seed from Belfast.'

'And what's the name of the variety?' he asked, without the slightest hesitation or embarrassment.

I savoured the moment.

'Papal Blessings!' I said.

AUNTIE
Norma MacMaster

My mother, the eldest of the three girls, never liked Aunt Tilly much and we never quite knew why. But we did understand that in their early years the young Tilly was different from her other sisters. They read books; Tilly used make-up; they knitted gloves and socks; Tilly contrived gaudy, useless scarves which she flung carelessly over her shoulders; they married nice men, stayed in Cavan and became pillars of society while Tilly did the outrageous thing of running away to London to train as a nurse. Now, it wasn't that my mother didn't admire that profession and its galaxy of ministering angels but there was a war on and Tilly, being the flighty thing that she was, was sure to come into contact not only with men, but with foreign men, who, wounded or not, were bound to make a dent in Tilly's life; or perhaps it was that Tilly was the secretly envied one who'd escaped the dreary drumlins, who'd hoisted her petticoats, as it were, and leaped across the sea like some gaudy bird that had never belonged there in the first place.

But Tilly kept her virtue as far as anyone knew and finished her nursing course, sending my mother a large photo of herself, triumphant in her nurse's uniform. This my mother framed and set on top of the piano.

'Tilly's mellowed,' she confided to my other aunt, 'settled down at last', thankful, perhaps that the wild one never returned to prove her right or wrong.

Instead, years later, when Tilly retired, she wrote gaily, inviting my mother to visit. Now this was something of a shock because, although letters had been dutifully exchanged ever since her departure so many years ago, her sisters had never seen Tilly in the flesh. All but forgotten, she'd never married, so was bound to be very well-off and, well, who knew…

So was my mother now, just a little hastily, packing a case and bringing me along too? 'We're going to England to visit my sister,' she told the neighbours proudly. 'Tilly's retired, you know… trained in one of London's big teaching hospitals.'

She avoided mentioning that her sister's address was Gravesend, a place of doubtful repute in my mother's mind perhaps because she always imagined it to be full of drunk but handsome sailors.

When we reached Gravesend, we found Tilly's street huddled among hundreds of little terraced houses. My mother fairly bounced along the footpath.

'You'll like each other, I hope,' she told me, 'Tilly's led a noble life really, is a credit to us all now but, oh dear, how the years passed us by.'

Now we were at Tilly's house. The door was shut tight. Not a sinner about; nor the faintest stirring of a net curtain. There was just a bit of paper stuck up crookedly with a tack. It read starkly: 'Gone to the bookie's. Back in five minutes.'

A RUB OF THE RELIC
Gerry Moran

I could not count the number of exams I have sat in my lifetime. Yet I never sat one of those exams alone as one should. Never sat in those scarred, timber desks with brass-topped, idle inkwells, on my own. To my fellow students I seemed to be alone. To the supervisor, I most certainly seemed to be on my own but the truth is – I always had company. I was always surrounded by saints, saints of the Catholic Church, established saints, latter-day saints and favourite family saints. Or rather, my mother's favourite saints.

It is a recognised fact in our household that not one of our family got through an examination on his or her own merit alone. We each of us – my three sisters, my brother and myself – had assistance. Divine assistance. Divine assistance that was brokered for us by my mother's prayers and devotion.

My mother's preparation started weeks, sometimes months in advance – rosaries were said, masses were offered and novenas made. Shrines were visited, candles were lit and in the dim light of hushed churches all around Kilkenny, a host of saints was petitioned and implored for its intercession in the academic trials that lay ahead of us.

The real ritual, however, commenced on the morning of the exam itself and would be repeated daily until the last test paper was handed up.

Calmly and reverently my mother would take down her precious horde of relics from a discreet corner high up on the kitchen press and begin the ceremony. Carefully unwrapping the soft tissue covering, she would make the sign of the cross on our eyes, our lips, our hands and finally our temples with each relic all the while whispering aspiration after aspiration to the particular saint in question. The relics most favoured by her were those of Saint Gerard Majella (a special friend of hers), Saint Anthony (who never let her down) and Blessed Martin De Porres whose relic was given to her by a saintly Dominican, a close friend of the family.

When my mother's ritual concluded, we were handed the relics, blessed ourselves with them, kissed them and carefully placed them in a shallow tin box next to our pens and pencils and mathematical instruments. We dutifully repeated the ritual in the examination hall before the start of each test. What the supervisor or our fellow students thought of our antics, I have no idea.

However, so intense was our belief, so strong was our faith that we never cared to ask or enquire.

To paraphrase a recurring theme in Dale Carnegie's *How To Win Friends And Influence People*; if the saints are for us, who could possibly be against us?

Not one of our family, I am glad to report, ever failed an exam. Whether this was due to the rub of the relic, natural intelligence, hard work or a combination of all three, I'll never know. This much, however I do know if I dared to produce those same relics and re-enacted my mother's ritual the morning of my son's exam, I think he would look at me in bewilderment and wonder what class of witchcraft I was practising.

THE AGE OF REASON
Thaddeus O' Regan

The first time somebody stole something from me, I was about three. It was a yellow tipper lorry, a scale model. I can still see it in my mind's eye. I know who took it too.

At school, the nuns taught us about stealing and while there were some aspects of morality that I found a little complicated, I hung onto the fact that all would sort itself out when I reached the age of reason. Sister Mary Conception assured me that between seven and eight I would be in a position to work things out for myself.

In the spring of nineteen fifty-nine, when I had reached seven and a half, one of my father's closest friends suggested that I accompany him on a trip to Schull.

'Travel broadens the mind,' he assured my father. 'He'll be company for me and sure 'twill be an education for him.' How right he was.

We set off in a shiny, green Morris Minor down the winding road to Schull. I chattered on endlessly, fulfilling my part of the bargain. The driver certainly could not have fallen asleep. My youthful mind delighted in the ever-changing vista unfolding before us. My mentor provided a modest commentary – when he could get a word in. What really caught my imagination was the Fastnet Lighthouse. We could see it far out in the distance, like a rocket rising from the shimmering sea. He told me about the keepers who lived out there for weeks on end and how, in stormy weather, nobody could reach them at all. I was quiet after that. It made a very vivid impression on me.

In Schull, we parked outside a large emporium that sold practically anything anybody could ever have wanted. I was mesmerised by the variety. What I really liked were the souvenirs. West Cork was just beginning to awaken to the possibilities of the tourist industry and the owner of this shop was at the forefront of such development. There before me were replicas of the aforementioned Fastnet Lighthouse attached to every conceivable object. There were 'Fastnet' vases, 'Fastnet' paperweights, 'Fastnet' letter openers and myriad items each adorned with the lighthouse logo.

Seeing my interest, the owner approached.

'Is it your first time in Schull?' he asked.

I nodded affirmatively.

'Well, we must give you something to remember us by,' he said, as his eyes ranged among the rows of souvenirs.

My heart leaped. I would have a present to take back to my parents. My first major excursion beyond the boundaries of my native heath would end in triumph. He smiled and picked up a small bakelite ashtray with a silver painted plastic model of the lighthouse mounted on it.

'This was damaged in the unpacking,' said he, 'but you'll not notice.'

I did notice. A large chunk of the ashtray was gone. The thing barely stood upright. I could not help noticing. I muttered a 'thank you' and continued my curious wanderings between the shelves.

I was incensed – well, as incensed as one can be at seven and a half! It would be years before I read and understood the word 'patronised', but even then my youthful intuition felt I had been wronged. I continued to prowl meditatively around the shop until it was time to go.

I sat in the front seat of the Morris Minor, clutching my memento carefully in my hand, as we bid farewell to our host. We drove east through the town and my mentor glanced sideways at me saying, with an exquisite blend of sympathy and encouragement, 'that's a nice little piece'.

I nodded.

He continued, 'pity about the crack though. That spoils it.'

'What crack?' said I, placing a perfect souvenir on my lap.

He laughed loud and long and returned to such merriment many times on the journey home. He was tickled, he said, that one of the most astute entrepreneurs in West Cork had been foiled by a mere seven-year-old.

I smiled. I had reached the age of reason.

BIRTH-SHARING
Tadhg Ó Dúshláine

Do you remember *Helga* the first technicolour sex education film to hit this country in the mid sixties? Remember the excitement, the sensation as John's Ambulance Brigade members patrolled the aisles, and ambulances stood by outside the cinemas across the nation to attend the weak-hearted and the fainting, as the facts of life and birth in all its gory detail was publicly revealed for the first time?

For us teenagers it blew the theory of the stork and the cabbage patch and the millions of angels flying around up there in heaven waiting to be born and when your number comes up, it's down the hatch and out the tube like the lotto numbers.

We've come a long way since then and sex education is now as much a part of the Junior curriculum as tables and spelling, and partnership is the 'in' thing, not just in education and employment but from the very beginning in the labour ward.

My wife and I were on sabbatical leave in America in the late 1960s, when the traditional taboos surrounding childbirth began to topple. Expectant mothers and fathers went hand-in-hand to pre-natal classes to learn all about partnership in birth, contractions, breathing exercises and stopwatches.

Íde told me not to take all this theory too seriously, that in the real life situation a lot of this went out the window when the pain came and not to take it personally if she cursed me from a height as I mopped her brow, and held her hand trying to soothe her and she in the throes of it.

'Tis like a hard camogie match,' she said, 'hanging around beforehand is the worst part, the real business is all blood, sweat and tears and when it's over you're just knackered.'

She was right. The build up to the big day was desperate. Clíona was in no particular hurry to leave the security of the womb and had to be induced. It was a long night of sweet nothings and empty chit-chat about house renovations and holidays and the best films we ever saw as we attempted to run down the clock without a mention of labour or birth or baby, as we had done on the births of our first two. To make matters worse, next to us was a young expectant mother on her first, in all her finery there, looking her best, while her husband, a vet, thumbed through a massive illustrated tome of gynaecology, smiling and nodding wisely and reassuringly to his wife as if to say, 'no bother, been there, done that, a piece of cake'. This guy had it all apparently, theory and practice.

Then all of a sudden Íde felt something stirring. Clíona had decided her time had come. Fast. Yer man, the vet, looked horrified as we were whisked off to the delivery room where all civility, gentility, decorum and etiquette went out the window. We were down to the fundamentals of life here and the actions and sounds were suitably primitive; screams and grunts and passionate pleas while beads of sweat, not of the romantic Keatsian variety, like bubbles in a late disturbed stream, mingled with tears and running noses of pain and effort. And then the exquisite slimy beauty of it all as Clíona popped out like a pea and we hugged and sighed in relief and exhaustion.

Soon afterwards they brought us tea and toast and as we sat blissfully content and grateful for the miracle of life, we heard the clatter next door. Apparently things had begun to happen for the vet's wife immediately after us and as he sat there on the stool, holding his wife's hand in one and his handbook in the other, he took fright at the real thing, fainted and fell backwards and clocked himself on the hard tiled floor. Alarm bells sounded and when they got him out of the way to the Accident and Emergency room, his wife had no bother getting on with the real business in her own natural way.

When I met him that evening on the stairs he was no longer carrying *The Partner's Complete Guide to Birth* but a huge bouquet of flowers and I gave him a wink and a nod, as much as to say: you know, sometimes a little learning is a safer thing.

THE HARMONICA PLAYER
Patricia O'Reilly

The nuns in our school were great believers in extra curricular activities, specifically chosen to quieten our rampaging hormones. Mostly the experiences were fervent nuns and priests returned from the missions with yellow skin, sad eyes and a joyous belief in God. Full of depressing stories of deprivation in darkest Africa.

When we learned we were to have a visit from a harmonica player, we were far from impressed. And rated it on par with the returned clergy.

On the appointed day we assembled in the concert hall, sitting in rows on the wooden choir steps. The double doors swung open. It was Sister Cecily, who was in charge of music. Behind her came the harmonica player.

He was just gorgeous. Tall. Dressed from head to toe in black. With the greasiest, quiffiest haircut imaginable. And he had on Brothel Creepers, the to-die-for shoes of the day. These had extra thick, black soles.

He sashayed up the length of the hall. With each step his pelvis thrust and his shoes squelched on the blond of the parquet floor.

I tucked my legs in as far as they would go to hide their fatness, accentuated by ribbed brown lisle stockings and laced-up shoes. All around me girls were straightening up their shoulders, tightening their belts and sticking out their bosoms.

When the harmonica player reached a point about six feet away from the steps, he stopped. And smiled. Flashing white teeth, brown eyes and tanned skin. A collective gasp ran through us and the blood coursed through our veins.

From the pocket of his very tight trousers he eased out a harmonica, held it to his mouth and ran his lips over the instrument. We nearly expired. Then he played a few virtuoso pieces, which included lots of individual eye contact which made us blush, and hip-swaying movements which had us squirming on the wooden steps.

In a rich Cockney voice, he told us we too could learn to play the harmonica. Anyone could. But it did require practice. There was no point in even starting unless we were interested and had the necessary dedication. He paused. Looked from one to the other of us. He had us hooked.

Harmonica playing was a skill that would have us in demand at all sorts of parties and social functions, he said. Though looking at us, he reckoned our smiling Irish eyes would bring us anywhere. A cough from Sister Cecily cut short his patter.

Only seven and six pence. We could think about it until this day next week, he told us. None of us needed to think. The harmonica had assured our futures. Our parents parted with the money, delighted at our sudden burst of cultural enthusiasm.

A week to the day, hair shampooed, eyes bright with anticipation, belts tightened to show off our figures, we re-assembled. The man who came through the double doors, carrying a box of harmonicas, was small and thin with yellow skin and sad eyes. He was a harmonica-playing priest home on holidays from the missions.

THE CARD SCHOOL
Ger Petrie

There were seven of them. Five middleclass but quite extraordinary housewives, and two spinster civil servants and they got together every Wednesday at 8 p.m. for over thirty-five years to discuss their lives, put the world to rights and above all to play penny poker.

They descended on our home every seventh week with lots of maniacal activity and kissing; all talking loudly at each other with nobody listening. Then all in to sit at the long table in our dining room. Up went seven large handbags, out came an assortment of naggins, beers and packets of ten fags. Coats off, drinks poured, fags lit, some semblance of order ensued.

'OK girls, five minutes now for mastectomies, hysterectomies, children, grandchildren, college degrees and Leaving Cert points.'

This usually came from an unmarried lady who was champing at the bit to get started and boxing the cards at a frightening speed, her eyes glittering in anticipation. At this a crescendo of noise rose up and my father hiding in the adjoining room sucked on his teeth with irritation, turning up the radio and in later times the TV in a useless effort to drown out the racket.

There was a language all of its own spoken on the evenings. Usie, Nusie, Consie, Mosie, Marsie, Sheesie, and Sparks (loosely translated from the players' names: Una, Nuala, Connie, Mona, Mary, Sheila and Kay).

Then they settled down to the real business of the evening 'Deal out, Nusie', 'Shut up, Consie', 'Mosie, did you hear yer man died suddenly – I'll have one please.' This was overtaken by 'Two people were killed on our road last weekend – three for me' then 'My friend is very ill with shingles and she might die and throw me two there and God make them lucky'. 'Oh God, were none of yous ever at a wedding?' this came from my Mother who, when she had enough sad stories, used to stem that tide by saying to the last contributor 'Here's the cup, you win this week's most tragic story!'

'Right girls, into the diddly this time and nobody be shy.' This was a collection for their Christmas outing. One lady was assigned each year the duty of 'Diddly Minder'. This consisted of browbeating the others to contribute extra to several pots during the evening, minding the money for the year (usually spending it and having to replace it with lots of whingeing and whining) and organising The Outing when the time came.

Off again – cards are dealt – 'Sheesie where did you get these cards, someone must have died in this chair, I haven't got a card all night.' Noise level rising, falling, silence, blue haze drifting, long ashes suspended. 'Check Mosie', 'Bet thruppence and Sparks say a prayer for my cousin in Carrick-on-Suir, she got a kick of a horse', 'See you and I'm praying for nobody this minute, I'm losin' me knickers' and on and on through the evening, shrieks punctuating every pot making my Father leap up in his chair, the highest decibel finally driving him out for a pint.

All the highs and lows of their lives discussed and chewed over. The congratulations, the sympathising, the camaraderie, all filtering through the dealt hands and diddly pots. They all discussed and knew intimately husbands, kids, parents, neighbours, friends and local tradesmen. If any of the housewives dared to whinge about her husband, a glare would shoot across the table from the elder spinster who'd spit out 'Shut up – you thought you'd never get him!'

They dissected and parsed, marvelled over and curtly dismissed, all the while expertly dealing, calling bets, counting, winning, losing until supper was announced. This was a signal for all to light up together and as there wasn't a decent inhaler among them, smoke was exuded copiously from mouths, nostrils and even ears. Such a thick fog descended that when supper appeared it needed fog lights for identification.

Supper consisted of a wonderful display of double-decker sandwiches and a gala exhibition of fruit flans, cream cakes, eclairs and meringues which in today's world of low-fat would send a cholesterol expert spiralling into a total decline with horror.

After supper came the last three pots. 'Legs ups' they were called. We were never quite sure what they were but peeping through the door, as kids, we were bitterly disappointed that not a leg in sight appeared on the table or even up in the air! After the final pot was won with a deafening roar. Coats were produced, bags collected, complete with empties installed, and with one mass kiss they went out into the night. My father and probably all the neighbours within a two mile radius sighed with relief as the lovely silence descended once more. Seven whole weeks before they'd be back.

BOBBY, NOBBY AND ME
Tom Rowley

When you are twelve you don't expect to find yourself the subject of a fairly damning sermon at 11 o'clock mass on a Sunday morning in a small County Mayo parish. And who do you think landed me in the clerical dock? There were two people to blame, neither of them known religious heretics.

There was Bobby Moore, captain of the English soccer team that won the World Cup in 1966. And Nobby Stiles of Manchester United who played alongside him on that team. Nobby was small and tenacious and was regarded as one of the all-time hard men of soccer.

It all began innocently enough late in 1966. I had been left in charge of the house and farm for a few hours and I was finally able to get stuck into a book that had arrived in the post that morning. I was soon interrupted by the arrival of a priest who was in the parish for a few weeks as a replacement for our normal parish priest.

He was in the front door and on his way down our hallway before I had time to act. As he headed down the narrow corridor he came face to face with Bobby Moore. Bobby stood close to six foot, a commanding figure in the full football regalia of England. The Bobby who was forever on his way out of our hallway had arrived in sections in Football Monthly magazine. The first month, the colour centre spread began with his football boots and socks and so on, until by the fifth month you had Bobby's neck and head and the picture was complete.

I decided to stick all the sections together on a sheet of plywood and cut out the exact shape of the footballer. A bit of wood was added at right angles at the bottom and Bobby was ready to take his place standing as a life-size replica in our hallway.

So, as the priest made his way in he came face to face with the ever smiling Bobby. 'Who or what is this?' he demanded. I was shocked that there were people on this planet who did not know who Bobby Moore was. I proceeded to give him a pocket history of the England skipper. I noticed the more I told the priest, the more agitated he became.

He swept past me into the kitchen. I felt relief. Here I was sure I was back on safe ground. Over the fireplace hung a large picture of the Sacred Heart. On one wall was a colour calendar from the Holy Ghost Fathers showing the fruits of their missionary work, the mantelpiece had a statue of the Child of Prague with head intact. At the side of the dresser sets of rosary beads hung in readiness. I felt the balance had been restored. Religion and true devotion were back on top.

And then he spotted the book, *Soccer my Battlefield* by Nobby Stiles. He flicked through the pages. The chapter headings were enough to tell him this Nobby was no saint. The illustrations in the centre of the book provided more graphic evidence of Nobby's exploits as a player. Nobby sliding along the ground as a white shirted opponent screamed. Nobby smiling into the camera, the gaps between the still intact teeth evidence of the times when opponents had managed to strike first.

The priest tossed the book to one side. He preached to me in rising tones. He finally warned that I would never be any good if these were the types I used as my role models. Bobby was given a glancing elbow as the priest swept out of the hallway, but like the good defender he was, he solidly stood his ground.

Then Sunday morning – 11 o'clock mass. I never expected the outburst from the altar. But out it all came again. Adoring false gods. Worshipping false images. The pagan-like icons that were replacing God in the life of this young boy who lived only a stone's throw from the church. If he had come down from the altar and branded the word 'idolater' on my forehead he could not have made it clearer who the lost soul was.

Bobby and Nobby remained a part of my life for many years to come. The priest left a few weeks later – I like to think a little wiser. At least now he knew who Bobby Moore was.

A PRESIDENT'S LADY
Richard Stokes

About twelve years ago, I was commissioned to write a booklet on Áras an Uachtaráin. It was to be a means of creating a wider appreciation and awareness of this beautiful heritage building. It would also be a useful guidebook and memento for visitors.

I duly produced a text which recounted the history of the building, how it had been built in the eighteenth century, used as the Viceregal Lodge and then restored and refurbished as the President's residence.

To go with this narrative, there were to be photographs. These were taken by James Bambury, whose work for the Office of Public Works and for Bord Fáilte had received great acclaim over the years. In the Áras he had a rich treasury to choose from: beautiful plaster work on walls and ceilings; specially designed Donegal carpets; fireplaces rescued from houses in Mountjoy Square; a good selection of paintings including Derek Hill's delightful painting of President Childers sitting on a tractor on Tory Island – a lovely combination of portrait and landscape.

Outside, there were fine vistas, shaded walks and solemn statuary to be photographed. Rambling through the grounds, I came upon a beautiful statue in a most unlikely location. It was of a female nude, almost hiding itself at the edge of a shrubbery. It was spotted and speckled from exposure and, in its delicacy, seemed more suited to an indoor location. How had it got there?

I did some further research and found that it was originally located in Iveagh House and had come with the gift of that house to the nation from the Earl of Iveagh in the 1930s. During the war, de Valera had taken on the External Affairs portfolio for a time in addition to being Taoiseach. On going to his office at Iveagh House, he had been confronted by this statue and, apparently, was not entirely comfortable with such a display of nudity. The lady was duly transferred to Áras an Uachtaráin which was then being made ready for our first President, Douglas Hyde.

In 1959, of course, Dev became President. Upon entering the Áras who did he see but herself standing as bold as brass in the hallway. Despite his failing eyesight, he recognised her and is reported to have said, 'An bhfuil an bhean sin fós ar mo thóir?' (Is that woman still following me?), whereupon she was consigned to the wilderness of a distant shrubbery. There she languished through the years until I came upon her.

Well, I finished the booklet and naturally chose a photograph of the statue for inclusion. The booklet was never published, why I don't know. Maybe it offended someone and was sent to some official shrubbery. Perhaps it may yet see the light of day.

I wonder about the statue too. Will it be brought in to its rightful place in the elegance of the Áras? Will that 'comely maiden' ever become one of Mná na hÉireann?

THE CHRISTMAS PUDDING VISIT
Michael Judge

One of the more grisly rituals of my youth was the Annual Christmas Pudding Visit.

Although it had nothing to do with religion, this was a penitential pilgrimage that should have qualified for at least a plenary indulgence. It was unremitting gloom from start to finish. It took place every Christmas Eve in an unending hour between breakfast and dinner.

My mother, God love her, was a kind woman who forgave readily and very seldom lost her temper. However, something strange always happened to her on the occasion of the Pudding Visit. She ceased to be the gentle lady of the rest of the year and became instead a bristling, barking sergeant-major.

Before setting out, we children were lined up in the hall and inspected – faces, hands, teeth, ears and shoes. This was usual and didn't bother us very much.

But we also had to *smile*.

'What are we?' Mother barked.

'Happy, Mammy.'

'What are we going to do?'

'Enjoy ourselves.'

'How will people know that we're enjoying ourselves?'

'We're going to smile.'

'Well, come on. Show me.'

Our faces contracted into a fixed simulation of a smile.

'All right. But if I see as much as a hint of a puss on any of you –'

The threat was left unfinished, but it hung ominously in the air as we marched out the door and down the street. Thus began the Annual Christmas Pudding Visit to the Three Witches of Dunkin Road. (All names have been changed to protect the innocent.)

Our first stop was at Mrs Dooley's house, next door to our own. Mrs Dooley was a large woman with a green apron, a pimple on her nose and a cat called Oscar. She made grey pudding. I don't know how she managed that, though my father, who incidentally never came on these visits, insisted that Mrs Dooley wouldn't waste stout on any pudding while she had a mouth on her.

Eating Mrs Dooley's pudding was difficult (grey is not the most attractive of food colours) but eat it we had to, and wash it down with tepid, flat lemonade. Sometimes, when the grown-ups weren't looking, we tried to feed the pudding to Oscar, but the cat, with more sense than loyalty, absolutely refused to have anything to do with it.

Somehow we survived the ordeal.

'And what do we say to Mrs Dooley?'

'Thank you, Mrs Dooley.'

The next stop was five doors further on, the home of Mrs Dunne.

'Smile!'

'Happy Christmas, Mrs Dunne!'

Mrs Dunne was small and birdlike and always wore black. My father said that this was because there had been two earlier (now later) Mr Dunnes. Mrs Dunne made purple pudding. Even my father could offer no likely explanation for this remarkable feat, though he did manage to infer that it had something to do with the passing of the two Mr Dunnes. In this house there wasn't even a budgie, and so the purple pudding had to be eaten in its entirety. The big problem there was that it *tasted* purple and there was a genuine difficulty in forcing it to follow Mrs Dooley's grey pudding.

By the time the Dunne visit ended our spirits were really flagging.

'Thank you, Mrs Dunne.'

'Smile!'

'We *are* smiling, Mammy.'

'I've never seen a smile like that!'

'It's a purple smile!'

'Wait till I get you home!'

The journey across the road to the house of Mrs Doyle was like the final assault on the summit of Everest. Mrs Doyle smoked a lot of cigarettes and I'm sure she swore when there were no children around. She was square, she had vivid red hair and she made black concrete pudding. This was the hardest of all to get down after the grey and the purple. It stuck in our teeth, it lurked in the crannies of our mouths and hurt our gums. We struggled manfully, while Mrs Doyle smoked and my mother coughed.

Finally it was over.

'Thank you, Mrs Doyle. Happy Christmas.'

We trudged sombrely back across the road.

'Mammy?'

'What?'

'Can we stop smiling now?'

IN A STABLE
Matt McAteer

'I once spent Christmas in a stable,' I told my grandchildren, as I sipped a post-prandial brandy, having done justice to the turkey, pudding et al.

'Was it the stable at Bethlehem?' asked Dermot Óg.

He had recently starred in his Primary One's Nativity play, and knew a thing or two about stables.

Though a collection of little angels, I try to overlook my grandchildren's worrying inability to appreciate my true age. However, placing me in a pre-Christian setting was a bit much, I thought.

'It wasn't,' I said shortly, and then told them how it had happened sixty years ago.

'In the mid-thirties, my father, a stone-cutter, had pinched and scraped for years to save enough money to start demolishing the old thatched cottage in

South Down where he was born, and replacing it with a two-storey, slated house. To this end he hand-cut enough granite slabs from the stone outcrops on his tiny farm to use instead of cement blocks. For the corners he chiselled large rectangular quoins. It must have taken years to prepare the hundreds of pieces required. He hired Jack Taggart, from County Armagh, a journeyman stone-mason and man of all trades. He lived with us until the house was built. Employing a neighbour's son to attend Jack, my father continued working in the local quarry. It must have been a crippling struggle to cover, from his meagre pay, the costs involved in the construction and the rearing of a family of four.

'My brother and I were involved in the labouring. Jack required immense quantities of chippings to fill in cavities between the granite stones. We brought these up the ladder, using as containers two old enamel chamber-pots. Jack, a noted raconteur and wit, had a voice like a fog-horn, which could be heard half a mile away. He would arouse the neighbours' curiosity as to the capacity of his bladder by roaring at frequent intervals, 'I need two more piss-pots, lads!'

'When the old cottage was knocked down to provide the site for the new building, the farm's barn and stable were converted into temporary, and rather primitive, living quarters. The stable was the bedroom for all, and I remember waking at dawn, cold, on a snowy Christmas morning, and seeing a large, net Christmas stocking fixed to the bottom of the brass bed. I was looking slightly down on it, for the bed sloped, as the bottom legs were in the 'group' – the local name for the sunken trough in the floor, used to collect the normal inhabitants' droppings.

'Though the commercial stocking contained little more than a thin card Snakes and Ladders game, an outfit for blowing bubbles, a sponge ball, a colouring book with crayons, and a whistle, I was overjoyed.'

'So you weren't born in a stable,' said Dermot Óg, a little regretfully, 'but you lived in one?'

I know he regards me as a silly oul' eejit. But as he stared at me intently, I dared to hope that there was a hint of growing respect in his gaze.

IF TURKEYS COULD FLY
Biddy White Lennon

The turkey, a forlorn looking beast with an address label around its neck, arrived 'on the hoof' in late December every year, a gift from our Tipperary cousins. The activities that took place in the dying days of the old year in Lower Abbey Street – it was the early fifties – would, today, almost certainly be the subject of an official enquiry. At the very least there would be reports filed with the ISPCA, with the ISPCC, and very likely with the European Union food police on the unauthorised rearing of wild turkeys by unqualified, underage persons in an unsuitable environment – to wit, a flat roof.

The flat roof was used by my brother and me as a play area, but had been designed (by the architect, Michael Scott) as a beer garden for the Abbey Bar, my father's pub. This roof, which overlooked the next door yard twenty feet below, was ringed by a low wall topped by a sooty, raised flower-bed, into which were rammed rustic poles. The theory was that vines, trained up the poles, would provide a leafy, scented, summer bower for customers, particularly the many actors and writers who gained entry by means of an iron fire escape from the dressing-rooms of the Abbey Theatre next door.

Now, on Christmas Day, exhausted by providing seasonal cheer in the bar, the family always took itself off to feast on goose, in Jury's or the Gresham. The turkey (I wonder did it breathe a sigh of relief when Christmas came and went?) was destined to become the centrepiece of the family's New Year repast.

For the week between Christmas and New Year, Frank's and my task was to feed and water the turkey, but not get too fond of it. Not that there was any real danger of that. From bitter experience, I can tell you that turkeys don't take kindly to being transplanted to a city centre flat roof into the charge of two children barely out of nappies. For several years, with blood-curdling yells that were probably heard in their native Tipperary, these wilful birds had shown more interest in eating us than the carefully prepared mash we offered. They spent the rest of the time gazing soulfully over the parapet, looking for an escape route.

Gangs of thespians, on the way in, down the fire escape, at all hours of the day and night, would pat the bird, and us, on the head, while offering sage advice on poultry rearing. That year they decided to feed the turkey with barley – in liquid form. In high good humour, perhaps in search of entertainment, some actors, who had better remain nameless, though they were led by Frank Dermody, invaded our roof space clutching bottles of ginger beer for us, and Guinness, in a bowl for the turkey. I can't remember that we objected. As a publican's children we never doubted that Guinness was good for you.

Now that year's bird was highly-strung when sober. Drunk, he decided, that if his end was nigh, he was going to take his tormentors with him. He flapped furiously, gobbled and screeched like the demon in the Irish panto next door, and practised kamikaze runs at the unguarded wall.

The actors roared with laughter and lurched back up the fire escape. With the instincts for survival of those accustomed to danger, my brother and I sang dumb.

On New Year's eve, Frank and I were always scrubbed clean and dressed in new clothes. Tradition, in those far-off days, decreed that the state you were in on the stroke of midnight was the way you'd stay for the year to come. Good humour was demanded of us, on pain of not being taken across the river to Christchurch to see in the New Year.

As the cathedral bells peeled out, standing in the seething mass of people, I know I heard the final screech of that turkey as he launched himself into eternity.

THE UNDERSTUDY
Fiona Coyle

The pupils were delighted. There was to be a grand Christmas pageant instead of the usual boring nativity play. The Form teachers were slightly more circumspect. The pageant that was planned was a highly ambitious undertaking involving the whole school. The idea was that each class, under the direction of its Form teacher, would produce an individual scene based on the Biblical events at the time of the birth and childhood of Jesus. The first scene would depict the Annunciation, then the Visitation and so on, concluding with the Finding in the Temple. All the scenes would be linked together with readings, music and poems.

I was Form teacher of 2E, a class of thirteen-year-olds, who were individually good-natured and happy-go-lucky, and collectively – well, boisterous, to say the least. They, to their delight, were chosen to present the pageant's finale – the Finding of Jesus in the Temple.

From early November we discussed the story and planned the staging and costuming. We didn't produce a script, the aim being to encourage spontaneity. I handpicked three relatively levelheaded and sober individuals to play the three principal characters, Mary, Joseph and Jesus, and so that everyone would feel included, each principal had six understudies. The understudies also acted the non-speaking parts of the elders, high priests and passers-by.

By early December it seemed that nothing was happening in the school except rehearsals for the pageant. The atmosphere was festive and the Form teachers dared to hope for a happy and uncomplicated ending. On the morning of the day the pageant was to be presented, calamity struck. Mary in the Finding of the Temple was ill. With a sinking heart I picked an understudy. The new Mary, when she had finished whooping and jumping with joy, said, 'Oh miss, I always wanted to be an actor.'

That evening the hall was filled with an expectant crowd of parents, visitors and several VIPs. Mother Prioress sat beaming in the front row beside the Parish Priest and the principals of the other local schools. The pageant started. As the various little scenes were presented the audience was appreciative, uncritical, regularly clapping encouragement.

I and Form 2E waited behind the scenes, all of us shivering with nerves and excitement. The new Mary looked angelic in a long blue skirt, white blouse and silvery stole, her hair a cascade of black shiny ringlets. Finally we were on. Jesus sat to the right of the stage surrounded by high priests, all talking and gesticulating nineteen to the dozen. Mary came in from the left, Joseph in tow. Mary was searching – she gasped dramatically when she saw Jesus.

'There he is,' she shrieked. She dashed across the stage and grabbed Jesus by the ear. 'Where have you been, you bloody wee brat?' she yelled. 'Just wait till I get you home!'

'But... but,' said Jesus, 'I had to tell these 'uns about my father's business.'

Mary's eyes flashed in the manner that won Katherine Hepburn an Oscar.

'Oh aye' she said. She swung around, pointing at Joseph, 'Well, what he knows about business wouldn't take too long to tell.'

A Sense of Presence

HOLDING COURT
Mae Leonard

She's there again. That Woman. I grasp the edge of the counter with the tips of my fingers and lift myself high enough to see her.

'Hello love!'

I drop back down again in my confusion at being spotlighted. That woman would surely speak to me again so I hide myself in the space under the counter hoping that she'll forget about me and start talking. She's a great talker.

'Givus a Woodbine, Ka, and put it on the book.'

My Auntie Kathleen gropes under the counter for the open packet of Woodbines. I push it into her hand. She flicks the top open and withdraws a single cigarette. I know the ritual so well, I hand the matches to her – she snaps one into flame and leans over the counter. I hear That Woman draw in a deep breath, exhale with mighty satisfaction, cough a great chesty rattle and then she begins to tell one of her stories. I watch the grey-blue column of smoke rise above the counter up into the air, it swirls magically and I think of a genie. The sulphur of the match added to the smoky smell means that she can stay a long time telling the latest episode of her eventful life.

I'll never forget that. I'll never forget That Woman. She trots out all sorts of tales while she enjoys the Woodbine right down to the smallest bit. So closely does she smoke the cigarette that her upper lip is permanently brown – as iodine coloured as her index finger and thumb.

Sometimes I sneak along to the other end of the counter to observe her undetected. In my six-year old eyes, she's a large lady with a moon-shaped face that has threads of broken veins purpling it. Her tweed coat is shorter than the skirt, which hangs lankly some inches below it. The buttons are strained over her broad chest giving her a slightly humped appearance. A woollen headscarf holds the pepper and salt hair in check.

Other customers come into the little shop. They buy their few groceries – bread, milk, butter, sugar and tea and go off on their business. That Woman remains and continues her conversation with my Auntie Kathleen, entertaining those who care to listen. I think That Woman is the most interesting person alive. She has time to tell yarns to 'beat the band', as Auntie Kathleen says to me and to me she's a storyteller to the power of brilliant. When my mother comes to collect me, I'm reluctant to leave.

Occasionally I'm sent down to That Woman's house in the Lane, with a box of leftover vegetables or bread. I think her family has a wonderful time. They don't have to wash and they have a house that doesn't ever have to be cleaned or anything. There's plaster, like chalk, crumbling off the walls and you can pick it off to draw pictures on the path. The bottom of the front door has been gnawed into a jagged edge like a lace border. There's a combination of smells, smoke and dampness, that is acceptable to me because it's part and parcel of That Woman.

Now the world knows her as Angela, she of The Ashes. But she'll never be anything but Mrs McCourt to me.

IMAGES OF CONSTANCE MARKIEVICZ
Ivy Bannister

In 1914 at the age of forty-six the Countess Markievicz posed as Joan of Arc to raise funds for the Irish Women's Franchise League. She stands, dramatic in her armour, sword uplifted, eyes glowing with divine fervour. It's a witty photograph that reveals, I believe, how clearly Constance Markievicz identified with her sainted predecessor, another selfless, cheery nationalist bent upon sending the English packing.

The image must have horrified Constance's mother, Lady Gore-Booth of Sligo, who didn't want a rebel heroine for a daughter. For in earlier years, when Lady Gore-Booth could shape her daughter's image, Constance was always pictured in the conventional, ascendancy way. At twelve, she was painted as the well-dressed daughter of the big house, her back aristocratically straight, as she keeps watch over her younger sister.

By eighteen, she was photographed as a debutante, exquisitely formal in snowy white, gloves to the elbow, a fan and dainty satin pumps. Through presenting her thus at Dublin Castle and in Queen Victoria's Court, Lady Gore-Booth intended her daughter to find her destiny in marriage to another moneyed member of the Protestant ascendancy, and in half-a-dozen healthy offspring to perpetuate her class.

Young Constance had different ideas. Liking nothing better than a wild gallop across the countryside, she remained unimpressed by her swarms of suitors.

'Jam, jelly and bread,' she snorted into her diary about one. She made another toss his hat into the air for her to shoot at. And when a third slipped his hand onto her thigh at a formal dinner, she lifted it gleefully into the air, announcing, 'Just look at what I've found in my lap.'

Fortunately, Constance was blessed with an artistic ability that enabled her to break from expectation. It began as a few lessons during the season. Then, after persistent badgering, she was allowed study art full time at the Slade in London.

Now with Lady Gore-Booth safely distant in Sligo, the young woman began to forge her own image. She had herself photographed – smocked and smoking – in her studio, a dishevelled Bohemian chaos. Her mother turned a blind eye, hoping perhaps that the phase would pass, and that time might see her daughter's return to the stately fold.

Instead, the industrious art student was accepted by the Atelier Julian in Paris, where she bought herself a ring and declared herself married to art. Now, at the ripe age of thirty, Constance did fall in love, totally inappropriately, with a penniless Polish Count, another art student, who, although six years her junior, had already been married, and was a father and a Catholic to boot.

Blithely, Constance commemorated the event with a photograph, upon which her mother must have gazed with horrified fascination. For in the photograph, Count Casimir's arm is draped informally around Constance's waist and they are both dressed in bicycling gear. It was a daring, even shocking pose for 1899 for Constance's knickerbockers reveal her legs completely beneath the knee.

To my mind, this splendid, happy photograph marks a point of no return, shattering forever her mother's picture of Constance, declaring in black and white that whatever Constance soon-to-be Markievicz might choose to do with her future, it would be both whole-hearted and unpredictable.

THE DOCTOR'S DILEMMA
Frances Donoghue

In 1865, before the days of tabloids, a sensational story hit the headlines in the English press. The background to the story was this.

A young man qualified as a doctor at the University of Edinburgh in 1812. He was a slight energetic youth with a pale face and red hair. After graduation the young man promptly joined the British Army as a Hospital assistant, but he wasn't long advancing himself. Within three years he was a distinguished surgeon and was posted to the garrison at Cape Town. His reputation grew rapidly. He performed the first emergency Caesarean operation on the wife of a Cape Town merchant – saving both mother and child; an accomplishment which came thirteen years before such operations were performed in England. And the grateful parents named the child after the young surgeon: James Barry.

Barry spent a long and busy life in the army – the next 58 years in fact – in a series of postings from Africa to the West Indies. His initiative and spirit were formidable. He challenged authority on matters of principle again and again and usually won.

At the outbreak of the Crimean war in 1854, Barry was close on sixty years old but took care of 500 sick and wounded on the island of Corfu. Before retiring five years later he became the Inspector General of Hospitals with the matching rank of Major General. All in all, a glowing career in a fairly predictable pattern. Now comes the point where the predictability fell apart, in spectacular fashion.

The morning in 1865 when James Barry – old, frail and alone – was found dead in bed, a cleaning woman was called in to prepare the body for burial. Shortly after, a commotion broke out and she ran from the room in hysterics. Major General Barry's body was that of 'a perfect female' she declared. Indeed, she had more colourful information to impart. The stretch marks seen on the major general's stomach were characteristic of a woman who had borne a child.

The newspapers had a field day. There was a rather awed recognition of the extraordinary determination which enabled a woman to function for forty years as an officer in the British service, to have fought at least one duel, and carry a high public profile in the pursuit of professional goals. Said the Manchester Guardian in its elegant way: 'An incident is just now being discussed in military circles so extraordinary that were not the truth capable of being vouched for by official authority, the narration would certainly be deemed incredible.'

James Barry – that's what the tombstone calls her – is buried in Kensal Green, in London. Who was she? Who were her parents? Who was the father of her child and what became of the child? There are no answers.

A simpler question to ask is 'Why?' Presumably because she was born a century too soon. She had the intelligence, ambition and determination to be a doctor and an outstanding one, and the early nineteenth century put that out of a woman's reach. She paid an appalling price in evasions and disguises of all outward expressions of her nature to achieve her ambition, and she got away with it.

Sadly, her achievement has never been acknowledged by the medical profession. If you look up the first woman to qualify as an MD, it is alleged to have been one Elizabeth Blackwell, at the Geneva Medical College in New York in 1849 – thirty-seven years after James Barry left Edinburgh clutching that precious diploma.

DESPERATELY SEEKING CHARLOTTE
Sylvia Sands

It's an ongoing joke with my closest friends, that when introducing me to anyone new at parties, they warn 'Now Sylvia's fine… just as long as you don't mention *Jane Eyre*, *Wuthering Heights* or *The Tenant of Wildfell Hall*.' Well all right, I'll own up then – I'm not so much a Brontë buff as a downright Brontë bore. One languid literary acquaintance announced, 'Oh yeah… *nothing* dates you more than a pash on those dreary sisters!'

Now I love them all, but it's Charlotte and her book *Jane Eyre* that really have my heart – which dates me indeed, for yes, I spent my youth listening for the sound of hooves and waiting for Mr Rochester. Strange isn't it, the people who inspire you? Well as I'm something of a depressive, over the years, Charlotte Brontë and her brave and lonely struggle with isolation and the bereavement of her mother and all five siblings, has strengthened and steadied me. So when last summer several kind friends – possibly in an effort to cure me of Brontë-mania – clubbed together and sent me to stay in a three-hundred-year-old hotel in the village of Haworth in Yorkshire, where the three sisters and their brother, Branwell, grew up… it was Charlotte I hoped to discover.

Odd then, that in the Brontë Parsonage Museum, it was the black horsehair sofa where Emily died that had me holding back the tears; it was the old china bowl and wooden rolling pin lying on the scrubbed-to-whiteness pine table where Emily made bread while learning German from a propped-up book that took my breath away. And upstairs, despite Charlotte's tiny muslin dress and gentle green and white wedding bonnet (in which parishioners said she looked like a snowdrop), it was Emily's narrow, bitterly cold bedroom overlooking the graveyard out to her beloved moors, where Heathcliffe and Cathy and warm hearted Nellie Dean had been created, that held me, head bowed in silence.

And as for the moors themselves – over which I rambled and climbed each day to Top Withens, the site of *Wuthering Heights,* every sweep of blue hill, every bird tumbling in the sky, every dramatic crag and darkling rock, all the vast-going-on-forever sky, cried, 'Emily, Emily!' just as in her one book Cathy had cried 'Heathcliffe, Heathcliffe'.

'I'll find Charlotte in the family church,' I thought. But in an encounter of pure surrealism at Morning Prayer, sitting in the pew next to me, fixing me with a basilisk stare, was one of the rooks that caw and circle the tall trees in the churchyard. 'Emily,' said his beady eye to me. For it was Emily who constantly brought home wounded birds from the Moors – including a Merlin hawk – and nursed them back to flight.

So though, it was brave Charlotte who I went to Haworth to find, it was the mystical, reclusive Emily I met at every twist and turn. Charlotte, of course, specially loved Emily, and considered her – as do modern scholars – the true genius of the family. Now that I'm several months back home in Belfast, I do not love Charlotte any less but I sort of wonder if back in Haworth, she stepped softly into the shadows as if to say to me, 'Meet the greatest of the Brontës – my dear sister, Emily.'

THE POET
Francis Harvey

Picture, if you can, a boy who at that time wanted, more than anything else in the world, to be a poet. A boy sitting at an upstairs window overlooking green fields, a wide river full of salmon, an ancient town and bridge, a gapped greystone eel-weir, and, in the distance, mountains and the sea. Picture as well in bed in that room a man time had beached among the blankets and pillows like a dying seal beached by the tide. A very old man who keeps telling that boy, over and over again, about how when *he* was a boy he once saw, and only once, a now long-dead poet walking through the fields by the winding banks of the river that flowed past outside and of how the poet had stopped to have a word with him and to give him a hard sweet to suck.

And in that room, after all these years, the boy, who is now a man, can still smell the compounded smells of sickness and new-mown grass. In that room with its big brass bedstead whose shining convex knobs reflected the distorted images of both of them, the boy, who is now a man, can still hear the old man repeating the story of his childhood encounter with the poet as he sits there looking out at the fields where the poet had walked, sacred ground to him, as were the river and the waterfalls and the bridge and the eel-weir and the town. And he would imagine he could see the figure of the dead poet clambering maybe over a low limestone wall or stopping to look at one of the waterfalls between whose white cascades stood the house in which all this was happening so many years ago. And he would begin to whisper the names of the places the poet had hallowed with his presence, Tullan, Camlin, The Commons, Bulliebawns, Coolmore, Kildoney, Portnason, The Knather, and The Mall, while the old man, in a voice that had begun to quaver with weakness and age and yet was still audible, not hearing him but seeing his lips move, would ask him what he was saying. And when he'd tell him, he'd begin to recite a stanza from the work of the poet he had once encountered on the riverbank and whose poetry he knew by heart, and the boy would join in a voice as low as the voice of the waterfalls in summer, both of them unaware that it might be the last time they would ever do this together. Both would recite a single stanza, for this was all the old man was capable of now, from William Allingham's *Adieu to Belashanny*.

Farewell to every white cascade from the Harbour to Belleek;

And every pool where fins may rest, and ivy-shaded creek;

The sloping fields, the lofty rocks, where ash and holly grow,

The one split yew-tree gazing on the curving flood below.

DARLING DAISY
Monica Henchy

Strange how a chance phrase can dredge up a flood of memories from your subconscious. This happened to me some time ago when I visited Warwick Castle. Now administered by Madame Tussaud's, it shows a panorama of English history and contains the most life-like figures of the main players in English society and politics. But it was only when we reached the bedroom where the figure of Frances, Countess of Warwick, was having her hair dressed, that a real butler wearing white gloves appeared and explained the scene. He told us that when the Prince of Wales, later to be Edward VII, visited the castle his room was always close to that of the Countess. Her nightly glass of milk was left in a prominent position outside her door. If the milk were untouched Edward could not enter, but if half of the milk had been drunk then his 'Darling Daisy', as he always called her, was ready. When I heard the phrase 'Darling Daisy' it immediately rang a bell in my memory. Where had I heard it before? And then it all came tumbling back. I had heard this very phrase in Lady Warwick's other residence, Easton Lodge in Essex, over sixty years ago. We were living in Essex and my father, who was secretary of a small poetry society, arranged through a friend a visit to Easton Lodge as Lady Warwick liked to be known as a patroness of the arts. There was an aviary with 500 birds and a pony sanctuary so I was brought along as I loved animals.

When I returned home from Warwick Castle after my recent visit I ran to look at the family album. Yes, I was right. Two of the photos still survived. Photographed beside her famous lily pool were some of the poets with Lady Warwick in the centre, and there I am in the front, clutching a peacock feather and looking as bored as only a five-year-old can, and quite unimpressed that the Countess has her gloved hand protectively on my head.

And who was this famous lady? Born in 1861, Frances Maynard, called Daisy because of her cloud of blonde hair, was the heir to Viscount Maynard and the great house at Easton Lodge. Disraeli seeing her at the theatre suggested to Queen Victoria that this beautiful girl with an income of over £30,000 per annum would be an ideal bride for her youngest son, Prince Leopold, but Leopold explained to Daisy that his affections were otherwise involved – much to Daisy's relief as hers were too. At twenty she married Francis Greville who was heir to the Earl of Warwick. It was the society wedding of the year with chief guests, the Prince and Princess of Wales. The marriage register was signed by the Prince of Wales who seven years later was to become Daisy's lover.

When her husband became the Earl of Warwick, Francis and Daisy moved from Easton to Warwick Castle where Daisy gave the most lavish parties. However, the extravagance of one of the balls she gave was harshly criticised in a socialist journal called *The Clarion*. This infuriated Daisy so much that she travelled to London to remonstrate with the editor. But instead it was he who converted her to socialism and, from then on, she devoted herself to good causes, founding a home for disabled children and a technical college for women. She campaigned for the Labour party and even fought – and lost – as Labour candidate for Warwick.

Her motto was: 'Our only understanding of money lies in the spending not in the making of it', and she certainly threw it around like confetti. Her extravagance led her to bankruptcy which she tried to overcome by writing her memoirs and including Edward's love letters to her. But the Palace quickly got an injunction preventing her from publishing the royal letters. However, she still succeeded in writing a colourful account of her life without them!

Such was Daisy's personal charm that her patient husband, despite his misgivings, stood by her in all her difficulties. She returned to her beloved Easton where she could now entertain her socialist friends such as the Webbs, Bernard Shaw and Ramsay McDonald. She lent her cottage to H.G. Wells who brought celebrities like Arnold Bennett, Charlie Chaplin and John Galsworthy. Even Lily Langtry, her predecessor as mistress to the prince, was lavishly entertained.

But back to the photos. This portly figure with a huge hat and enveloped in a fur stole bears little relationship to the willowy slender figure of the 1880s but the aristocratic pose is still there. And on the day that photograph was taken I can remember going home in the car. There I was, a five-year-old, listening to the adults telling stories about Daisy's romantic escapades. At the time I was puzzled why everyone was laughing so much. But now I know!

EATING AN ICE CREAM CONE
Cyril Kelly

It was a sweltering day and the sash-windows of our third class were opened as wide as possible to gulp any stray puff of fresh air. Outside swallows were arcing like black bolts of voltage against the blue sky. Master McMahon had had to call on all his stamina and wizardry to keep forty of us on our collective mettle since early morning. But, as the minute hand of the school clock flicked towards three, there was one delightful twist left in the day.

Pressing the blackboard firmly against the easel, he wrote the title of the story we were getting for homework, namely 'Eating an Ice Cream Cone'. Then turning to face us and, without uttering a word, he pushed up the white cuffs of his shirtsleeves as far as they would go. In the expectant hush, he slowly undid the strap of his rectangular watch and placed it on the table.

From that moment his stern eyes no longer needed to demand our attention. He had become a nine-year-old boy approaching the high windowsill of our classroom to buy a cone. Nobody in the class dared to blink, I hardly allowed myself to breathe. We saw him proffer his money up to some shopkeeper who must have been as gigantic as Fionn McCumhal. We were parched as we waited for him to be served. Occasionally the raucous call of a rook ripped the backdrop of silence which was the only prop for his performance.

As our Marcel Marceau turned away from the counter, we were entranced by his widening, expectant eyes. We salivated as, firstly, he licked his lips and then fastened a fond smile on his upheld fist. We, too, agonised on how best to tackle this cone which had materialised before our hungry eyes. Should he lick the quiff of soft ice cream that drooped with a cowlick at the apex, or should he tackle the fronds melting over the crisp edge of the cone?

Forever the *agent provocateur* against predictability, he suddenly raised the ice cream, got his mouth under the golden tip and snipped off the plain bit at the end. The crumbling cone crackled in every inner ear and brought more water to our teeth and we watched as, manfully, he tried to suck the ice cream through the small opening in the end.

The other classes were already on their noisy way out of the building but Master McMahon remained motionless, with his knees bent for balance, his head thrown back and his face upturned towards the ceiling. Frozen for a moment in that pose, he was the strong man in the circus, the base of the human pyramid, supporting the combined expectancy of forty spellbound boys. As he resumed sucking for ice cream, his cheeks grew more and more hollow. We could feel the ice cream offering stout resistance and we were craning forward on the edges of the benches, almost asphyxiated with anticipation, our cheeks also concave with phantom pain.

At last with a resounding pop, his cheeks relaxed and we knew that he had, finally, sucked an air hole through the dense ball of ice cream. The relief in that classroom was audible. What an expression of Dennis the Menace satisfaction Master McMahon had on his face! As he put on his watch again and before we could stretch out of our trance, he pointed to the words on the board and said:

'Tomorrow I'll give the price of an ice-cream to any boy who makes me taste the flavour of vanilla from his story.'

Ten years later, as a student teacher, I was assigned to Bryan McMahon's class for three weeks in May. One afternoon, when he had just given the class their story for homework (Oisin returns from Tir na nÓg), himself and myself were walking out of the school. Our footsteps resounded in the empty building. When we reached the gate the swallows were windsurfing the thermal rollers above the deserted playground. Bryan looked back at the building.

'You know,' he said, 'after all my years, the challenge is still the same; a child's mind is like an oyster. But unlike the pearl divers of Polynesia, the teacher can only open the shell with a blade called the imagination.'

COLLIE
Áine Mac Carthy

When my parents came to Monkstown in the years immediately following the last war, it was a quiet place. Rising in tiers to overlook Cork Harbour were the homes of many retired people whose genteel manners and customs were largely of a bygone era. As children we liked to visit a particular friend and neighbour of my parents called Miss Collins. I remember a huge hydrangea tree, which bloomed pink in summer, growing outside her door. To pass under the great bush meant a shower of drops after the rain as one bent low and parted the branches. My father offered to cut it back for her but Miss Collins liked it that way. I suppose having spent all of her working life in the centre of London, she enjoyed the wildness of it.

Although polite and always on our best behaviour with Miss Collins, we enjoyed her company. She was a gracious lady with a great smile that, even in her advanced years, lit up her face. She always called us 'my dear'. In fact she called everybody 'my dear' in her polished English accent and she liked us to call her 'Collie' as her friends in London had done.

The house reflected her refined taste with good quality furniture, some paintings and of course a photograph of her brother on the wall. At the end of her life Collie's great library was divided among her friends and I am pleased to have some books on my own shelf signed and dated by her.

Intelligent and well-read but, in spite of her considerable charm, Collie had strong opinions and liked to have things her way. She was a lady who spoke her mind. When my brother Daithí was born and given the second name of Micheál, having been born on the feast of St Michael, Collie did not like his name and told my mother so, declaring, 'Of course, my dear, I shall always call him Michael. I am sure you understand why.'

True to her word Daithí was always Michael to Collie. Out on the road with our baby brother we soon learned to accept that she would look in the pram and ask 'How is baby Michael today?' and as Daithí grew up he had to get used to being addressed as 'Michael my dear'. My mother explained this was because of her own brother killed during the civil war. We knew very little about her younger brother and the story of his death was not a very comfortable topic in our house. We were quite familiar with our country's recent struggle for Independence, with both parents telling many stories from their own youth such as watching the burning of Cork by the Black and Tans. Like many others of their generation however they had no stories for children of brave men and deeds of the civil war. To them it was a subject laden only with shame and regret and spoken of as little as possible.

Our friend lived to a great age but it was many years after her death that I, as an adult, found out for myself the full story of the life and death of Michael Collins, brother of Hannie, affectionately known as Collie to her friends.

THE DAY I MET PELE AND LIAM BRADY
Niall McGarrigle

I'll always remember the day I met Pele and Liam Brady. This happened in a back-garden in Santry during the winter of 1970, when I was ten years old. The occasion was my cousin's 13th birthday party. My cousin had told me about this fellow who lived near him who was so good at football, he could take on a whole team on his own and still beat them. I told him to pull the other one, that it had bells on it. Little did I know.

The main event of the party was the football match. The teams were picked. It was Liam Brady and a fellow called Pele Butler against the rest. Ten against two. Pele was skinny as a matchstick, he wore thick-lensed glasses, and he seemed to lack any trace of co-ordination. The worst footballer ever to grace any back garden, my cousin said.

There were whoops and shouts when Liam Brady tipped off. He ducked and weaved his way through the forest of opposition players, the ball never budging from his magical left foot. He came towards me; someone shouted, 'Tackle him'.

I was the last line of defence. The ball was there, all I had to do was kick it clear. Everyone was watching. This was the moment. Time seemed to stand still. I lunged into thin air. With a drop of a shoulder that was to become so familiar to millions around the world, Liam Brady changed directions. I looked around in time to see the ball whistle past our goalkeeper. Pele Butler let out a roar that very nearly stripped the paint off the gutters.

The game ended when Liam Brady said that he was 'knackered'. Needless to say, we lost. Inside, I heard my uncle say that hoards of people left 11 o'clock mass early on Sunday mornings just to watch the young Brady lad play.

Four years later, I went along to Dalymount Park to watch Liam Brady's debut for Ireland in that famous 3-0 victory over the USSR. His hair looked like a burst cushion but he was using precisely the same shimmies he used in that back-garden, and they were demolishing the cream of the USSR.

In 1979, Arsenal beat Manchester United 3-2 in one of the most breath-taking FA Cup finals ever. Liam Brady laid on the last-minute winning goal with the most sublime of passes, and straight after the match, on live TV, a suave interviewer asked him how he felt. 'I'm knackered,' the bould Liam replied.

FLYER IN SILK STOCKINGS
Frances Donoghue

Flying, in those dangerous years before we were all doing it without a thought, attracted vivid individualists of both sexes. They were people who had the talent to captivate the world's attention, and when they got it, to manipulate the subsequent publicity with charm and personality. Curiously, they were often good-looking people, which contributed to the 'star' image. Look at the list: Lindbergh, Earhart, Amy Johnson.

Sophie Pierce from Newcastle West in Limerick was in the same mould. A pretty woman, she was always photographed in that classical mannequin stance with one foot extended elegantly at a slight angle in front of the other – even if the outfit she was wearing was a leather flying jacket and a Biggles cap with earflaps. In 1928 when she flew from South Africa to London – the first solo flight from an overseas dominion to England – she emerged from the cockpit at Cairo in silk stockings, white gloves and a smart cloche hat brought along specially for the benefit of the newsmen and their cameras.

Sophie came to flying with a major track record already as the woman who had broken down the barrier of sex in sport. She held a world record herself in athletics with a high jump of 4'11" and did major pioneering work to admit her own sex to a field dominated by men. She wrote articles for newspapers on health, beauty and fitness, she published a book on athletics for women, she was asked by the International Athletics Federation to present the case for women's inclusion in the Olympic Games. When women were finally admitted into the Games in 1928, the groundwork had all been Sophie's.

On the flight back from a sports congress in Prague she was making agreeable conversation with an RAF captain when he offered to arrange some flying lessons for her. Perhaps she was ready for a new challenge after the pioneering negotiations for athletics. She accepted his offer with enthusiasm and so found her passion for the rest of her life. It did not escape her feminist politics that civil aviation was an ideal career area where women could assert their equality with men – physical size and strength would not be an issue. By 1925 she was a qualified pilot but her efforts to make a career of it met with the familiar brick wall. 'Women shall be excluded from any employment in the operating crew of aircraft engaged in public transport' was the ruling. Moreover, all candidates 'must have successfully undergone a medical examination at which he must have satisfied the following minimum requirements as to physical fitness. He must be of the male sex... ' No ambiguity there!

Of course Sophie took the establishment on. The tactics she had employed to gain the admission of women to the Olympic Games were brought out again. Lobbying (she got the backing of Lady Astor, the first woman MP), acquiring every conceivable qualification in her new skill, publishing a book on women and flying, keeping herself in the headlines by stunt flying, exhibition flights, a parachute jump of 15,000 feet. This final tour de force almost cost her her life because the plane's engine failed and she had to stay standing on the wing while the pilot made a forced landing.

The South Africa-England flight had huge publicity value, of which Sophie made the most. When she circled Croydon aerodrome with the faces of the large crowd turned up to meet her, she did a little loop over the landing field first to give them a little extra thrill. Predictably, the objections to being hired by a commercial airline vanished in the light of the stardom and she became a pilot with KLM in 1929. She was, however, used far more for demonstration flights and lectures – even a promotional film – than for ferrying the mail.

With a sad irony, the dazzling flying career came to a premature end in 1939 – not by plunging from the skies, but by falling down the stairs of a tramcar and dying of her injuries. Sophie was forty-three. She was cremated and her ashes were scattered over her hometown of Newcastle West.

THE REAL BIG TOM
Padraig McGinn

Now and then I watch the school children playing football. Their heroes are Giggs or Beckham, their favourite teams Manchester United, Arsenal or Liverpool. What a change television has brought about! When I was their age, our heroes were home-brewed: Big Tom and John Joe O'Reilly, Joe Keohane, Paddy Bawn Brosnan or Brendan Nestor. The voice of Michael O'Hehir on radio made them giants in our imaginations and we followed the fortunes of Cavan or Kerry or Galway county teams. There wasn't a soccer team within miles of our town, and we thought soccer was a game for mammy's boys.

When we played cowboys and Indians or cops and robbers, the biggest and toughest boys in our street always had to be the cowboys or the cops and the rest of us were the Indians or the baddies. Of course the baddies were always captured or shot. And when we played football in Caraher's field or Ward's meadow, they were always Cavan and we were Kerry. Cavan always beat Kerry in Ward's meadow.

We knew the names of all the famous footballers and it was quite common for the members of both teams to give running commentaries on the game as it progressed, calling themselves by the names of their idols. My idol was Big Tom O'Reilly, from Cornafean, but I was never allowed to be Big Tom. That honour was strictly reserved for the top buck cat on the Cavan team and I was destined to be always on the losing side, Kerry or Galway. The captain of our side might call himself Joe Keohane or Paddy Bawn. I could be anyone I liked after that but Big Tom would scatter me on his way to scoring a goal or breaking up an attack.

We all knew how the real Big Tom kicked a dead ball from all the talk about him although none of us had ever seen him play. He placed the ball and stepped back ten or twelve paces. Then he took a few running steps forward, gave a little hop to adjust his stride, like a show jumper meeting a fence, a few more running steps and WHAM! The ball went sixty or seventy yards up the field or over the bar, as the situation required. Or so we liked to imagine. The essential part was the little hop in the middle of the run up. This often led to arguments and rows.

'You're not supposed to be Big Tom.'

'I never said I was.'

'Well you shouldn't be doing his run up.'

'That's my own run up.'

'You're a liar.'

'I'm going home.'

'Go home to your mammy.'

Eventually I did see the real Big Tom. It was near the end of his inter-county career and he was playing full-back for Cavan against Fermanagh, in the Ulster final. He didn't have many kick-outs from goal – Cavan won easily – but he did the little hop in the middle of his run-up, just as I had been doing all those years ago. I was glad to know that I had got the steps right, even if I was never allowed to be Big Tom in Ward's meadow.

THE GIRLS
Aodhan Madden

They came every Monday night for supper. Mother called them 'the girls' but Alice and her sister Mary were well past their prime when they used to sit by our fireside on winter nights, nibbling roast beef sandwiches and revelling in the gossip of the parish.

On the surface they were the epitome of maidenish rectitude. We all had to be on our very best behaviour when 'the girls' arrived with the customary bag of assorted sweets. They came after the Monday evening devotions in the parish church. They seemed to exude a certain odour of sanctity and their visits always began with a recitation of what we came to call their 'sorrowful mysteries' – all the aches and pains and disappointments which had beset them since the week before.

There was only one man in their lives – and he was the great comedian Jimmy O'Dea. The very mention of his name and their sad faces would suddenly light up with illicit pleasure. Mother always knew precisely when to introduce the subject of Jimmy O'Dea into the proceedings. Just on the point when Alice or May was getting carried away by some painful bunion or a lingering cold, she would strike, cutting the self-pity like a knife through blancmange. I can still hear their laughter pealing through the house as they described the latest sketch that their hero had adorned. The more risqué the sketch, the more hysterical was their laughter.

Alice and May followed Jimmy O'Dea's shows everywhere in Ireland and Britain. They planned their holidays to take in shows in places like Scunthorpe or Newcastle or Birkenhead and every new sketch was reported back to our fireside with a breathless delight that seemed like madness.

The highlight of their year, of course, was the Gaiety pantomime. Every St Stephen's night they set off in their taxi dressed up to the nines like two opera dowagers. They always brought with them a huge box of chocolates which they munched in the parterre while they waited like two over-grown and over-excited schoolgirls for the orchestra to strike up and their hero to appear.

They brought me along with them one year. I was about eight and had never been inside a theatre before. I remember the huge excitement as the great red curtain slowly rose to reveal a world of Arcadian magic. The pantomime was 'Babes in the Wood' and the stage was a riot of colour as dancers tumbled out of fairytale windows and a girl dressed like Robin Hood sang 'Younger Than Springtime' from *South Pacific*.

Then suddenly, the whole theatre rocked with laughter. May almost leapt out of her seat with excitement.

'Look at him. *Look* at him!' she squealed.

Jimmy O'Dea appeared at the top of an illuminated staircase. He was wearing the most outrageous dress I'd ever seen and on top of his head was a gigantic contraption that looked like a wedding cake. He moved down a step and the theatre roared again as little candles flickered on the cake. Alice and May were now clutching each other and screaming with delight.

But what fascinated me was the strange garden gnome face beneath the wedding cake and those great dark octopal eyes which slowly moved across everyone in the theatre and then homed in on me. Jimmy O'Dea then winked a black feathery wink and a mischievous smile crept up his face. He passed some remark to the audience which sent Alice and May into further convulsions. Then the orchestra struck up again and O'Dea continued on down the staircase.

So this was their hero, this little man in a ridiculous frock! I was a little bemused that the two grown women had given their hearts so completely to such strangeness. And yet, as the pantomime continued, I found myself drawn increasingly to this man, to the huge black eyes, to the comic outrage in his voice, to something unsettling yet funny in the way he moved about the stage as a woman, in the way he communed with each one of us personally.

In the taxi going home Alice and May sat back in silent pleasure. Then May whispered one word out the window to the passing night.

'Magic,' she said.

HUMANITY DICK
Barbara McKeon

When we found a lost little cat wandering around a car park, we took it to the Galway Society for the Prevention of Cruelty to Animals, where it would be taken care of until either its owner was found or it could be re-homed.

We then went into Neachtain's pub for a well-deserved pint, commenting on what wonderful organisations animal protection societies are. And to think it all began right here in Galway. Perhaps even in this very pub, we mused, for Neachtain's on Quay Street was the town house of Richard Martin, whose humanitarian work to alleviate the suffering of domestic animals led directly to the founding of the R.S.P.C.A in London in 1824.

Born on the family estate at Dangan, County Galway, in 1754, Richard Martin was to become famous as Humanity Dick, a nickname bestowed on him by King George IV. He was from an illustrious old family that had come to Ireland in the eleventh century. By the sixteenth century the Martins, one of the fourteen tribes of Galway, had established themselves as wealthy landowners with vast estates covering most of the county. To keep a hold of these lands, Richard had been brought up Protestant. He was educated at Harrow and Cambridge and groomed to stand for Parliament so he could fulfil his father's wishes and fight for Catholic Emancipation.

In 1776, aged twenty-two, he became MP for Galway and took his seat in Westminster, where he began a long and momentous parliamentary career not only fighting for the rights of the disenfranchised, but for the rights of animals. For this he received much ridicule from the press and pamphleteers and was laughed at by the ruling elite who cared little what suffering animals endured, as long as it wasn't the adored lapdogs of wealthy ladies.

Martin was appalled by the atrocities he witnessed in the knackers' yards of Whitechapel, and in 1824 he introduced the Slaughter of Horses Bill, for the reasonable care of horses prior to their slaughter. The Bill was defeated in Parliament but a month later a meeting of concerned individuals took place in a London coffee house at which was established a society to fight for the proper care of all domestic animals, the Society for the Prevention of Cruelty to Animals.

Martin was also known to intervene physically whenever he saw acts of cruelty, such as restraining a sheep drover in Smithfield market who had deliberately broken a sheep's leg. On another occasion, he avenged the wanton shooting dead of an Irish wolfhound owned by his friend Lord Altamont by challenging the perpetrator, an arrogant young aristocrat, George Robert Fitzgerald, to a duel. This was a serious challenge, for Martin had also a famed reputation as a duellist, be it swords or pistols, which had earned him another sobriquet, Hair-Trigger Dick. He is alleged to have fought over one hundred duels, including one that caused the death of his own nephew.

When asked one time why he cared so much for animals, Richard Martin replied, 'Sir, an ox cannot hold a pistol.'

Humanity Dick died in Ballinahinch in 1834, ten years after founding a society that has spread world-wide, and for which countless numbers of domestic animals and pets and their owners are forever indebted.

ON THE TILES
Anne McSherry

My father was a vandal, a graffitist. He used to write and draw on the tiles surrounding the fireplace. In the Dublin suburb where I grew up, all the houses had the same tiled fireplaces in the dining room. Those tiles were perfect for writing on – smooth, cream and matte-finished. He used a short stub of pencil, which he always kept behind his ear. It might have been only a shop-bill that he wrote or a calculation of the number of rolls of wallpaper needed for a certain room or a quick sum to check that he hadn't paid too much income tax!

But usually, it was more exciting. For us, his pencil was the key to the world's mysteries, the tiles the place where those mysteries were laid bare.

He drew for us the solar system: a spiky sun at the centre, the planets in tight ovals. The Earth, with a curved arrow over it like a halo, was shown spinning on its axis, as Copernicus had described. By the light of the fire, he bravely attempted to prove Einstein's theory of relativity with complicated mathematics; he even tried to draw the great man's concept of curved space. He drew pictures to illustrate the Northern Lights, the Aurora Borealis, and told us that Aurora was the Roman goddess of dawn. With little diagrams of tilting Earths, he showed us why autumn days are shorter than summer days. When the tiles beside him filled up, he would lick his thumb and wipe it all away – a fresh slate.

He wrote poems on the tiles. 'Fear no more the heat o' the sun…'

He taught me that poem by the fireside. When I had one verse by heart, he'd lick his thumb and erase that verse, and so I would start on the next. Long tracts of *The Ballad of Reading Gaol* and *The Deserted Village* were spread on the tiles, like bolts of precious fabric unfurled, uncurled. A line he wrote from Omar Khayyám stays with me still, 'the moving finger writes and having writ, moves on… '

He wrote puzzles and conundrums on the tiles before going out in the mornings; we would work on them during the day, and write an answer before he returned. We became vandals too! He loved woodwork: he would draw dovetail and housing joints in cross-section on the tiles and demonstrate how the pieces should fit together like a jigsaw.

My father has long since gone and that house has been sold and somehow I am sure the new residents do not write on the tiles. I often wonder though, if all the words he ever wrote might still hang there in the air around the tiles like a mist. Maybe on a winter's night, they whisper their truths and secrets to the stranger sitting at what used to be our fireside.

I HEAR YOU CALLING ME
Marie MacSweeney

I admit to being a bit of a sceptic where car boot sales are concerned. I distrust the tall tales of those who claim to have captured prize pieces at such events – a Meissen plate, for instance, unrecognised as such by the seller, and secured for just a few shillings, or a fine porcelain vase which made its way from the orient over several, history-laden centuries, and was then offered to bored punters for peanuts. Such bargains never come my way. And why on earth, I ask, should they always bypass me?

Recently these thoughts came unbidden to my mind when I was invited to support a car boot sale, and were instantly dismissed when I heard of the charity involved. I turned up at the venue, wandered around for a while until I came to a stall carrying a selection of records. After a nostalgic rummage among the 78s, I moved to more recent times – and vinyl LPs. It was there that I found my treasure – an early recording of our own Irish tenor, Dermot Troy. It was made by the Avoca Record company of Brooklyn, New York, and included such favourites as 'She Is Far From The Land', 'At The Mid Hour Of Night' and 'The Lark In The Clear Air'.

When I played the record later that evening I was both thrilled and saddened to hear again the voice I had heard sing out over those famous crowds in Crumlin many decades ago.

You see, although born in Wicklow, Dermot was regarded as a 'home-grown' boy by the people of Crumlin. And after a short career in the R.A.F. he began to nurture his vocal talent, studying at the Royal Irish Academy of Music and winning the prestigious Caruso Competition in 1952. As a result he was invited to join the Glyndebourne Chorus, and this was followed by a three-year stint at Covent Garden. He also carried out a successful tour of Germany over a period of several years, and his playing of Lensky in Tchaikovsky's

Eugene Onegin, performed in April 1962, was his last performance. He died in September of the same year at the tragically young age of thirty five. But on one of Dermot's visits home, his fame having preceded him, crowds collected outside his home in Cashel Road in Crumlin. And I was among the many youngsters there, attracted by the glamour and excitement of the occasion, and determined to help provide a decent 'Welcome Home' for the local boy-made-good. For his part, Dermot repaid his friends, neighbours and fans by singing for us. He stood just inside the open front window of the upstairs bedroom and sang, his sweet powerful voice rising like a prayer, on the evening air.

I can't recall which songs he selected on that balmy night, but in listening to my newly acquired record, I fancied he finished up with the song 'I Hear You Calling Me'.

> 'I hear you calling me.
> You called me when the moon hath veiled her light,
> before I went from you into the night.
> I came, do you remember, back to you,
> for one last kiss, beneath the kind stars' light.'

AS OTHERS SAW US
Bernard Share

Lord Byron was here, of course. But then so were Hemingway, and Stravinsky, and Charlie Chaplin and Noel Coward, and Nabokov, and Ustinov, and even a few of the wandering Irish. Louis Brennan, eccentric engineer and inventor, is buried here, as is Edmund Ludlow, Cromwell's brutal commander in Ireland. Yes, this singularly picturesque stretch of Switzerland's Lake Geneva – Montreux, Vevey and the hills behind – has attracted more than its fair share of the illustrious. And not only for tax reasons. It is very much, as Olda Kokoschka put it to me, at the centre of things; you can be almost anywhere in Europe within a couple of hours.

After the statue of Chaplin, the tomb of Edmund Ludlow, the shuttered, undistinguished house of Noel Coward, the hotel where Nabokov holed up after the success of *Lolita*, the chance of a live encounter was not to be missed. Realising, however, that my knowledge of the Austrian artist Oscar Kokoschka was embarrassingly minimal, I had trawled a local bookshop for information, emerging somewhat surprised, not with a volume of art reproductions but with a solid paperback of imaginative and colourful autobiography recording his peripatetic experiences in Vienna, Berlin, Cyprus, Stockholm, Jericho...

and Ireland. I felt, in spite of the book's title, *Mirages of the Past*, on firmer ground.

Olda Kokoschka welcomed us into the house a bit beyond the Château de Chillon which she and Kokoschka – she referred to him always by his surname – had built when they settled in Switzerland in 1953.

'This is the room where he worked,' she told us – a room, though he died in 1980, still hung with his paintings.

'When we built this it would have been quite easy to make light from the roof,' she explained. 'He didn't want it because he said it would look like a work room, "like somewhere I *have* to work! I want to work when I feel like it!" '

There was something about that approach to the daily business of creation that kept coming back to me as Madame Kokoschka began to talk about her late husband's involvement with Ireland. She had met him in her native Prague in 1938 when he was already in his fifties and, though thirty years his junior, married him after arranging their escape to England from the mounting Nazi terror which was particularly directed at the school of 'degenerate' artists which he represented. Before leaving Britain after the war they had visited Ireland together 'for a long weekend', as Olda Kokoschka recalled. She remembered being taken to see round towers, and meeting Jack B. Yeats, who, she said, 'was charming, very sweet. We went together to a regatta.' Yeats, himself no mean writer, must have delighted in the brief encounter with a fellow multi-talented spirit.

It was a much earlier visit, in 1929, long before his marriage to Olda, that, as she put it, had aroused Kokoschka's great sympathy for the imagination of the Irish.

'He was a storyteller,' she said, 'he depended on an audience, and when people were interested or impressed he made it very much richer.'

So his 'letters of a traveller in an imaginary world' as he described them, were not to be taken entirely at face value. Did he really, one wonders, persuade the curator of Dublin's National Museum to let him try to get a note out of an old Celtic horn and, having failed, to send for a musician from the Municipal orchestra, who could do no better? The stories became even more bizarre when, in the course of another visit, he travels west to an island which remains unidentified but sounds on the evidence not a million miles from Aran. This was 1945, but the Ireland he describes seems to be set firmly in the realms of some mythical past. He falls in with fiddle-playing, whiskey-drinking vagabonds, donkeys more real than living man and a formidable red-headed Irish woman, 'with a prehistoric look about her,' he writes, 'like a flesh-and-blood Valkyrie'. Kokoschka's Ireland is a fascinating product of his own unique vision and the spell which the country quite clearly laid upon him.

As we talked, Olda Kokoschka recalled other Irish associations, in particular visits of the Abbey Theatre to London with the plays of Synge when they were still living there during the post-war years. And I realised, rather guiltily, that I had failed to ask the prescribed questions about the artist's life in Vienna café society, his tempestuous love affair with the widow of the composer Gustav Mahler, his first world war service with the Austrian cavalry, the school of painting he founded in Salzburg, his expressionist plays which are sometimes still performed, or indeed about a dozen other facets of the life and work of this remarkable man. But this unquestionably cosmopolitan lady, with a life in half of Europe behind her, had seemed content to talk of a country they had touched but briefly, but which had clearly touched them, leaving its mark, however lightly, upon them.

'Ireland, the Emerald Isle,' Kokoschka had written in 1945, 'is green like the colour of hope. In my experience it is the only promise made by Cook's Travel Agency which does not turn out to be a fairy story.'

LAUGHING AT THE ENEMY
Sheila Smyth

Outside the town of Tallow stands the beautiful Georgian mansion of Lisfinny. Near it stands the ruin of Lisfinny Castle, a tower house dating from Geraldine times. Sedately, they both look down on the quiet meanderings of the River Bride. A hundred years ago, this extensive property was owned by the colourful Jasper Douglas Pyne.

In 1888, orders were sent out that Pyne should be arrested. Home Rule MP for West Waterford and a tireless agitator for land reform, Pyne had infuriated the RIC (Royal Irish Constabulary), by publicly speaking out against their actions in Mitchelstown; the police had fired into a defenceless crowd and killed three people, a sort of nineteenth century Bloody Sunday.

Leaving the comforts of his Georgian mansion, Pyne took up residence at the top of his ancient tower house to escape arrest. With the help of his many followers, he destroyed the entrance to the castle and then proceeded to block the high, mural stairway with an endless stream of ploughs, harrows and hawthorn bushes. The police made only one abortive attempt on it.

Pyne stocked his larder with ample provisions and even kept a goat in his eyrie for his daily supply of fresh milk. A man of ingenuity and humour, he rigged up a pulley system whereby he could sit in a huge bucket and lower himself to within feet of the heads of his supporters. From this vantage point, he could address the devotees who came daily to hear him.

Word of the dramatic self-imprisonment and the witty speeches spread throughout the land, and soon thousands flocked to the banks of the Bride. The RIC boiled with indignation, for the irreverent Pyne made jokes at their expense from his dangling pulpit, and they couldn't get near him.

One dusky winter evening, they decided to pounce. But, unknown to them, their plans had been uncovered.

Waiting until the bucket was within two feet of Pyne's audience, they charged. Mysteriously, at that very moment, a herd of cattle broke out of a nearby field and, mingling with the multitudes, completely foiled the sudden rush.

After much shouting, confusion and wasted time, the police were relieved to see that Pyne had remained in his swaying seat. Perhaps they could still haul him in and arrest him. He showed no signs of leaving.

Clutching ladders and ropes, they shouldered their way through the unobliging crowd, and eventually reached the man who had tortured and teased them to the very limits of their patience. Imagine their fury when they dragged down the bucket and found, not the irrepressible Jasper Douglas Pyne, but a realistic-looking effigy.

Their quarry had escaped from the other side of the castle during the mêlée, jumped into a jarvey car on the Fermoy Road, and travelled to Cork where a fishing boat awaited him. That night, he sailed for France.

If, on a dark, winter evening, you stand beneath Lisfinny's ivied walls, it's said you can sometimes hear the sound of distant, mocking laughter.

MALCOLM
Richard Craig

Far from Skibbereen, Paddy and I were in Fort William. The war had just ended and we were enjoying the new freedom of travel abroad. This was the beginning of our first walking tour of the Scottish Highlands.

We decided to head as far north as possible before seeking a place to shelter for the night. Our rucksacks and boots were new and we were disappointed that nobody observed our good looks and how fast we walked. As it grew dark the surrounding mountain seemed to become larger and more mysterious. Being inexperienced we had overloaded our rucksacks and we were not accustomed to the weight or the newness of our boots. As a result our walking pace slackened due to painful feet. The wind rose to gale force and the rain poured down, battering against our faces and sapping our youthful enthusiasm. We decided to seek shelter.

We were both relieved and somewhat apprehensive as we approached a farmhouse where lights were still burning. A stout, pleasant-faced middle-aged lady opened the door and I let Paddy do the talking.

'I am Paddy Mulroy from Skibbereen and my friend and I wonder if we could sleep in your barn?'

'I am Mary MacDonald and you certainly can sleep in the barn.'

Soon we were in the barn happy to be lying in warm hay. It was the first time I had lain in hay and been covered by it. I fell asleep listening to the snores of the collie dog also sharing the barn but concealed by the almost total darkness.

Paddy, already washed and dressed, wakened me in the morning. Using the freezing water from the trough at the side of the barn, I washed, shivered and rubbed my skin hard with the towel. Suddenly I caught sight of a young man. He wore a khaki uniform and the beret and footwear of a commando. He smiled at me as though in welcome. I was about to call a greeting to him when he completely disappeared.

Back in the barn Paddy looked at me and asked, 'What's happened to you, you look as if you've just seen a ghost?'

'Perhaps I have,' I answered.

Seeing us approach the farmhouse, Mrs MacDonald opened the door and called on us to enter.

'Come in and have some breakfast,' she said.

We sat in silence enjoying the boiled eggs, toast and mugs of sweet steaming tea. Observing Paddy with a wistful look, Mrs MacDonald said.

'You boys remind me of my son Malcolm. He was your age when he went to the war.'

I had just been examining a framed photograph near me. It consisted of a group of young commandos looking bright and happy. My attention was drawn to a tall young soldier, he was wearing sergeant stripes and looked both handsome and fearless.

'Do you know those boys in that photograph Mrs MacDonald?' I asked. 'Somehow I get the feeling I have seen one of them somewhere.'

'Which one?' she asked and I pointed to the sergeant.

'Yes!' she said. 'That was Malcolm my son. He was a very brave boy and took part in many raids on the French coast. He was killed in Normandy on D-Day 1944.'

THE MULLINGAR MOSAICS
Mary Russell

In Mullingar Cathedral, there is a mosaic, executed by the Russian artist Boris Anrep, which when lit up, gleams like a cloth of gold. The mosaic was commissioned to celebrated the Marian Year of 1954. The subject is the Presentation in the Temple by St. Anne of her small daughter, Mary. It is the figure of Anne which dominates the picture, tall – much taller than her husband – she stands in the forefront giving an encouraging hand to her child. Anne wears a blue gown and over it hang the graceful folds of a red-lined yellow cloak. The child's gown is white shading into a blue which glimmers when caught by the light.

The whole piece stands about sixteen feet tall and maybe eight feet wide and it is only when you get close to it that you have some idea of the intricacy of the work, the skill of the executor and the scale of his undertaking. The tiny pieces of mosaic dance with light – brilliant red and orange alongside turquoise and yellow, the glaze of each piece sharp and clear. Using my hand to span one section, I counted 25 pieces, each minute square having its own place in the huge scheme. And on the tiled steps where the priest stands, I measured 440 pieces in one step alone.

This wasn't the first mosaic by Boris Anrep that I have seen. On the floor of the vestibule of the National Gallery in London is a series, also by him, entitled *Modern Virtues*. One of the virtues is based on a real woman and has its own story to tell.

It was in 1914, that the young Boris met, in St. Petersburg, the twenty-five-year-old poet Anna Akhmatova. He fell in love with her – as most men did – and though she valued his art and friendship, she was never able to match his passion. He was already building up his career in London but returned to fight for his country during the 1914-18 war. He begged Akhmatova to leave Russia and settle with him in London but it was a choice never open to her. Russia was her home and Russian her language. To leave would have meant a double exile. One of her poems to him touches on this:

> I have been silent since morning
>
> About what my dream sang to me.
>
> For the red rose and the moonbeam
>
> And for me – a single destiny.

Anrep left Russia forever although he never forgot Akhmatova. The virtue for which she is the model, in the National Gallery in London, is Compassion – a quality which shines through all her poetry.

In 1966, forty-nine years after Boris Anrep left Russia, the two met again when Akhmatova came to England to be honoured by Oxford University. He was nervous about meeting her, fearing that he would see himself grown old in her eyes. Akhmatova, though also vain, had been through too much to worry about such things. By then, she was a regal seventy-seven. That meeting, he said, 'was like being ushered into the presence of Catherine the Great.'

MEETING LAURENCE OLIVIER
Vona Groarke

My mother once had a drink with Laurence Olivier. It was a story I loved. Not that Laurence Olivier could hold a candle to David Essex or Donny Osmond in my young mind, but at least he was famous, good-looking and a definite movie star. This was a scarce commodity in Ballymahon – no matter how wide the main street, it was no Sunset Boulevard, and despite its best efforts, the River Inny never managed a majestic film-score sweep. When my primary school class was picked to star in a television ad about the Safe Cross Code, we imagined ourselves as Hollywood-bound. And in truth, we were probably the nearest things the town ever had to film stars. So to me, my mother's brush with celebrity was a tale of fabulous glamour and showtime glitz.

She had recently finished in secretarial school, where her strongest memory was of the night all the girls rushed to the dormitory window and broke into a round of the rosary with what they believed would be their final breaths, as they watched a flurry of German bombs rain down across the strand. Her first job was in an architect's office. One and six a week with just enough to cover digs and a slice of black bread for lunch. She would walk from Portobello Bridge to O'Connell Street and home. For her, that year was characterised forever by the feel of wet feet and the smell of damp on her lodging's walls. That, and of being introduced to Laurence Olivier, and hearing him speak her name.

Her architect boss had been employed to work on the set of Henry V, which was filmed in County Wicklow. At the end of the shoot, a lunch-party was thrown, to which she and her boss were asked. And so she found herself seated at a trestle table in an erstwhile film-set, with Laurence Olivier standing above her. A gentleman and a mannered host, he was ordering drinks for the guests. My mother had taken the pledge and was sworn off alcohol, so when he asked her what he could get for her, she pointed to a brightly-coloured sundae at another table and said, 'Mr Olivier, I'd like one of those.'

It seemed too sweet and it made her a little dizzy, but when he came round to ask again in that succulent voice of his, if she would like another, she thought it hardly polite to refuse the hospitality of a man so commanding, so well-spoken, so blue-eyed. After three gin cocktails, for that is what they were, my mother felt unwell. She rose from the table, reeled slightly on her feet, and was steadied by the accommodating hand of Olivier himself. Mortified, she excused herself from the company and took the bus back to her room in Portobello, slipping past the landlady's stern enquiring eye.

In the future, that afternoon would assume a magic glow. Not so much for her, but for myself, for whom the story was a detail from another life, in which my mother was not much older than me but yet had seen history happen in a bomb-lit sky; had survived the desolation of those damp, rented rooms; and had been made tipsy by Laurence Olivier in the star-filled hall of a castle in Agincourt.

A Sense of Pathos

O FOR THE WINGS OF A DOVE
Bryan Gallagher

He was standing behind me at the football match and he was shouting. Shouting those coarse meaningless phrases one sometimes hears at matches.

'Bury him!'

'Get stuck in!'

'Bog him!'

On and on and on.

I turned round to look at him. He had the flushed face and bloodshot eyes of the heavy drinker. His hair was thin and receding, he had the beginnings of a beer belly and he sucked deeply on the cigarette butt he held in his cupped hand.

'How're you doin',' he said, 'you don't know me.'

'No,' I said.

'Well you should,' he said, 'you taught me.'

'Oh,' I said, and turned away.

And then through the cracks in my memory a face looked in, the face of a young fair-haired boy with the voice of an angel singing on the stage in the local feis.

And I remembered how the adjudicator had called me over and asked to speak to him saying that he should have his voice trained, and the young boy was talking to some girls and said he couldn't be bothered.

I turned back to him.

'It was you, wasn't it,' I said. '"O For The Wings of a Dove".'

'Jaysus, I hated that f-ing song,' he said.

And that, I thought, was that.

At half time there was a tug on my sleeve. He signalled me to come with him.

I thought I knew what was coming and wondered would it cost me ten pounds or could I get away with five.

In a quiet part of the stand he stopped and put his mouth close to my ear.

I could smell his drink-laden breath and the stale tobacco reek. And in a cracked hoarse voice, my God, he started to sing.

'O for the wings of a dove

Far away, far away I would roam'

At first I was embarrassed, wondering who was watching us, but then I listened, fascinated. The intonation was perfect, even in the awkward intervals of the second half of the song. The nuances of expression, even the *rallentando* and *diminuendo* at the end, he observed them all, exactly as I had taught him a quarter of a century before.

'Well,' he said when he had finished, 'you never lose it, that's what you always said, you never lose it.'

We got talking. He was home for a few days from England. Yes, he was married but separated. He had a couple of children, somewhere over there. He was going for a few drinks after the match, did I want to come.

We parted. At the end of the match I watched him leave, an arm carelessly thrown around the shoulders of his drinking companions. He turned to wave at me.

'You never lose it,' he shouted.

'You never lose it,' shouted the golden-haired boy with the voice of an angel.

SAILING WITH MY FATHER
Ivy Bannister

I only saw my father sailing once, and that time, he was an old man with Alzheimer's disease, and there wasn't any boat. It happened like this.

That my father loved sailing was part of our family lore. He'd had his own boat – two boats, in fact – long before I'd ever come along. A photograph proved it, a splendid old black and white snapshot with 1942 scribbled on the back, a decade before my birth. There he was, younger than I'd ever known him, smooth-faced, a boyish thirty, his immense, capable hands wrapped around the tiller. How splendid he was, that young stranger with his bulky chest, a white nautical cap perched on his head. How serious his face, caught up, as it was, in the intricacies of sailing, in searching out the shifting balance between wind, wave, tide and sail.

Everything was perfect in that photograph: the handsome young man; the gleam of the sailing boat; the blur of waves and dreamy horizon, capturing forever that rapturous idyll in my father's life before work and young children made sailing a thing of his past.

But things were very far from perfect on the day that I finally saw my father sailing, half a century later. My father had Alzheimer's disease, and it did not sit easily with him. Every morning he'd march off to the little beach, a few hundred yards from his home, carrying a rake and a garden chair. There he'd roar angrily at what he discovered. Seaweed. Deposited in quantity by the overnight tides. Vigorously, he'd begin to rake. Too vigorously. Nothing would stop his frantic labours until the job was done, until all the seaweed was gathered into a tidy pile. Then, thankfully, my father would sit for a while, staring out at the water.

On that particular morning, I followed my father to the beach. I had my own son in tow, a six-year-old tot. I'd given the boy a kite to keep him amused. The kite was Japanese, of simple but clever design, a sure and steady flyer.

In my son's inexpert hands the kite responded to a quiver of breeze and swooped up. Up and up it soared, the string running speedily through his fingers.

I looked at my father, but – lost in his illness – he took no notice of his grandson.

After a while, my son had enough of his kite and wandered off to chase the waves.

Again I looked at my stony-faced father.

On a whim, I handed him the kite string. My father pushed it away.

'No, Daddy,' I said, wrapping his fingers round the string. 'You take it. Try it. You'll like it.'

So he accepted the kite, and then, bit by bit, his dead eyes began to light up, as the kite tugged and pulled, as the wind swooshed, and after a while, his ancient mouth stretched into a forgotten smile.

That morning, my father, an elderly man with Alzheimer's disease, flew that kite for all that he was worth, and as I watched him, I saw a young man again, in his prime, out on the glittering water, feeling the wind, finding the balance. And before my eyes, my father sailed that kite right on into the afternoon.

THE GARDENER
Denise Blake

We always visited my grandmother for our holidays. The same scene greeted us year after year. After an endless journey we pull up at her two-storey house. The front door bursts open and Granny runs out whooping with excitement. She examines us for the year's growth, wraps us each into her apron-covered bosom, sprays us with kisses and pushes us towards the house.

While she is welcoming us we can see a man working in a nearby field. He has a wild grey mane of hair. He wears black boots laced up his ankles and black clothes. He stops digging and leans on his shovel. My father walks over to him and shakes his hand. They exchange a few words about our journey and about the weather.

The man's name was Dennis. Every day of our holidays he would walk up to us, hand us each a Kit Kat, smile and walk away. I thought Dennis was Granny's gardener.

My grandmother had had a hard life. She had been married to my grandfather who died suddenly leaving her with three small children. She had to fight the State, the Church, and every financial institution in order to give her sons a good life. Eventually she remarried. As I grew older I realised that her second husband was Dennis, the gardener.

They had an unusual relationship. Granny's house had four bedrooms. She filled the spare rooms with lodgers – civil servants, guards and bank clerks. Dennis didn't sleep in the house. He didn't live in the house. He lived in a shed. The shed was black corrugated steel with a tin roof.

In the mornings Dennis called at the back door. She handed him a list of whatever messages she needed. An hour later we heard the rhythm of their conversation. Granny sitting in a chair, Dennis filling the middle of the kitchen. He told her stories from the village – who was dead, who was marrying, the latest saga in a feud and whose son was emigrating. After a half-hour Dennis went off to work.

He cared for the garden, coaxing fruit and vegetables to full growth – potatoes that burst into balls of flour in the pot... pods of peas that tasted like exotic sweets... lettuce... berries... apples... a whole gallery of food. Dennis gathered the ripest produce and handed them in the kitchen window.

At meal times, Granny called him. He came to the window and she handed out a tray holding his dinner and a glass of milk. He went to the shed and ate alone. His only company was the wireless.

When I realised that Dennis was Granny's husband, I was curious about the way they lived. I asked around and was told that things happen in a marriage.

Granny and Dennis both had their private loves. She grieved all her life for her first husband. Dennis's love was different. He had been born on a small island. His whole being belonged to that island. He married Granny and he wouldn't desert her. Responsibility was an entwining weed that rooted him to the ground. He lived on the mainland but grieved for the sea. They had a partnership, a friendship. He grew the best from her garden. She turned it into wholesome meals.

They're both dead now. My grandmother is buried with her first husband. Dennis is buried in the same graveyard. His plot is right at the edge, along the sea, looking out at his island.

TURNING POINT
Denys Bowring

My father's ship was torpedoed during the second world war. I was twelve years old at the time and I was not really alarmed because the daily news was full of infinitely worse events. Dad's ship had not even sunk.

He had joined the Royal Navy when he was sixteen, during the Great War, and he served through both world wars, until 1946. Three of my uncles were also in the navy. At the time I'm thinking of, Dad was a Chief Petty Officer Gunner. Part of his job was to aim the guns in his turret at what the gunnery officer told him to hit. Dad said that his ship's success or failure depended entirely on his aim. He was a man who took great pride in his work.

So I grew up impressed by what my father did, but I never felt close to him. He was a forbiddingly big man, five feet eleven and around fifteen stone. His uniform was always beautifully pressed and spotless. During his brief visits home on leave he was bursting with energy and never showed the slightest hint of self-doubt. He always knew what to do next. He somehow lacked the human frailty of other kids' dads, who were often tired and sometimes out of work. He seemed remarkably unapproachable and I was all the more intimidated because, when I misbehaved, my mother occasionally threatened to tell my dad when he got home.

Once he was on leave during what we thought was a hot summer, but he shivered in his greatcoat after the tropical heat of the Indian Ocean. He was back again in a freezing December, perspiring copiously in his shirtsleeves after escorting a convoy to Murmansk.

My mother's youngest brother, my favourite uncle, was killed when HMS

Kelly was sunk. But my dad always came home again. He was just his usual brusque self when he told us how his ship had been hit by a torpedo whilst escorting an Atlantic convoy. They had brought their damaged vessel safely back to port. And that seemed to be that. Until, after he'd gone back to sea, my mother showed me a photograph, taken by a shipmate, that was to become a turning point for me. It changed my understanding of my father and of much else as well.

He was pictured slumped on a box-like structure on the ship's deck, in his shirtsleeves, with his head in his hands. His posture suggested abject depression and even fear. His hair was uncombed; his collarless shirt was creased and dirty. He looked like a man who had lost all hope. The horizon in the photo seemed to be sloping sideways, but it was the ship that was tilted at a perilous angle.

Listing like that, it would have been impossible to bring her big guns to bear if they were needed. It must have been a truly terrifying voyage home, with the ship moving only slowly; a sitting target for any passing U boat. And my dad could only sit and wait until they reached port or sank.

As I looked at that picture, I realised for the first time that my apparently all-powerful father was, beneath a lot of bluster, a frightened, vulnerable human being. That realisation was a shock to my young mind. It took a long time to get used to the idea that a brave man could also be a frightened one.

NOBODY'S CHILD
Rita Curran Darbey

I watched her play, she was no more than four years old. She shovelled sand into her bright coloured bucket until it was full, then with both hands lifted the heavy bucket and turned it upside down. She reached across for her red spade and with it patted the bucket gently on all sides while she sang a little nursery rhyme. Then very carefully she removed the bucket to reveal a perfectly formed shape. She squealed with excitement and clapped her hands while her father scooped her up in his arms and swung her high. Eventually she wriggled free, eager to repeat her performance.

As she refilled her bucket I watched the golden sand turn dark and muddy before my eyes. The long colourful beach shrank in size to that of a small back yard, the only colours were those hanging out to dry in a triangle from a two per-back window. The smell of fresh sea air became the stench from an eight-family tenement house.

A child was playing in that back yard. She scraped at the heavy clay with a piece of glass chaynie, loosening enough earth to fill a shoe-polish tin. She spat in it, mixed it around with her finger, spat in it again until it was smooth, then turned it upside-down and waited. She banged on the tin with her narrow little fist, then sang:

> 'Pie, pie come out,
> I'll give you a bottle of stout,
> If you don't come out
> I'll give you a kick in the arse.'

She lifted the tin slowly and watched her efforts crumble.

'Mummy, Mummy,' cried the little girl on the beach, she twirled around and around, making an umbrella display of her red frilly dress. Her parents watched in rapture.

The child in the back yard found an old wash-pole, she put her big sister's hat on it, stood it straight against the wall and asked,

'Mammy, will you buy me a new dress, a red one like Molly Delaney's?'

'I will Chrissie,' replied the child to herself in a grown up voice.

'And,' she added, 'new boots too and… and a pixie to match.'

The child became excited and tried to straighten the tilting washpole.

'A pixie!' she repeated, 'and maybe… maybe a pair of hornpipe shoes…' The washpole fell, hurling the child back to reality. Slowly she picked up her sister's hat and through her sobs she cried, 'I want a red dress so I do, and a pixie to match.'

'Lunch!' called the little girl's mother. Her father lifted her onto his shoulders and carried her to the picnic laid out on the rug, they all sat down to eat.

'There'll be goodies if you finish,' coaxed her mother.

The child in the back yard turned to the wash-pole and asked, 'Mammy can I have a piece of bread and jam?'

'Yes you can, Chrissie,' replied the child out loud.

She smothered a red chaynie with muck, then another one and stuck the two together. She pretended to eat it.

'I love bread and jam,' she told the pole.

The pole didn't answer and the child fell silent. She sat back on her hunkers, and stared into the greyness of her surroundings. Her stomach rumbled. The grey wall became blurred and the child ran crying, looking for her big sister Bridie and knew she wasn't fibbing when she said she had a pain.

The little girl gathered her bucket and spade from the sand. Her mother shook the crumbs from the rug before folding it away and tidied the cups and plates neatly into a basket. The little girl yawned, then held up her arms to her Daddy who stooped to pick her up. She curled her arms around his neck and rested her sleepy head on his shoulder. With their bags all packed they walked away, taking with them my bruised memory. I watched until they were but specks on the horizon.

WHEN THE TAR WAS RUNNY
Shane Fagan

When I learned a boyhood friend of long ago had passed away in England, a special sadness pervaded my thoughts. Tommy was the 'second link' in a childhood chain… and now, it was broken.

A few days later, these same thoughts were in my mind as I parked the car near the old bridge that spanned the Boyne.

I'd driven past it a thousand times, never giving it a second glance, but now, on this tranquil evening, I would search for something… something I hoped had endured the decades.

The old bridge had changed little; weather-beaten but unbowed, it stood defiant, a veteran of countless engagements with the elements.

As I walked, my memory began tumbling through the years. Back forty summers to that scorching hot day when as nine-year-olds, Tommy, Joe and myself set off on our first long walk in the 'country'… a walk that would become a wondrous odyssey!

As the town receded behind us, so our excitement grew. It was the first day of the long summer holiday, the liberation put wings on our heels. We frolicked and pranced along the narrow winding road, until rounding a bend, we caught sight of the 'bridge'. Never in our lives had we seen anything like it!

A silvery web of intricate steelwork, it shimmered majestically in the hot afternoon sun. We had come upon a magical vista… an enchanted place. Time stood still that day, as we climbed and swung on the latticed girders.

With an agility akin to a troupe of spider monkeys, we grew ever-more daring.

Names, dates, love messages and things we didn't understand were all etched deeply into the steelwork… an earlier generation was showing the world they'd passed this way.

It was decided we also would leave our marks on history. Joe and I had old penknives. We prepared to engrave.

Tommy, the innovative one, was watching from the road. His shrillness pierced the pastoral setting.

'Look boys,' he yelled, 'the tar... the tar is runny, get sharp sticks, we can write with it.'

So it was, twigs became our brushes, the tar our paint, the bridge our canvas. The names were painted on an unobtrusive girder.

Then Joe, with a profundity rare in one so young, painted linked circles around the names. These chain-links would never break. We were friends forever.

I'd reached the bridge, my thoughts returned to the present. I began my search.

A few minutes later, I found what I sought, faint but legible, I was gazing upon the tarry 'masterpiece'.

I was recalling how, less than a dozen years later, we were to disperse over the globe. Joe lost his life tragically in America, he didn't see thirty and now, Tommy...

I alone had returned.

To some passing travellers, the old bridge simply spanned a river. To others, it was a keeper of secrets from a simpler time. To me, it was a monument for lost friends, and that long-ago summer... when the tar was 'runny'.

CHATTIE
Sam McAughtry

My mother had ten children; four of them died aged between one and four. Of the survivors, five were boys and one, Charlotte or Chattie, was our sister. She never married and no wonder, for she only had the slimmest of chances to meet boys in the usual way. In the Thirties only the Catholic churches ran dances in their church halls, so that was out for us, and Mother believed that ordinary dance halls were dangerous, morally and physically. Coming out into the cold night air after several hours of dancing, she thought, opened the door to the risk of TB and that was equivalent to a death sentence in those days.

I think that Chattie would have risked death to learn dancing for, in her job in Gallagher's tobacco factory, the girls around her seemed to talk of little else. An example of the forces that kept her away from dancing and meeting boys was the attitude of our Rector, the Rev. R Dixon Patterson, to the subject. One evening in our Church hall, the Church Lads' Brigade seniors were meeting on the same evening as the Girls' Brigade; someone had brought a portable gramophone, a jazz record was playing, and couples were dancing the quickstep, when in on top of it landed the Rector.

'Stop this ungodly business at once!' he shouted, rushing to lift the needle off the record.

'Don't ever let me see this place desecrated like this again,' he said sternly. When he walked out he left thirty youngsters looking at the floor, burdened with guilt. Chattie was one of them.

We five boys were waited on by Mother and Chattie. They did the housework, washed the clothes and the dishes, and on Sunday morning, Chattie and Mother made our breakfasts and carried them upstairs to us. Indeed, I had one brother who would stay out so late on a Saturday night that he would have all three meals in bed on a Sunday, reading the Sunday papers in between.

Chattie had a friend called Margaret. Three times a week the two of them would go out to the pictures, arm-in-arm, and arm-in-arm walk home again. In this way the years passed.

In the war she had one or two dates with British soldiers; one even called at the house a few times, and tucked away the odd feed, but there was always with soldiers the chance that there was a wife across the water, so nothing came of it.

After the war a man called Billy came into her life, but it was a funny kind of relationship, for he only visited her at our house, and the two of them would sit in the parlour for hours, until midnight, when he would go off home. I don't know how they met, but Chattie was very fond of him. However after about five years of this, she broke this one-sided affair off, and it really seemed to wound her, from what we boys could see. Naturally, nobody but Mother and Margaret knew the ins and outs of it. All through the years of his visits, we'd been too shy to ask about Billy's intentions.

The war took one brother away for good, Mother died soon after, and when three of the remaining got married, Chattie looked after the bachelor survivor in the same way she'd cared for us, but in 1965 she was taken to hospital: it was the worst kind of news. After some weeks Chattie was sent home to die, and she died as she had lived, quietly, almost shyly, on a roaring, blustering February morning.

In 1995, thirty years later, I was opening the door of my car in Belfast, when I was spoken to by an elderly man. I didn't know him at first, then he introduced himself. It was Billy.

'Poor Chattie,' he said. 'I was very fond of her you know.'

I didn't ask how they had broken up.

'She'd wanted to see me, when she was ill but I couldn't.'

'You what?' I said, wide-eyed, 'you couldn't go to see her on her death bed?'

'Well you see,' he said, 'I didn't want her to see me so well, when she was so bad.'

I left him, standing looking after me. I drove away, and he was still in the mirror, looking. All the time I kept stealing glances at him in the mirror until, in the end, I couldn't see him any more for the tears.

BOARDING THE BUS
Maeve Flanagan

'Let me off at that new shop on Stephen's Green,' I said to the bus driver as I boarded his bus one very busy Saturday. My car was being serviced and I was off to town to spend some blissful hours among the shop's glasses, lamps and throws. I rarely take buses; I didn't know what the correct fare to town was, that was the reason I mentioned my destination with such precision. I lived to rue my honesty.

'Which shop Mrs?' the bus driver asked irritably as the queue behind me grew.

'The new English shop at the top of Grafton Street,' I replied, my own irritation mounting at the idea of such clarification being necessary. How could the man not know the shop I was speaking about? Conversations at coffee break among my women colleagues had been of nothing but this shop and its wares for weeks. The bus driver was young, too young it seemed to me to hold a driver's licence – yet he wore a wedding ring. I heard my voice resonate throughout the silent bus; seated passengers stared at me. I didn't like what I heard. My voice rang out clearly, sharply and authoritatively. I reeled in shock.

'That couldn't be my voice,' I thought, 'I don't sound like that'.

But far worse than the tone was that the voice I heard was the voice of an older woman. I had gone to bed the previous night young and invincible. And suddenly that Saturday morning I had become someone with a blowsy matron's voice, rapping out commands on public transport.

'Pound,' barked the driver, clearly wanting rid of me. Seated upstairs I considered the stinging revelation. When had all this happened? Had an evil goblin come during the night and changed me? Or had the process begun long, long ago without my noticing? Creaking floorboards or the wind howling in the chimney on winter's nights could still terrify me just as much as they did when I was four. Surely that meant that I was still young? I didn't deserve to have a matron's voice lobbed at me out of the blue on a beautiful Saturday morning when raggy clouds danced across the sky above the dome of

Rathmines Church. The bus inched into Stephen's Green. I stepped over the long, long legs of the Celtic Tiger cubs which blocked the aisle of the bus. Once out in the street though I didn't go into the shop. I didn't feel like fingering fabrics or sniffing huge yellow garden candles and dreaming of long summer nights.

BONGO AND THE BULB
John Carmody

Sometimes when I'm walking through my neighbourhood I feel a twinge of sadness. I think back to my childhood and early teens – the good old days when glue was plentiful and you had to shave your head with a Wilkinson – not like those trendies you see today with their number 1s and number 2s.

In the evenings twelve or so of us would stand at our well-worn corner (for we were corner boys and that was our job) discussing topics that most interested us, like football, cider, and the size of Mrs Murphy's bra. Many of us agreed that it was most likely the heavy-duty industrial type – probably reinforced with steel girders and small planks of wood.

One evening the conversation turned to electricity and the body's electricity.

'Would you have enough to light a lightbulb?' asked Bongo whose head was always shaved but this had more to do with pest control than fashion. The youngest of eight and of our group, Bongo wasn't exactly a rocket scientist but he had a curious mind.

'Yeah but you'd have to generate it,' answered Pablo who *was* a rocket scientist – well, when it came to street-smarts that is. Bongo had an intense look on his face – we all knew that some major scientific breakthrough was about to be made.

'I'll be back in a minute,' he said with a determined look on his face.

We watched as he walked across the street and into his house. The light went out in his living room and we could hear his father shouting at him.

'What are you up to now you shagging lunatic – how am I going to do my jigsaw – what in the name of God are you doing with that sellotape?'

We heard no response from Bongo so we knew that whatever was going on in his brain was serious and there was no way he would be distracted by anything or anyone, included his father.

We shushed each other into silence and tried hard not to laugh as Bongo appeared at his front gate with his father's tall-lizzy bicycle and a lightbulb sellotaped onto the top of his head. The tape ran all the way down the side of his head, under his chin and up the other side to form a complete circle. He made sure it was secure and would not fall free once he was sweating.

He cycled slowly about a hundred yards up the main road and came back towards us as fast as his legs would take him.

'Is it lightin'? Is it lightin'?' his teeth grinding because he couldn't open his mouth.

'It's lightin', it's lightin',' we shouted as he passed us like Apollo Seven. He repeated this a number of times to make sure the initial test run wasn't a fluke. Of course every time he passed our shouts of approval convinced him even more that his calculations were correct.

Eventually he stopped and we surrounded him like a pit-crew offering many cheers and claps on the back. Drenched in sweat and breathless, Bongo managed a few words.

'There's no law-boy can pull me now. I'm off into town for a spin!' and off he went. Everyone cracked up with laughter as we watched him cycle off into the distance.

I've often wondered what people thought as they saw him cycling through the streets of Limerick – a young guy on a tall-lizzy bicycle with a lightbulb sellotaped to the top of his shaven head.

So why the twinge of sadness? Because many of those lads are dead now and I have no doubt that there are one or two more who will yet see an early grave. Between murder, suicide, alcohol and drugs... it all began with foolhardy innocence – all we ever wanted was a laugh.

THE POETRY LOVER
Bryan Gallagher

The routine was always the same.

His wife would open the door to my knock.

'Can I have a lift with John on the lorry to Belfast on Monday please?'

'The college boy wants a lift,' she would shout in sideways.

'Six o'clock sharp,' she would say to me and close the door in my face.

The neighbours said she was a sharp woman.

They also said that *he* wouldn't wait for the Pope, and more than once I stood on the road watching in impotent frustration as his tail-lights disappeared in the direction of Belfast and the rooks, woken by the sound of the engine, cawed in the trees overhead.

Sometimes I did make it on time.

The lorry engine was governed at 28mph and it took us three and a half weary hours to get to Belfast.

But what used to really infuriate me was his unvarying predictability. My eighteen-year-old mind could forecast everything he would do.

When I got in he always said, 'Is that door closed?'

And that was all.

At Fivemiletown chapel he blessed himself and for the next mile said his morning prayers, moving his lips silently. At the same crossroads every morning, he blessed himself again and then, with great care and deliberation, he got out a plug of tobacco and a knife, cut and teased the tobacco, filled his pipe and lit it, all the while steering with his elbows while we trundled through the twisting roads of South Tyrone. I watched every move out of the corner of my eye in seething youthful irritation.

And always when we came to the town of Augher, he would look over at me and say, 'Augher, Clogher, Fivemiletown, eh?' clearly expecting an answer, and I would mutter 'That's a good one'. Or 'Oh indeed' but he always seemed dissatisfied.

And then one morning, I said, 'Sixmilecross and seven mile round.'

He looked sharply over.

'What?' he said angrily.

'That's the rest of it,' I said.

'Augher, Clogher, Fivemiletown,
Sixmilecross and seven mile round.'

He glared at me balefully but for the next few miles I could see that he was turning it over in his mind.

A few weeks later we gave a lift to a local woman and when he came to Augher he said to her,

'Augher, Clogher, Fivemiletown,
Sixmilecross and seven mile round.'

And the next week I said,

'Cookstown, straight and long
The drink is right but the price is wrong.'

'What was that?' he said sharply and I repeated it.

A couple of weeks later as we drove out of the yard, he said,

'From Carrickmacross to Crossmaglen,
You'll get more rogues, than honest men.'

And I replied,

'It wasn't the men from Shercock or the men from Ballybay
But the dalin' men from Crossmaglen put whiskey in me tay.'

And he said,

'That's a good one.'

And then I taught him,

'Thomasina from Ballymena
Could dance on her toes like a ballerina,
But she married a man from Cushendall
And now she cannot dance at all.'

And he said,

'That's a great one', and laughed chokily through his tobacco smoke.

And one April morning as dawn whitened the drumlins of the Clogher valley we said all the rhymes one after another and we ended with the one about Fermanagh.

'Lisnaskea for drinkin' tea,
Maguiresbridge for brandy,
Lisbellaw for woppin' straw
And Derrylin's the dandy.'

And we sat in companionable silence for the rest of the way winding through Tyrone and Armagh to the city.

'You'll be up next week,' he said as I got out.

'I will,' I said.

I never spoke a word to him again.

That week, he slumped over the steering wheel in the yard, dead of a massive heart attack.

I was amazed at how devastated I felt.

In the graveyard, his wife said as I shook hands with her,

'He said you were the best of crack, that you had great rhymes.'

But she spoke in a puzzled, resentful way and I knew she would never understand.

The new driver was just a few years older than myself and we talked young men's talk of dances and footballs and girls.

But it was never the same again.

THE SINGER SEWING MACHINE
Vona Groarke

It arrived one year to the day after her death, hauled in by two removal men who set it down as carefully as they could, and asked, a little fearfully, if I wanted it upstairs. I had asked her for it, she had left it to me, and I wanted to have it near. The lid of it makes a tabletop. When I raised it up, the smell – of metal, oil, leather, wood and thread – brought it back.

This was the scent of long ago; afternoons in the family room, spent in failing light; me at my lessons and her, sitting up at the window, at work on the sewing machine. The sound the sheets made when she pulled them open with her hands was sharper than the hum of the treadle and the whirr of the wheel. It would break the quiet rhythms of the room: the fire and its shadows on the brasses, the spruce trees etched in darkness on the glass, the dog, whining gently to come in.

It could be more than twenty years ago, or it could be now, here in the new home I have made. With one push of the treadle, one push of the wheel, the needle rises and drops as it always has; it is another winter afternoon. I sit at the Singer in failing light, and I have laid in yards of cotton to make curtains for the room where my children, not yet born, will one day sleep.

I am no seamstress, though I learned at school; made nylon aprons and a towelling teddy for the missions with the other girls. I could have bought the curtains ready-made, but something of those afternoons, their ceremony and lull, is not lost on me. Perhaps it is the feeling, unacknowledged, that I can make those moments hum again, and somehow that by doing what she did, I'll revive the steady rhythm of her life.

Hers was the last hand to touch this sewing machine. I know she has threaded it for me: gone into the family room, now cold and packed with boxes, past a hollow grate, the chair where I would sit over my books, my knees drawn up. She has gone into this room where she so rarely goes. She has sat at this machine in failing light, and remembered with her hands and a white card held behind, how to wind the thread from reel to bobbin to needle to eye to reel. She knew I would not know how, and the sewing machine would be finally undone. So now, one year after her death, it stands in my house, primed for use, not with the white thread she so often used, but with black she knew would suit most of my clothes.

There is a drawer to the front, shallow and neat. Inside, I found an array of buttons from twenty years of my family's clothes. I could have told her life from them: buttons from best dresses, slacks for everyday, small pearls from my father's shirts, a spare from the winter coat she loved, two peach ones from her dress for my sister's wedding, the summer blouses, the widow's black. I laid them out, the colours and shapes of them so lively, so bereft. These days, my son and daughter play with them: one day, they are medals, the next day, coins. I tell them about her as they spin and barter the bright discs, her life, her stories, the patterns that she stitched in all our lives.

THE LONELIEST JAZZMAN OF THE TWENTIETH CENTURY
Michael Harding

I knew him twenty years ago; he lived in the hills, alone in a two-storey house, with his tin whistle, his conjuring tricks, his deck of cards, and his mysterious picture of a lady with a German Shepherd dog. The eyes of both the lady and the dog followed the observer round the room.

Magician and entertainer, jamjar bottom spectacles, brown hair in a wave that Elvis Presley would have been proud of, Phil Bernard was an old bachelor. His house was full of derelict rooms, and the local children said his hair was full of boot polish. The musty kitchen, the smell of turf, the dirty frying pan and the fly paper hanging from the ceiling. And in the middle of it, was this erect, dapper man in a three piece brown herring-bone suit. Phil Bernard was a performer and a professional; even the white leather texture of his face sported wee smudges of rouge on either cheek.

He played the tin whistle as if it were a saxaphone. Jigs and reels if you wanted them, but he was happiest with big band numbers, he often dispensed with the whistle preferring to sing out the chorus with the physicality of the lead in a Broadway musical. In a kitchen tossed to the wind, with upset frying pans and a broken down refrigerator, Phil Bernard was the original jazzman. The only jazzman, in Gowlan, Cornaha or Glangevlin.

He often stood at the back door in a storm, where he kept his stack of empty porter bottles, and looked out on the sallies clinging to the ditches and the rushes clinging to the hill and he'd say to me, 'Jeepers Michael, aren't we living in an awful goddamn part of the world to be sure.'

He must have been, underneath it all, the loneliest jazzman of the twentieth century.

The trolley that brought Phil Bernard into the world took the wrong turn, and delivered him to the wrong address; Phil Bernard's ticket was for New York or Boston, not the Cuilcagh Mountains in the nineteen hundreds.

He whispered Carnegie Hall like a mantra, bringing it into existence by saying it. His dream an open stage, the instrument resting by his side, the audience on their feet, and he the performer, he the star, taking a grave and deep and humble bow. Instead he got public houses, parish hall concerts and wedding receptions, but every song he sang, he sang as if he were truly on that stage in Carnegie Hall, and the children who said he had boot polish in his hair had him at all their weddings and they loved him without measure.

I saw him some years before he died. The kitchen was darker; he sat on the seat of an old Cortina, staring at the wall. He was white-haired and completely blind. We talked about telephones. By now the children of the children were in Queens and Brooklyn. They rang him up the night Sinéad O'Connor played in New York, and promised to send him the tapes. Phil Bernard never stopped loving music.

He died in a nursing home in Fermanagh. The trolley took him away; took him on to another life, another destination. All I pray for is that they get it right this time; that they drop him out there in New York, in the goddamn right spot, that someone puts a damn good instrument in his hand, and that there is applause without end.

THE WHITE, WHITE ROSE
Peter Jankowsy

There is almost nothing around here that could compare with the whiteness of this rose. Certainly not the whitewash of the cottage where the bush stands, it only serves to highlight the absolute white of the rose. If I look out at the sea – the foaming breakers there, in the sunshine, they come close, but they flash, and are gone, while the roses hold their gleam all through the day, through dawn and dusk, even in the darkest nights I can make out their luminous shimmer. 'Stella Maris', the pole star, the type is called says my book, where we turn to when we have lost our bearings, and I can't think of a more suitable name. The blooms are not bunched together, but regularly spaced, each one resplendent in its own white shine against the rich green foliage. It's not a noble rose, belonging, as it does, to the Rugosa group; the branches are encrusted with thorns, picking one guarantees you will be wounded.

But pick them you must, if only to admire at close quarters their immaculateness, the elegance of the five green sepals, like fingers holding up between them something white, fragile and precious. The petals, silvery-veined, slightly crinkled and thus of a many-faceted white in the light, are of course the flower's first glory, an untrammelled, loose assemblage of the lightest tissues, of host-like translucence. The smaller ones, towards the middle, even when fully open, still half-hide a sprinkle of gold-dust. In its very centre, the light-green stigma or, as the Germans call it, the 'scar', the female part of the blossom, surrounded by its golden wreath of male stamens – the focus and purpose of the whole splendid show. From the depth of these parts rises the second glory of this rose, a most beguiling fragrance, delicious, but delicate, the flower is bathed in it. This you only fully realize when you have a few of them in a vase indoors; in the open air the constant breezes of the island tend to dilute the richness and subtlety of the smell.

I put four of them into a water-glass on top of the fridge standing opposite the open-fire place and dominating the room like an altar. Each time I pass by them, I receive a gentle waft of perfume, like an earthly blessing, or as if the air suddenly smiled. At night I take the little flower arrangement with me and place it beside my bed – why should they sweeten the night-air unappreciated? And again – each time, during my tossing and turning, there is this scent, like a silent, loving presence.

Is it any wonder, then, that as a man, and on your own, your mind starts remembering feminine moments, the girl who always, always smelled of roses, the woman bewitched by them, that from the depth of your memory, or your longing, there rises the aura of love-making. Those glowing glances and heart-stopping encounters, promises hoped for and perhaps even promises kept, the ever evasive nature of fulfilment and all the enhancing and then again stultifying power which, for the man, lies in what Goethe called the Eternal Feminine.

There was very little of that in the life of the man who planted the rose and dwelled in this cottage until a few years ago. His name was half-female, John Lizzey, after his mother Elizabeth, an unusual combination on this island of Michael Joes, Charley Brians and Paddy Micks. He farmed and fished, he never married and lived together with his sister, a woman knowledgeable about plants and herbs. After her death, when he lived alone and was an old man, he was popular with certain continental lady tourists who enjoyed his gentlemanly manners, his earthy sarcasms, his lack of cant and wealth of anecdotes, and who showered him with their easy charm. That, as far as we know, was all of the Feminine he had in his life.

Although in no way given to sentimentality, he loved his rose, and by always having a few of them in the house, I only follow his example. He died a few years ago, peacefully, in the middle of the wildest hurricane in living memory.

Now I sleep in the bed he died in, and sometimes at night, for a few seconds, the two of us are united in the scent of his rose – the man who is sleeping for good now and the insomniac, the rooted island-man and the man between two worlds, the man who never entered the labyrinth of love and he who did, and came out at the other end, bewildered, a wounder, wounded.

Oh, the living breath of the white, white rose!

CROWNING GLORY
Francis Harvey

They say that a woman's crowning glory is her hair and in her case that was certainly true. She had this magnificent head of long black hair that, when she loosened it, fell almost to her waist but which, as I remember, she mostly wore in a bun spiked with hairpins on the nape of her neck. And in childhood, it appears, she used to wear it falling around her neck and shoulders in cascades that in time would grow as white as the cascades of the Donegal river beside which she used to play.

But whatever way she wore it, whether loose or in a bun, I always knew that she was inordinately proud of her hair. One of my most ineffaceable memories, and I have as many memories of her as there were once corncrakes in her father's meadow or salmon in the river alongside which she played, of a woman who was born into a vanished world of horses and carts, jaunting cars, summer roads and wayside flowers white with dust, is of the way she would, when she was preparing for bed, unpin her long black hair and brush it and comb it until it shone like patent leather.

One summer's day, when she was a child, she and one of her sisters were playing on the riverbank close to a salmon pool where once, you could hear, on windless evenings anglers hate, the hiss of their wet lines slicing the butter-soft golden air. One fine summer's evening it somehow happened that she overbalanced and fell into this deep pool. She was in immediate danger of being carried away by the current only for the fact that her sister, having failed to grasp some part of her body, an arm, a leg, anything, as she was going under, managed in a last, almost despairing effort, to catch some strands of her hair and succeeded in pulling her towards the bank and then dragging her out on the grass where she lay, panting, exhausted, like one of the salmon generations of anglers had landed in the same place.

Was it any wonder then that she who owed her life to her hair, would always cherish it with such a fierce passion and would continue to brush it and comb it every night of her life until, in old age, she became incapable of even this labour of love. Was it any wonder that, as she lay on her deathbed, and those who were looking after her had unthinkingly cut her hair and I was one day confronted with this white cropped head on the pillow, was it any wonder that I instantly knew that in depriving her of her hair they were depriving her of something which even the river had failed to do so many years ago. Surely enough, this woman, who was my mother and to whose hair, its length and its strength, I owe my very existence, died not long after that.

THE LAST OLÉ
Bill Kelly

It is a mid November night. A sharp breeze comes in off the Atlantic and threads its way through the buildings and into Eyre Square. Padraig O'Conaire sits on his stone seat and doesn't feel the cold. O'Conaire has his back to the wind and we do likewise. Through the swing doors and into the pub. On the television screen, high above the heads of the patrons, the picture is coming from Brussels. The last Olé has just started.

There is standing room only and even that is tight. A couple of young lads burst through the swing doors and the man minding the entrance lassoes them with his arm. They produce ID and he lets them through. They do the equivalent of a handbrake turn and lock into a position below the television. The television sound is high but is completely drowned by the noise in the pub. All we can be sure of is that the lads in green are Irish and the ones in red are Belgian. To and fro across the twenty eight inches of the screen the play moves. It is Saturday evening and the pub spectators have been warming up all afternoon.

The ball flies across the Belgian goal and we sway with it. The first Mexican wave in the pub sweeps a small man off his high stool and in under the counter. He re-emerges suggesting his mishap is an ominous sign. This man is a prophet. Two minutes later Belgium has scored a goal. Like a lull in a great storm, for a few seconds the pub falls silent. Outside the wind is picking up, the windows moan a little. Here in this city in the far west of Ireland, with our backs to the Atlantic, we don't hear the words, but we read the sign language. The screen is full of red flags. They replay the goal. Over and over and over. Like a judge repeating a death sentence four times. The swing doors push open like a gaping mouth and two lads leave. But the play resumes, the appeal is on.

A tall man, wearing a hat, steps in front of the small one on the high stool. The small one taps the tall one on the shoulder.

'Take off your hat and maybe I can see over ya.'

For a second or two I feel that a fight will take over from the football. But the action on the telly focuses their attention. It is in Brussels that someone is injured and being carried off. Behind me, two elderly men are sitting in a corner at the back. Locals, they come here on quiet nights when a place in the World Cup final is not at stake. They look like men under house arrest in their own pub.

Back in Brussels the rain is pouring down. Someone shouts that that should be good for the Irish. Another prophet is among us. No sooner said than done. Ray Houghton gets his thatch to a ball and the Belgian net is shaking. The pub explodes. Even the men under house arrest in the corner stand up to see what is happening. A new Mexican wave takes off and I get half a pint of beer down the leg of my trousers. How fickle the pendulum of joy and sorrow. The man with the hat throws it against the ceiling and it almost knocks over another man's pint on the way down. No one cares, times are good again. But not for long. The Belgians score again, the pub has been given another anaesthetic. The stunned silence returns and you can see the hope flying out the doors and out over Galway Bay. The dream of France '98 is over. The phrase books go into retirement. This pub will no longer be on tour.

The long afternoon of warming up has softened the brains and some are now crying into their beer. In dribs and drabs we trickle out into the Galway night. Memories flood back. Rome, New York, Orlando. Football madness on the streets of Dublin on balmy summer nights. But tonight the dream has died.

It is now spitting rain and the wind has a cutting edge. Eyre Square wears the mantle of night. The crowds spilling onto the streets scatter in all directions. The bond has been broken. Defeat is not a unifying force. The dream of a little nation doing big things is, for the time being, over. In another time and another place something new will lift us again. Far away in Brussels the lights are going out. The last Olé has sounded.

THE TELEPHONE AND THE CAMEL
Thomas J Kinsella

The telephone pole always smelling of creosote in the ditch opposite our house was a symbol of status and impending prosperity in the late fifties. My father called it 'our pole'. We were proud of it because the wire from the pole to our house proclaimed to all who passed by that we had a telephone. After a shower of rain in spring the wire was lined with hanging silver droplets, and in autumn with thronging twittering swallows, prior to their African sojourn.

For some time, that wire was the only one on the pole before others began to appear. Everyone knew that a new phone was being installed in the neighbourhood when the big green P&T truck and its crew of lines-men appeared at the pole.

'Did you hear who's getting a phone?' my father would ask, and as the wires on the pole increased, his sense of importance decreased.

The phone itself was a heavy black apparatus with a handle on the side, and a shrill ring as loud as a modern day fire alarm. It sat on top of a small table in our hallway. Calls out were made via an operator at the local telephone exchange who was contacted by turning the handle. Three minutes per call was the allotted time for a trunk call, after which the operator came on line and asked 'Do you require more time?' Some of the operators were identifiable by their voices and my father would comment on them, depending on the amount of leeway given beyond the allotted three minutes. Sometimes he appealed to the operator saying, 'I'm nearly finished', and she would leave him on for another while free of charge. These were the good operators, according to him. The bad ones had no mercy.

One of my mother's brothers worked for Irish Shipping and occasionally he rang from foreign lands. When his call was expected all my uncles and aunts assembled at our house, the time of the call having been synchronised by letter. All waited in silence. If the phone didn't ring at the appointed time someone would exclaim from the abiding silence.

'He must be finding it hard to get through.'

Phone calls were not taken for granted in those days.

On one occasion he rang from Egypt. As usual we queued in the hall to speak to him. My turn came, and in a faint voice barely audible above the crackle on the line, he told me he had a camel for me.

For three months until he arrived home I waited, wondered and dreamed about the promised camel. Restless nights of childish excitement slowed the time even more.

Where will I keep it? I thought.

Will Father allow me to have it?

What will my friends think?

Eventually my uncle arrived home. He lived with my grandmother. The night before his arrival I didn't sleep at all. In the morning I went to see him. On meeting him, he swung me around in a friendly bear hug and said, 'The camel's upstairs'. I became suspicious. However, in a child's mind, favourite uncles can do great things and my suspicions were momentarily assuaged, somehow.

He ran up the stairs and I followed. Before I was halfway up he emerged from his bedroom, and in his hand was a cream coloured leatherette camel, with gold reins, and a maroon cloth with gold flecks covering its hump. My disappointment was so great, I began to cry. My uncle was baffled. In his goodness he had brought me the toy from a port in Egypt, little did he realise that this would be the first major disappointment in my life.

MOLLY
Aodhan Madden

This is a ghost story. There can be no other way to describe it. It all began on a late summer's day in a busy suburban street. I had just got off the bus in Phibsboro when I thought I saw her. She was standing in the porch of St Peter's Church. She seemed to be staring at me. There was a lot of traffic between me and her, yet that stare sought me out and held me. Then the bus passed between us and she was gone.

That couldn't be Molly, I thought. She was dead ten years at least. Yet I found myself walking across the road and into the church – just to confirm that I had made a mistake. The church was empty.

I decided it was merely some trick of the imagination and so I went off about my business. I was still a little troubled though; that strange intense stare followed me all afternoon.

After a few days I had almost forgotten the incident, but then late that Sunday evening the phone rang. At first I heard nothing. I was about to put the phone down when I heard a low sobbing sound coming, as if from a great distance. It was an old woman crying. My blood turned cold. I thought of Molly. I slammed down the phone.

Was this some nasty hoax?

Molly and I had no particularly strong bond – she was hardly even a friend, just an elderly neighbour whose lawn I sometimes cut in the summer. I went to her funeral out of sense of duty really, she being the last of an old and respected family. There was no obvious personal context here for a hoaxer to exploit.

The two events had to be coincidental.

I had never given much thought to Molly before. Even in life she was a shadowy figure; in death, she disappeared all together. She had no living relatives, no close friends. The few people at her funeral were all neighbours.

Some time later there was a knock on the front door. It was a solitary rap and at first I thought it was the wind. I looked through the spyhole; there was nobody there. Yet I had this funny sensation that someone had been there; a vague trace lingered.

I ran upstairs to look out the window. She was standing at the garden gate. I couldn't see her face. All I saw was an old woman beating her sides in a slow, rhythmic movement that suggested great distress. But as soon as I saw her the movement of her hands merged into the swaying of the myrtle bush in the garden and her image seemed to melt into the shadows.

It had to be the wind; the rap on the door, those indistinct movements at the garden gate. People just don't come back from the dead.

I still could not get Molly out my mind. I began to remember her toiling away in her garden, grimly pulling out weeds.

'Rain coming,' she would say, pointing to the sky, even in the sunniest weather.

There was another detail which I saw now and never noticed when she was alive. She never actually looked at me in all the years I passed her in her garden. Her head was always tilted to one side, her eyes avoiding contact with the world.

She was always sweeping leaves outside her front gate and even late at night I sometimes saw her bent over her broom, already ghostly I now thought.

I decided to call to her house recently. It is still derelict and the front garden overgrown with weeds. I sat in the morning sun thinking about her near the end, sitting on her own window ledge with a heavy coat draped over her shoulders as she watched me mowing her lawn.

Was it possible, I thought, that the key to all this lay in the very private reality of Molly's own life? Was it possible that she was reaching out from some forgotten and anonymous place, claiming the right to be remembered?

I sat for ages in her garden. On summer evenings she sometimes sat in that drawingroom window looking out at the world passing by. Did I ever wave back to her then? I wondered. Or did her very familiarity invite indifference? I'm sure I must have passed her in her window right through my childhood and nothing ever registered, nothing save the vaguest impression of her being there.

'Rain coming, Molly,' I heard myself saying out loud. Of course she cannot hear me now. But sometimes I like to think that the odd word, the odd remembrance cast into the great silence of eternity might calm her troubled progress. I would remember Molly and place some humble marker on the forgotten space she once occupied.

CUBAN JOURNEY
Sam McAughtry

I was in Cuba to visit my father's grave, the first member of my family to go looking for it, in 1984, thirty-three years after his death. He had been taken off his ship to a small sugar port, near Santa Cruz del Sur, in 1951, where he was to die of peritonitis the same day. In Havana airport I was two hours in the passport inspection queue, but I didn't mind: there was Cuban noise and chatter, and kissing and hugging all around, and travellers came and went. I was full of excited curiosity, but the lady in the airport reception area who allocated hotels wasn't long in softening my cough.

'Hotel Deauville, Havana,' she said, 'and that will be three hundred dollars, please.'

Lovely, I must say. I had only three hundred and fifty bucks. In my stupidity I had assumed that the newspaper for which I was to write about my journey, had pre-paid my hotel. I had no plastic money, no credit: I was on the floor, practically a pauper, with ten days to punch in, on five dollars a day. Ah, well, I needed to lose weight anyway. The Cuban PR people weren't happy about my poverty. Hard currency is the oxygen of the country. But there was something more pressing: I wanted to know if they could actually pinpoint my father's grave. Their embassy in London had been vague, whilst still giving me press accreditation. Well, young Alba Holder told me that she knew where it was, and that, in three days time, she would take me there, and she and her Cuban colleagues all laughed at the way I lifted her and swung her around, on hearing this.

'You are not very English,' they said.

'You're right there,' I said.

For three days I wandered around Havana, drinking coffee at street stalls, eating mostly fruit, talking to pensioners outside their apartments, and workers in the streets. The Cubans granted me credit, and I took an official car down to a glorious beach, empty, except for young men and girls who looked like Californian film stars. Seeing my Marks & Spencer shirt and shorts, girls rushed over to me, smiling and pointing; it wasn't me that interested them, it was the camera around my neck. As the boys stood back, watching, the girls all the way along the beach posed excitedly for pictures. I ran out of film, and kept clicking anyway, trading the deception for the innocent pleasure it was giving to the gorgeous Cuban girls.

Alba Holder and I flew down to Camaguay, in the middle of Cuba, where a party official put us into an old American Ford and set off along the dusty road, past fields where lean, alert, straw-hatted *caneros* (sugar cane workers) rode horseback with as much assurance as Hollywood cowboys. We were going to Amancio, I was told; my guides would go no further. The Cubans were refusing to reveal all; I was just hoping that the suspense would be worth it. Certainly, when I became impatient, the soothing way that they put their fingers to their lips promised satisfaction in the end.

In Amancio, a dusty, sleepy town straight out of a Sergio Leone film, I was entertained by the local party officials and given cool orange juice. Then we all went out and walked, almost ceremonially, down the main street, for a hundred yards, until we came to a small, brick building beside a pair of gates.

It was the *cementaria*, the graveyard. I was motioned inside the building. On a table, a large book lay open; a chair stood ready beside it. My hosts stood back, deeply respectful. I studied the list of names, entered in copperplate writing. I found him, easily, halfway down the page. Mark McAughtry. It stood out amongst the names of the Cuban dead. He had passed away at 10.30 am on the 6th of October, 1951.

The ground on the grave was black and hard and cracked. All over it lay the leaves of a nearby giant casuarina tree. Tiny cedars were dotted at random among the gravesites. The committee turned away, as I placed flowers on the grave, stood silent above my father's remains.

He was fifty four years at sea, in the engine room, and survived being torpedoed in two world wars. But he couldn't live at home after Mother died so he falsified his age to stay at sea. He was sixty nine when he died. Now I knew where he lay, and how he came to be there. After a proper period of mourning, I turned back to the committee. The chair of the committee, a black woman, offered her hands to me and I took and held them. Alba Holder photographed me by the grave, then we all turned and went slowly back again, out of the past, out of the shade and into the bright, bright Cuban sunlight.

FLOOR
Susan Zelouf

I can't stop staring at our floor. Twelve by twelve-inch square multi-coloured Chinese slates laid on a diagonal throughout the house – very French country. Wild colours: blue grey, dove grey, charcoal, mushroom, rust, salmon, pinks, purples, golds… like the stages of a serious bruise. The colours come up best when the floor is clean, which is rare, but it's a floor we can live with – we chose it because it passed the boot test.

Before we moved in, I had visions of chalk white walls, pristine cream carpet, Portland stone, and surfaces. Our stuff would be put away discreetly. We'd only keep what adhered to a strict aesthetic code: if it isn't both useful and beautiful, we'd get rid of it. Shoes would be left at the door, Japanese style.

The road to hell may be paved with good intentions, but if the Devil wears lace-up work boots like my husband, keeping that surface spruce will end in tears. The slates, ridged, chipped, gouged by the quarrier's pickaxe, each different as snowflakes, didn't show up the dirt. Our tiler went to work.

Like his father before him, our tiler was an excellent tradesman; he had a waiting list. Slate, a fine-grained metamorphic rock pressed into service after thousands of years bedded into a mountainside, is not easy to lay and Ger was particularly skilled at working with it. He warmed to us after we noted, with excitement, that a few of our slates had fossil ferns and leaves. He told us of a job where a slate with a fossil fish went unnoticed, and wished he'd kept it. He promised to look out for slates with fossils for us, if he wasn't in Australia by then. Sometime, he'd go back to Australia with his young family, and work on a fishing boat, which is what he really wanted to do. Above all, he didn't want to die in Ireland.

He did die in Ireland, suddenly, leaving his family and friends shocked and grief-stricken, his waiting list in limbo, the heat and light of Australia fading to slate grey. I can't stop staring at our floor, cool beneath our bare feet, mud-caked yet still beautiful; a permanent job. It's as if it's always been there, and will be when we go on.

IN LOVING MEMORY
Rita Normanly

In years to come, when they speak of Pat Tom Andy, I will not remember this day. I will not remember this funeral, this wet and windy graveyard where his children and his neighbours huddle together for warmth.

When I look back, I will always see Pat in his hat and his working clothes, walking over the street to the old house. He might be going to split potatoes for planting or to get a bucket of mash for a cow after calving. He might turn in the gate beside the turfshed if there's a load of turf to be thrown in or on a frosty morning he might be going down the garden to the hayshed to get a backload of hay for the cattle.

I will not remember this funeral parlour, these silk flowers, this old man with the pinched white face lying in a coffin in his good suit.

When I think of Pat in his good suit I will see him cycling home late from second mass after having a couple of pints in O'Connors. He will be wearing his good hat and his red tie and he will be smiling to himself, remembering the yarns that were swapped at the bar. He will put the bike in the old house, take off his cycling clips and saunter in to his dinner.

I will not remember him in his sick bed, waiting for the priest to call on Friday or for his grandchildren to visit on Sunday.

In my memory, I will always see him cutting a whitethorn hedge, tackling an ass and cart for the bog or driving the cows home from milking on a summer's evening.

For me, Pat will always be the one who directed the show the day the black cow went down in a drain. All the neighbouring men came to help and the children were banished to the top of the ditch. When the drama was over, the cow safe, the ropes wound up again, Pat got the bottle of poitín and the glasses and the men sat on the ditch and drank to the success of the operation. The men who pulled the cow from the drain long ago, have all gone before him.

In my mind, I see them all now, sitting on a sunny ditch. Make room for Pat Tom Andy there, he's on his way and he has a bottle in his pocket.

A FOOT IN THE DOOR
Nuala Smith

By October 1955, my father managed to make a complete pig's breakfast of things. His love affair with Guinness had led him to yet more creative accounting at work. Sacked again and at home, the last chance of hundreds, all used up.

Privately, Mother decided she'd coax him to leave, then, keep it that way. Like the people on the Titanic, she'd finally accepted that with Da's weight, our dinghy would eventually sink. There was work in England.

In November, he agreed to try Liverpool.

I went as far as the bus stop with him. There'd be a train to Dun Laoghaire, then the mail boat. It was drizzling and cold. Mist fizzled around the amber fog lights that were new on our road.

'Me oul pal,' he said by way of farewell, and he stepped onto the No.13.

I ran back home, sniffling, but stopped when I got in. Mother and my sister sat by the fire, their eyes fixed on the red, concave wall of late-evening slack.

We heard nothing from Da for ages. Then, a week late for Mother's birthday, but too early for Christmas, a package arrived. We watched her open it.

'Parcel them up! Send them back!' Mother cried, 'himself and his lipstick!'

Her lips were pursed into a thin line. No sign of lipstick on them.

We girls were shocked. As under twelves, the idea of getting a parcel, all sticky tape, brown paper and three stamps; opening it, looking inside; taking out its beautiful contents and *sending it all back!* Shocking!

We stood in the bay window of her bedroom and looked. She'd strewn its contents on the eiderdown. Two gold lipstick cases, both with raised pink tops. Each top had a magnificent bee with wings carved into it, these wings spreading down each side, protecting the magical contents. Like a royal seal, the letters 'HR' were engraved on the bases.

We – this fool's daughters – took one each and looked inside. Mine a luscious scarlet, my sister held something called 'Sunset's Kiss'. We tried swivelling them up and down from their golden hideouts. The tops were cut to perfect ovals.

With the lipsticks there was a buttoned manicure set in turquoise leather. Inside, a wonderful set of implements, each held in place by rucked, gold satin. I longed to try the dainty scissors with its curved blades.

'Waste of money!' our mother exclaimed, disgust in her voice.

'Typical of him!' she heaped on the fury, rifling through the wrapping. 'Here we are needing *everything* and he sends lipsticks and manicure sets!'

'But Mammy,' my sister protested, hopelessly smitten by the turquoise leather, 'would you not keep them anyway?'

'No! Back they go!' the tight-lipped woman was adamant.

A card had pink roses and a poem in squirly print, signed, 'Daddy'.

'This is the foot in the door,' she added by way of explanation. And then she bundled up the lot and we never mentioned it again.

THE QUEEN OF DUNCES
Michael Harding

I have a friend who lives in New Jersey. Went out fifty years ago as a boy, worked in hardware stores and is now almost retired. He has a daughter living in Greenwich Village, a nephew at Art College, and his daughter's boy friend makes movies, little movies, and promotional videos for perfumes.

From poor beginnings he has carved out a life. His family around him, retirement will mean the sidewalks and public parks of New York and New Jersey with the grandchildren.

The thought of finally coming back to Ireland has no attraction; it ain't home no more.

He remembers with pride being at the first run of *Philadelphia, Here I Come* on Broadway. He drove a broken-down banger all the way into the city, and he remembers the disgust in the eyes of the valet outside the theatre as his machine rumbled up in the line of black limos; when he got out he handed over his keys to the valet who said 'you want me to park it sir, or just dump it?'

Nowadays his local Hibernian club organises coach trips. It's forty minutes into Manhattan; you get a Broadway show, a drink, and you don't have to worry about the journey home.

So I asked him was he at *Dancing at Lughnasa*.

'Yes. We saw it when the Irish cast was in town. That was when to see it.'

He told me of the bus trip home that night; the lights of New York floating past the windowpane, and his astonishment at the beauty of the play and how he fell into a reverie of his own memories.

There was a frail little girl, shy and always frightened, and one day the schoolteacher found her to be in error with her sums. So he got the old clock, that the guts had long been dragged out of, and he put it on her head. Then he took a tongs from the fire and he placed the tongs in her hand.

'Get up,' he said, 'on the table.'

So she hopped from the floor, to the chair, to the table, and there he forced her to sit on a suitcase, with the tongs in her hand, and the empty clock on the crown of her head. He got the other pupils to dance around her in a circle, and made them bow down and kiss her feet, because, he explained, among all the dunces, she was the Queen of the Dunces.

They danced. They kissed her feet. And she shivered on the table top like a rabbit in a headlamp.

Now I know that the memories in *Dancing at Lughnasa* are warmer and more endearing, but I also know that the burden of remembrance is a single act, and that it is in the enhancement of that act and action that theatre finds its centre and power. And I suspect that people who have lived half a century in exile from their childhood can more fully appreciate the complete power of Friel's great play. But why did my friend recall that particular incident?

'Oh,' he said, 'that little girl is an elderly lady now; she works in the city in a book store, and just by chance, I met her in the foyer at the interval. I happened to ask her was she enjoying the show and she said she was enjoying it, very much.'

MAGNETS
Kevin Whelan

The first home I remember was Staff Bungalow number 3, in the grounds of Bradwell Grove Mental Hospital. My parents were psychiatric nurses; Bradwell Grove was the name of that part of the Oxfordshire Cotswolds we moved to from London.

During World War II, the hospital had been used as a base for the US army. Signs of the Allied occupation lay scattered in the long grass near the men's wards, odd bits and pieces from that monochrome time. We children picked up and inspected spent bullet casings, faded webbing belts, strips of khaki and helmets curiously riddled with bullet holes. Nearby squatted redbrick bunkers, choked with weeds and thick tufts of grass, but fun to scramble in and out of. Next to the bunkers were the oily rank depths of tank and jeep servicing ramps.

The Americans abandoned these ramshackle billets that stood windblown and sleepless except for a few dented lockers, metal bedframes and the broken halves of black Bakelite telephones. Inside the phones were heavy magnets. We'd never seen magnets before and wondered about them. How did they snap together like that? And why was it some resisted sticking together, however hard you pushed against them? These magnets would repel each other, as though some invisible force field wobbled in the air, preventing a connection.

One mile from the bunkers and the billets was a long abandoned airstrip. It too was choked with weeds and grass and dull dandelions that sprouted up through cracks in the tar runway. Looming over the lot was the control tower, tall and empty and peeling white and beautiful in the sun.

As with the army stuff we stumbled upon, the airstrip made me think of American movies and gangsters and cool blokes in flying jackets smoking fags and firing machine guns and laughing. The airstrip reeked of dead glamour and the musty smell of leather left too long in the scorching sun.

Occasionally, patients from the hospital would be drawn to us and want to go exploring. We weren't exactly sure what was wrong with them, but we'd heard, though not from our parents, that there were words to describe them. Barmy was one; nutters, loonies and headcases were others. We didn't know that they were mentally handicapped. Nor did we know of the wards inside the hospital filled with handicapped women and children.

Our mothers and fathers liked to see us playing with the patients. They had names that seemed to belong to another era: Bert, Ted, Arthur, George. They had razor short haircuts, the hair shorn very close to the nape of the neck, flecked with grey and combed through with a margarine slickness. It made them look much older than they actually were. Released from the wards we watched as they wandered around near the staff bungalows, a shifting mass in baggy suits that reeked of disinfectant, their tender faces either deeply tanned, or badly sunburnt, gazing into space, muttering and smiling at us, until as two kinds of innocents, we were drawn back to each other.

THE FROZEN MAN
Adrian Smyth

I once took a photograph, a black and white photograph, of a man waiting to cross the middle of Dame Street in Dublin. As I look at it now he stands on a traffic island as a blurring bus provides a backdrop which throws his own static pose into sharp relief. The shutter of my camera has frozen an image which has stuck in my mind these last ten years. Every time I come across this picture it stops me dead in my tracks and forces me once more to ponder its meaning.

The subject of the picture – this unknown man – stands with his body slightly angled to the left, his face in complete profile as he stares up the street towards Trinity College. He's wearing a flat cap, an outsize double-breasted suit with a wide pinstripe, under which I can see what appears to be a white tee-shirt. The pockets of his jacket sag slightly and his trousers, which neither taper nor flair, are wide and drop straight to his feet. He wears sandals but no socks. His right arm reaches across his lower chest and seems to be gripping the strap of a small knapsack which drops over his left shoulder. A bony left hand has reached up and rests across his right forearm.

In an instant, I pointed my camera, focused and shot. I know this figure struck me as unusual at the time otherwise I wouldn't have taken the picture, but as the years have gone by, the significance of this man and his reason for being in Dame Street that day – a reason I will never know – have grown in my mind.

Yet more than the clothes he is wearing, what intrigues me about this man is his face, his posture and most of all, what might be his past and future. He has the features of an old man yet he is not an old man. His emaciation has aged him prematurely. There is a mark on his right cheek and dark patches on his neck which could be shadows cast by bone and sinew or they could be bruises. Yet he looks too placid a man to have ever thrown or received a punch. With his lips tightly shut and his brow slightly furrowed, his gaze is fixed on something out of shot. Is he looking towards an uncertain future or simply on-coming traffic? I remember being struck by the frailty and isolation of this figure which might at any moment be sucked into the slipstream of a passing vehicle. He stands as if any minute he might sink into himself, and with his arms clasped loosely and forlornly across his chest he could almost be holding himself in place.

Yet these are all presumptions, because with my camera I would grab images and opportunities whenever and wherever I chose with little or no contact with the subject – in this case no contact whatsoever. I flip over the picture and I see I have written the words 'The Last Journey' on the back. I remember he looked so lost that day, so vacant and open that he could only have been a tourist, perhaps on his first and last tour of the capital cities of Europe. And when I look at him now, he has the look of a peasant. I imagine him having lived his life in some far-off European village, a man who had seemed destined to end his days within a mile or two of the place of his birth, but who had, through the kindness of some distant emigrant relation, been given the opportunity to fulfil a dream. Maybe he was a man with a long-held secret desire to one day quietly visit each capital city of his great continent for no reason other than to travel and experience.

I will never know who this man was nor why I came across him that day. Yet the probable truth of all of this speculation is that when I look at this picture now I see whatever I want to see. I project my own changing aspirations onto this stranger, and so the photograph continues to develop in my mind and continues to have a richness and fascination which deepens and bemuses with time.

THE MANY-SPLENDOURED THING
Thomas F Walsh

It is a cold Saturday afternoon in late December and I have climbed into the attic. I'm supposed to be looking for last year's Christmas decorations, but that's only an excuse. I have really come up here to escape the pre-Christmas bedlam below.

This silent room above a bustling world is, for me, like the still point of a turning wheel. It is a space between past and present, under heaven and above the earth, free from conflict and tension, where I can sit and think.

I don't know about your attic, but mine is a repository of all that is useless and precious in my life. Things I should have thrown out long ago but couldn't, artefacts that have survived as we moved from house to house. In a place barely penetrated by light or sound, they lie like ghostly guardians of the past.

I move apprehensively between the tea chests and cardboard boxes that lurk here in the shadows. Surrounded by old familiar things, I am wary of their power. A tattered schoolbag, a school exercise book whose soft pages once opened on a world of wonder, a tin box containing a white seashell. A smooth stone taken from a windy western beach. Why do we keep things? Why are these the things we keep?

As I look around me the slanted sunbeam from the attic window picks out a blur of white far back beneath the eaves, something half-hidden by an old plastic Christmas tree. I reach in to find a pair of angel's wings, made from two coathangers wrapped in white muslin. And Francis Thompson's poem comes to mind:

> 'The angels keep their ancient places;
>
> Turn but a stone, and start a wing!
>
> 'Tis ye, 'tis your estrangéd faces,
>
> That miss the many-splendoured thing.'

I am drawn back to a Christmas play and a little girl, at the tender age of six, about to make her acting debut as an angel. She has just one sentence to say, 'Do not be afraid, Mary'. She has practised it for weeks, flitting about the house wearing her wings and singing 'Do not be afraid, Mary'.

And now her big moment is approaching. She is bowing down in adoration, her forehead on the boards. There is an uneasy delay and then a slight commotion, as the teacher comes to rescue her. A shepherd has been standing on her hair. Now she trots towards the Virgin Mary and her baby, looking a little flustered.

'Do not be a-scared, Mary,' she says, caught midway between St. Luke's Gospel and *The Little House on the Prairie*. She smiles and moves away out of the light.

When she herself left the stage of this world seven Christmases ago, there were people who said 'she's an angel up in Heaven now, you know, you can be sure of that'. I must confess that it didn't mean much to me at that time. But now as I sit here in the gloom and ponder that Christmas past, their words come back to me, and so do hers, 'Do not be a-scared' and once again a happy memory shelters me from grief.

And then I hear a muffled voice calling me from downstairs where angels fear to tread. It is my son, who wants me to give him money so that he can buy me a Christmas present.

Who knows? Maybe he'll buy me something useless that will warm me with laughter in the winter's gloom of some far off future Christmas. It might even make it to the attic and become enshrined with all the other many-splendoured things.

A Sense of the Past

THE TOWERS
Sheila Smyth

Miss Martin came from Galway, and like the Connemara goats, she had high notions. In 1824 she married the nouveau-riche Arthur Kiely-Ussher. Since the fancy name of Kiely-Ussher was newly acquired and was an imaginative variation on plain old Kelly, and since her husband was thirty-five years her senior, the proud lady felt she had bestowed an enormous favour on him by agreeing to marry him. Perhaps the tight-fisted Kiely-Ussher felt so too, for in 1834 he allowed her to persuade him to build a new and magnificent home to replace the very ordinary one they lived in at Ballysaggartmore, County Waterford.

As the plans were being drawn up, Mrs Arthur Kiely-Ussher had a brainwave. Using all the wiles at her disposal, she wheedled her husband into building the entrance first. She had seen what had happened at Strancally Castle and she was determined the same fate would not befall her. Her sister had married John Kiely-Ussher, her husband's brother, and he it was that built the fairytale Strancally Castle overlooking the glorious Blackwater. When he was finished, however, there was not sufficient money left for gates worthy of such a stately pile, and her sister had to be content with riding in her carriage through an entrance that lacked a lodge and a gatekeeper.

Mrs Arthur Kiely-Ussher had always envied her sister's fabulous home at Strancally. Now, at least, she had the chance to own an equally beautiful castle, and in the matter of entrances she would completely outshine her sibling.

Fired with her jealous obsession, she persuaded her gardener, a competent architect named Smith, to design an amazing castellated bridge that spanned a gurgling mountain stream. Florid towers and turrets were silhouetted against the romantic background of woods and waterfalls. This was the main entrance, but it was not the only one. Further up the avenue, this ambitious woman insisted on another phenomenal Gothic building of massive proportions. On either side of the second arched entrance stood a lodge, each one large enough to house a good-sized family, and both were adorned with their quota of cut-stone castellations.

Mrs Arthur Kiely-Ussher née Miss Martin of Galway, was ecstatic with her follies. They spoke of wealth and power, a foretaste of the opulence that was to come at the end of the avenue, and even more importantly, they would make her sister pea-green with envy.

History doesn't tell us how her husband broke the news to her that his money had run out. Just as work was due to begin on the castle of her dreams, fate stepped in and decreed otherwise. History is also mercifully silent on her humiliation in the long years ahead as her guests swept up the impressively long and winding avenue, passed through the truly awesome entrances, and arrived at, well, a very ordinary house.

This plain building was demolished in the 1930s, but the follies remained. They are known today as simply 'The Towers' and tourists often stop when they see the sign on the Lismore Road. They are invariably astonished when they discover that these extraordinary portals lead to nothing, but they are also fascinated when they hear the story of the woman who had a castle with no gates, and her sister who had gates but no castle.

OPERATIC TRADESMAN
Gregory Allen

In the 1950s, I worked the beat in the south Dublin suburbs. During a boom in the building industry, new housing estates were rapidly extending the city boundary beyond the Dodder river, overrunning the grounds of abandoned nineteenth century villas. Official business would often bring a garda on site to pick his way over the builder's rubble.

A foreman was always glad to see a garda passing through. In the twilight years of a more leisurely age, I was cheerfully greeted by courtly tradesmen whenever I looked in to admire their work, and perhaps pick up a tip on some DIY job in hand at home.

Nothing so much characterised the age than the tradition among tradesmen to sing on the job. The old music hall ballads were still going the rounds. A snatch from the chorus of some well-known ditty to serenade a job well done, a skirting board nicely spliced, a door well hung.

'Who were you with last night/Out in the pale moonlight?'

Before the windows were glazed, a tenor voice would carry to the house next door, where someone was bound to reply, 'It wasn't my sister, it wasn't my ma/La-la, la-la, la-la-la-la!'

One carpenter verified his measurements in plain chant.

'Four by two, six feet four and seven-eighths!'

To which his mate responded with a triumphant 'Amen!'; especially when the last nail was driven in at knocking off time.

On a dog day, a man with an extrovert personality and a good voice would be asked to entertain his workmates. An evergreen something from Michael William Balfe, well-rehearsed at hoolies in the old days: 'The moon hath raised her lamp above/To light the way to thee, my love/To light... the way... to thee... my love.'

When the carpenters and the plasterers and the plumbers had moved on, and the painters arrived, the real concerts began. The painters were the real songbirds. They had the acoustics of an empty house to exercise their vocal cords, seldom failing to hit the high doh as they primed and brushed the new timbers, and pasted and hung papers on clean, smooth walls.

I heard of a whistler among a gang working in a convent. Happy at his work, the warbler was performing with the passion of a blackbird on a telegraph pole when a distraught foreman remonstrated anxiously.

'Chippy, please! Remember where you are!'

No sooner had the rendition ended than the Reverend Mother appeared to say how delighted they'd all be if the performance could be resumed.

Nowadays, a garda passing through a building site is likely to hear a transistor radio fighting for supremacy against an electric drill or a screaming saw. The advent of the power tool – the pity of it – silenced the operatic tradesman forever.

THE PIGEON FANCIER
Larry Brassill

Jack was every city boy's dream of the ideal adult. I could not wait to meet him again. He worked on my aunt's farm in County Limerick and knew everything about nature, as well as the idiosyncrasies of such wild unknown creatures as otters, badgers and foxes.

And so, within days of the closure of our school in that summer of 1943, I was already on my way to the country. Wonderfully, little had changed since the previous year, but when I met Jack I found that he had developed a new and fascinating hobby – racing pigeons. He had built a loft for them in an old disused outhouse. Soon I knew all about them, how there were only two eggs in each clutch, with both cock and hen sharing equally in the hatching and rearing of fledglings. To complete this picture of wedded bliss, each bird took only one lifetime mate.

Jack explained that pigeons had been trained to carry messages as far back as Our Lord's time and could race for distances up to 500 miles at speeds of 60 mph. Races took place all over Europe. Extraordinary though it seems, this practice continued throughout the war. But how could the pigeons find their way home from so far away? Jack said that no one knew the answer to this, but they seemed to have compasses in their brains and could navigate by the sun.

Bud was Jack's pride and joy, a super racer. He had nearly died in January as he pined after his mate, who had been killed by a local hawk. Now he was about to have his first race since then, from Dover in three days time. Jack expected that Bud would fly home in about 12 hours, after his release on Saturday.

We were up at dawn on Sunday, anxiously scanning the sky, but no joy all day. Even cheerful Jack grew glum, as night descended. Had the hawk got Bud too? But we could not believe our eyes on the following morning. There was Bud in the loft, not on his own, but with a beautiful lady friend too. He had been romancing instead of racing! How had they met up? When we examined her leg we found that she did not carry the countermark of a racing pigeon but, instead, a small cylinder containing a hand-written note in a strange language. Jack gave them both to me as a souvenir and on my return home I placed them in a box of treasured possessions, there to remain undisturbed for a further thirty-five years.

Twenty years ago our daughter shared in a student exchange with a French girl Yvette, who was accompanied on her journey from France by her Grandad, Pierre. His hobby, surprisingly, was racing pigeons. I told him of my own past experience and resurrected my tiny cylinder from 1943. When he opened it his face grew ashen. Slowly he translated the message to us.

'Rocket launchers moving North towards Normandy. Suspect under observation by Gestapo. Hold further messages.'

He had instantly recognised that handwriting – his sister's final message from the French Resistance to British Intelligence in Dover, before she had been arrested by the Germans at midnight on 5th July 1943, never again to be seen by her family.

THE STRIKE AT BANDON WALLS
Tony Brehony

Strikes and lock-outs are not the product of twentieth century social unrest. They were with us long before James Larkin rallied the workers of Dublin to the banner of militant socialism. Look what happened in the year 1610 when Lord Cork decided to erect an elaborate set of walls to defend the West Cork town of Bandon from constant attacks by the rebel Irishry.

The walls were to be constructed mainly of black slate, about nine feet thick, varying in height from thirty to fifty feet. The area of town enclosed was estimated at twenty-six English acres. There were three castles to be erected also, each containing twenty-six rooms, the turrets and flanks to be platformed with lead and mounted with cannon.

This then was the ambitious building project about to be undertaken by Lord Cork when a militant leader of the workforce upset his programme by demanding an immediate increase in the masons' wages from two and a half pence to three pence a day.

'My members have been exploited for too long,' the masons' leader told a very irate Lord Cork. 'And no walls will guard the town of Bandon unless the just demands of the workers are conceded.'

The earl refused to be blackmailed by such idle varlets and he told them so in no uncertain terms. They could, he went on 'betake themselves to the devil out of Bandon and, by gad, he'd be damned in Hell before he'd bow before their impudent demands.'

Lord Cork withdrew to his stately home and the masons marched off the site.

As in all labour disputes, there were side issues. One unfortunate mason with a sick wife and a family to support decided that he couldn't afford to join the strike. Lord Cork, hoping that his good example would influence the others, agreed to let him work alone.

Days passed into weeks. Whatever about the pressures of hunger and misery on the idle masons, the political pressures brought to bear on Lord Cork to complete the defences of Bandon became unbearable. Suddenly he pocketed his pride and capitulated, agreeing to all the demands of the striking workers. They marched triumphantly to the site and started work at the new rate – three pennies a day.

As for the blackleg mason, his fellow craftsmen demanded that he be instantly dismissed but Lord Cork refused. That evening, however, the masons gathered menacingly around their erstwhile workmate and one of them, chosen by lot, hit him from behind with a pickaxe, splitting his skull and killing him instantly. They buried his body in the foundations of the walls and laid a course of masonry over it to conceal their crime forever from the eyes of man. They nearly succeeded.

It was fully two hundred years later that workers removing part of the old town walls came across a large flagstone. A quick tap of a pickaxe gave off a hollow sound. Visions of Spanish doubloons and buried treasures rose before their eyes, but further investigation uncovered only the mouldering bones of the unfortunate mason. His hammer and trowel lay under his broken skull as they had been placed the day the strike at Bandon walls had finished. And soon that was all that remained – the skeleton upon being exposed to air, crumbled into dust.

THE BURGHERS OF CALAIS
Dolores Stewart

I'm not exactly a philistine but anything more than twenty minutes in a museum or art gallery is likely to bring me out in a rash or, at the very least, is guaranteed to send me reeling through the nearest exit. But now and again, once in a while, something stops me in my tracks. This was the feeling I had while visiting the Musée Rodin in Paris. It was after I'd escaped into the garden that I saw it. Saw *them* – six large ragged figures, roped like animals and with flesh-and-blood wretchedness written all over them. Their expression and gestures told me a story of anguish and despair.

The plaque told me hardly anything, just the name of the figures *The Burghers of Calais*, a date of 1887 and the medium which was 'Bronze'. It turned out that they were the leading citizens, the burghers, of Calais one time when the French garrison town was besieged by the English.

This particular siege had dragged on for almost a year. By which time food supplies had run out and the defenders were down to eating rats. It was at that point that the leading burgher, Eustace de St. Pierre, turned the key in the gates and surrendered the garrison.

But by then, Edward the English King, wanted revenge.

He agreed, finally, to spare the population in exchange for the lives of the six leading burghers. They were to bring the keys of the garrison to the English camp, where they would then be executed. Those were the English terms. St. Pierre and five others were to be hanged.

It was this moment in history that the French sculptor, Auguste Rodin, was commissioned to commemorate in 1884. It was a moment etched into French consciousness – a moment of heroism when a single act of sacrifice saved all the others.

But Rodin saw things differently and evoked the group of six burghers in all their human frailty: the bowed shoulders of an old man, Eustache de St. Pierre; the clenched fists of Jean d'Aire, defiant in the face of death; the raised arm of Pierre de Wiessant, proclaiming the vanity of all things; the transfigured face of the youngest, Jean de Vienne, turning to the others on their way to Calvary; the despairing figures of Andre d'Andrieux, clutching his head and Jacques de Wiessant who tried to drive away from his eyes the image of a nightmare.

Rodin showed them trudging out beyond the walls to suffering and death: bareheaded, barefoot, roped. His figures were not heroic, but human.

The Parisian art world was unimpressed. Rodin's figures, they said, were dejected ones. And anyway, they lacked elegance. Those figures, their heroes, were men of clay. The sculpture was rejected.

But Rodin was no stranger to controversy. His figures were so life-like, their expressions and gestures so convincing that critics accused him of casting them from life.

It took ten years before his masterpiece, *The Burghers of Calais*, was finally put in place. Rodin's plan was to place the figures as if, he said 'they were setting out in single file from the Town Hall to Edward's camp like a living rosary of sacrifice and suffering'.

But the larger-than-life sized bronzes now stand where I found them, in the garden of the Musée Rodin in Paris, a monument to what might have been.

Yes, might have been. Because the Burghers didn't, after all, die. As luck or providence would have it, the English queen Philippa intervened. In a startling gesture, she knelt before the King to beg for the lives of the Burghers of Calais.

It took another two hundred years before the English were finally persuaded to go home; when that other English queen, Mary Tudor – so they say – died of a broken heart.

SPUTNIK
Seán Canning

Forty long years may have come and gone since, yet everybody remembers exactly where they stood in the chilly dawn of that November day.

How eagerly we scanned the dim horizon until suddenly, with all the dramatic flourish of a shooting star, it appeared right over our heads.

The Russian Sputnik, that very first man-made satellite was bleeping its flight path through the Irish sky.

The Class of 'Fifty-Seven was enormously impressed, standing on the front lawn of our boys' boarding school not far from Dublin.

There were some who vowed at once to become pilots; which at the time seemed a very logical first step. Others thought more in terms of Engineering with particular emphasis on rocket construction. But as I recall it, Research had the most enthusiastic supporters all fired up with important details such as the correct fuels to propel us into the heavens.

Not a whisper to be heard about that long coveted Double First in the Classics, Latin and Greek. A new star had arisen in the East whose name was Technology. Nothing from now on would ever be the same again.

For me however, the coming of the Sputnik struck a very personal chord. A few years before, I'd placed an ad for pen friends in an international teenage magazine. Finally a letter arrived with an unusual postage stamp. The enclosed photograph was of an attractive, dark haired sixteen-year-old. Lidia Gordeev was a Russian student with excellent English for which she gave full credit to Vera, her black American tutor at the Maxim Gorky Academy in Leningrad.

Our correspondence continued sporadically long after Lidia went off to study music in Moscow. I always replied by return. But there were inexplicable delays between Lidia's posting and my receipt of her letters. More irritating still, everything she wrote was extensively if amateurishly censored. A thick white substance was used to blot out particular phrases and sentences.

However, it was still possible to read the offending words by the simple expedient of holding the letter up to a mirror.

And what caused the Thought Police so much angst? Apparently these shadowy figures who controlled Lidia's environment were reluctant to let the rest of the world know that there were no potatoes in the shops. Or that Lidia simply adored the music of Elvis.

Whoever felt threatened by this innocent exchange and made the decision to end it, Lidia's simple, handmade New Year's card of twelve months before had been her last communication with me. Somehow I sensed as the Sputnik flew over that I would never again hear from her.

For the moment, however, school holidays were all that mattered.

As our train crossed the Shannon, donkeys and carts were still to be seen on the winding roads of Connacht. Cattle were haggled over at fairs held on the street.

None of us then could foresee a world that knew instantly by satellite how matters stood potato-wise in Moscow, what the Spice Girls wore in Barcelona, or how much a prime bullock might fetch in Ballinasloe.

In that New Year of 'Fifty-Seven, our hearts and minds were filled with study-free days and parties, and only the odd wistful thought for friends far away with exotic names and a lively interest in Rock 'n' Roll.

YOU COULD HAVE FOOLED ME
Maureen Charlton

In 1925 a Reader at the English publishers, Chatto & Windus, opening a package from Ireland, discovered to his great excitement that he had a literary scoop and very probably a future bestseller on his hands. For the package contained four leather-bound notebooks written in a fine Italian hand, purporting to be a novel written in diary form by a young Irish girl, Cleone Knox and giving a vivid and enthralling account of her life between 1764 and 1765. The diaries had been sent, according to the enclosed note, by a descendant of the writer who had discovered them among family papers.

According to the diary, Cleone was the daughter of Edward Knox, a rich landowner who lived in Castle Kearney in County Down on the Ards Peninsula. A widower, he was bringing up Cleone, her elder sister Cary and their brother Edward.

Cleone, a spirited and strong-minded girl of twenty, had become enamoured with a dashing but impecunious neighbour, a Mr Ancaster of whom her father did not approve and so, for reasons as much tactical as educational, he decided to bring Cleone and her brother on a trip to Europe.

And so the diary takes us from her native County Down on a marvellously brisk and entertaining Grand Tour of the spas and high society of eighteenth century England, Switzerland and Italy. There are brilliantly observed descriptions of the places she visited and the glamorous people she met and the many adventures and misadventures which were wont to befall travellers in that pioneering era.

The Knox family, it appears, were people of great eminence because in no time at all they are being presented to the King and Queen at Versailles where the King does her the honour of kissing her on both cheeks. An unparalleled honour as only the grandest people – Ambassadors and Royals – are so greeted.

With remarkable prescience and political maturity for a girl of twenty, she gives indications of foreseeing the French revolution, while on a more frivolous plane is given tips by a famous court beauty on how to keep her looks – by eating raw vegetables and not using too much rouge.

On to Switzerland where she is as much impressed by the cleanliness of its citizens as by the majesty of the Alps but totally unimpressed by Switzerland's then most famous resident, Voltaire, at his house in Verney. 'The great man received us in a chintz dressing gown, with a flow of brilliant wit. Sometimes affable, more often peevish. To tell truth, he reminded me of nothing so much as a chattering old magpie.'

The diaries end on a note of high drama in Venice when her brother Ned elopes with a nun. The nun's family being very rich and influential, are enraged, pursue the couple and the unfortunate Ned languishes in a Venetian jail for several days, being only rescued by diplomatic intervention at the highest level.

And Cleone's beloved Mr Ancaster whom she had left behind her languishing in County Down, miraculously appears in Venice and the postscript of the work informs us that they marry in Geneva, return to Ireland where they settle down and have twelve children.

Chatto & Windus were absolutely taken with the manuscript and went ahead and published it. On its publication this racy and romantic tale caused a sensation and became a best seller in England and the United States. The experts declared it to be a genuine eighteenth century diary, one of them even going so far as to compare it in importance with that of Pepys.

Six months later it was revealed that the experts had been taken in.

'Cleverest hoax of the century' rang the headlines in the Daily Express where the diary and its alleged author, Cleone Knox, were shown to be the work of a twenty-year-old writer, Magdalen King Hall. Though born in London, King Hall had Irish roots and had spent much of her youth and childhood here.

She went on to write more romantic novels and died in 1971, but none of them had the astounding success or displayed such an inspired melange of high comedy and meticulous historical research as *The Diary of a Young Lady of Fashion in the Years 1764-1765.*

If any of you happens to come across this slim volume on a shelf of your local library, be sure to take it down and I know that you will find it an enthralling read.

CLOGS TO CLOGS
George Ferguson

The firm of Timothy Eaton and Co has closed. Its lifespan was one hundred and thirty years. I walked through the Toronto store a few weeks ago and felt like a mourner. Perhaps it's because I'm a draper's son or perhaps it's because the founder of this great business was an Irish lad from Ballymena who made good that the romance of it has always fascinated me.

It was in 1854 when 20 year old Timothy Eaton left Ireland for the new world. Two years later, he opened a 12 x 14 foot log cabin store at Kirkton which was a trading outpost. For some customers it meant a day's journey. Business was by barter. The expanding Grand Trunk Railway passed Kirkton by and went to

St. Mary's instead. In time Timothy Eaton followed and determined to trade for cash only with no more barter. By 1868 he was ready for Toronto and opened the first of a chain of more than seventy department stores that reached from Winnipeg to Montreal.

It was the human face of Timothy Eaton & Co that touched me. I spoke with a sales lady. She began her working life there twelve years ago. The previous day, she had worked for thirteen hours marking down prices on the stock. Her father is eighty-eight. He came from Ballymena and worked all his life for the firm. The demise of the company has left them bereft.

I felt too ashamed to buy. Lovely goods were displayed beneath garish signs declaring '50% off lowest marked prices'. The saleslady told me the reductions would continue until the largest sign of all was satisfied 'Everything must go'. I was watching the lifeblood of a gallant merchant slowly drain away.

There will be many other mourners. Part of the legend is that any job applicant from Ireland would get at least a start in employment. The legend even includes the smiling Chinaman who announced 'me from Ballymena'.

There must have been staff affection and loyalty. When the company was fifty years old, they contributed to erect a larger than lifesize statue of Timothy Eaton just inside the main door of the Toronto store. Ever since, all who enter give a rub to Timothy's left boot in the hope that some of his success might pass on to them. The toe cap shines.

Few family businesses survive three generations. The first builds, the second spends and the third collapses. It's 'clogs to clogs in three generations'. Some cautious banker foresaw it all for he wrote on Timothy's now yellow credit file, 'Has put up and opened new building for clothing store. This may be a safe extension at present, but think it will not pay eventually.'

I made my purchase. It was handed to me in a high quality, purple carrier bag with rope handles and bearing the Eaton name. That will remain among my souvenirs long after the goods I bought are forgotten.

THE FATE OF THE *STEPHEN WHITNEY*
Sean Fitzgerald

The American sail ship, *Stephen Whitney*, sailed out of New York on October 18, 1847. With a cargo consisting mostly of corn, cotton and cheese, and with a total of 110 persons on board, she was bound for Liverpool. Captain Popham didn't realise it at the time, but his ship was to become instrumental in influencing the decision to erect a lighthouse on the Fastnet Rock a couple of miles out to sea from Ireland's most southerly point, Mizen Head. The voyage proved uneventful until the ship neared the Irish coast on Wednesday, November 10 when the weather turned foggy.

The ship hove to, and the sounding line was thrown overboard. When it was ascertained that the vessel rode on fifty fathoms of water, the captain decided that it would be safe to proceed – with caution.

About eight o'clock that evening, land was seen immediately ahead, and was identified as Crookhaven. Referring to the inclement weather being experienced by the crew, a contemporary newspaper journalist claimed 'it was impossible for even the keenest eye to descry the land which lay in treacherous contiguity'.

The mistake which was to prove fatal, was now to be made! A light was seen on land, the ship's Mate identifying it as Cape Clear Light.

'Not so,' said the Captain. 'Cape Clear is a revolving light, and is very high. So that must be the Old Head of Kinsale.'

Adjustments were made to the course, and the *Stephen Whitney* unwittingly turned into Roaring Water Bay – dotted with rocky islands, and about forty miles west of the Old Head.

About two miles from Cape Clear the jagged rocks on Western Calf Island awaited the *Stephen Whitney*. She hit them broadside, and within minutes ninety-two of those on board – including the captain – had perished.

The eighteen survivors managed to get ashore across the rocks, and made their way to some cottages they could see inland. The inhabitants of those dwellings, not quite recovered from the ravages of the recent great famine, rendered what assistance they could, and willingly shared their food.

Commenting on the suddenness of the occurrence one of the survivors told the same journalist:

'At half-past nine on Wednesday night as Chief Officer I was in command of the *Stephen Whitney* with an efficient crew; at ten o'clock I was shivering, almost naked, over a few sods of turf in a wretched cabin.'

The following morning hundreds of locals converged on the scene of the accident hoping to find something which would make their miserable lives that little bit easier.

But, so efficiently did the sea and rocks perform their task that no trace of the *Stephen Whitney* could be found.

Writing to *The Times* a couple of weeks later one of the survivors listed the names of the ships that had been previously lost along this coast, included the *Sirius*, reputed to be the first vessel to sail completely under steam across the Atlantic. In reference to his own recent experience on the *Stephen Whitney* he said, 'there has perished a noble ship, with her gallant commander and ninety-one persons, victims of the incompetency and the apathy of the Ballast Board of Dublin'.

He then pointed out that the Cape Clear light is 455 feet above sea level, and is therefore frequently obscured by fog, and so claimed that the proper position for that light should be on the Fastnet Rock.

The existence nowadays of a powerful flashing beam emanating from the construction on that remote rock suggests that he was listened to.

THE GAMES WE PLAYED
Maeve Flanagan

One of our favourite childhood games was playing Mass. I was the priest. I took the starring role myself because it was I who had thought of the game. We always celebrated these Masses at the top of the hall. Its cruciform shape resembled that of a church, and the evening summer sun filled it with gold light, just like any stained-glass window behind the high altar in a real church.

We paraded up and down the hall, two little girl acolytes, and one larger girl priest, clad in old tablecloths and sheets. I carried one volume of the Encyclopaedia Britannica for my Mass Book. We quaffed vast quantities of malt vinegar stolen from the kitchen and diluted to the colour of altar wine. At Communion time my congregation of teddies and dolls received Silvermints which we had sucked to just the right wafer thinness for Communion Hosts.

'Jabber, jabber, jabber,' I intoned in my home-made Latin.

'Wibbly wobbly, wibbly wobbly,' my acolytes responded.

And then we tired of that game. We scoured the real adult world for any little bit of pomp or ritual which we might incorporate into a new game, but found none. None that is until 1966 dawned and the whole nation plunged into an orgy of commemoration of the 1916 Rising. Suddenly the world was replete with possibilities.

Roger Casement's remains were brought back to Ireland and we were taken to see him lying in state. Nightly on the television de Valera inspected guards of honour, unveiled plaques, and laid wreaths. De Valera, tall, gaunt and almost blind, linked by his aide-de-camp... now he had definite possibilities for a new game.

And so we created our own 1916 Commemorative Spot in the back garden, a sort of Arbour Hill and Kilmainham Gaol combined. We hacked down great boughs of purple and white lilac and fashioned them into wreaths. I was de Valera, and my sisters were my aides-de-camp. I wore an old overcoat of my father's festooned with St. Patrick's Day badges for medals, and my sisters linked me round and round the garden.

We felt that there must have been some hitches at the real Commemorative Ceremonies. Leading an old partially-sighted man around couldn't have gone as smoothly as the television news would have had us believe. We started our ceremonies from the back door.

'Ten paces down, then five to the right, then you lay the wreath,' my sister instructed me. But de Valera was tall, his paces longer and invariably I ended up off course.

'Oh, no Mr President,' my aide-de-camp/sister would shriek. 'They're the gooseberry bushes.'

'Go raibh maith agat,' I would reply as she would try to steer me back on course. But not until we had recovered from helpless bouts of laughter.

The de Valera game lasted far longer than the Mass game, and it was much better fun. It lasted to the point where it seemed futile to replace it with another; adolescence and puberty beckoned and I left behind the games we played.

PICTURING THE PAST
Barbara McKeon

The photograph was taken in the summer of 1956. It shows children in a suburban garden holding hands, encircling a girl whose birthday it was, all wearing pretty party frocks, beaming up at the camera.

Over forty years later I have a copy of that picture. And I'm still friends with Beverly, the birthday girl.

That picture captures for me the essence of my growing up in Dublin in the

Fifties. For so many, that time meant poverty and despair, repression and ignorance. But my photograph reflects a different image; we were part of a new prosperous Ireland, offspring of professional and commercial people who owned their mortgaged houses, drove cars and sent their children to nice schools.

But more importantly, the photograph is significant because it encapsulates another aspect of the Ireland I grew up in. Of the ten little girls in the picture, three were Jewish, two were Protestant and the other five Catholics. We went to different schools and churches and learned the ethos of our separate religious identities, but we came home and played in each other's gardens. While we were conscious of our differences they rarely impinged on our friendships, having no more bearing than being on opposing teams for a game of tag.

Except for one potentially combustible occasion. On a summer's day, shortly before her birthday, Beverly was taking me and another friend, Maura, to the Macabi Club, a Jewish sports and social club near the Kimmage Crossroads. I had been to the club before but it was Maura's first visit and she felt a little apprehensive about entering a Jewish enclave. For some reason she chose that moment to tell Beverly that the Jews had murdered Jesus.

Beverly hotly retorted that Jesus himself was a Jew, and besides he wasn't the Messiah just a prophet and holy man. This piece of blasphemy staggered Maura, especially as we were passing the Holy Ghost Fathers at the time.

'Jews are doomed to eternal damnation in the fires of hell for not believing in Our Lord,' Maura solemnly warned.

Then, looking at me, added in equally regretful tones, 'So are Protestants for not believing in Our Lady.'

That led to a good old, stand up, ecclesiastical knockabout that involved a bit of hair pulling and a kick on someone's shin. An adult cycling by ordered us to behave ourselves and the holy war ceased abruptly.

In festering silence we crossed the Kimmage Road and were about to enter the club grounds when Beverly pulled off a theological masterstroke.

'Catholics aren't allowed to be in here,' she announced, as Maura's jaw dropped open, 'but Protestants are,' she added triumphantly, grabbing my arm and hauling me off towards the clubhouse.

Maura's eyes were brimming with tears as we left her standing outside the gate, thirsting after the promised lemonade.

There was no intentional sectarianism, just words and attitudes that had filtered down from the grown-up world. A world we would one day inherit ourselves.

It took a week and a packet of Matzoth biscuits to patch up that row, but we were pals again in time for the birthday party that was to be captured in a photograph for all time.

LIFE UPON THE WICKED STAGE
Ted Goodman

For the first six years of my life I moved in the company of actors and even if they were not, for the most part, great actors (though one did make it to Hollywood) the people of the towns and villages of Ireland flocked to their dramatic presentations in the 1930s and 1940s. I am talking, of course, of the 'fit-ups', those troupes of strolling players who presented their very individual versions of everything from Victorian melodrama to the latest offerings from Hollywood.

The expression 'fit-up' well describes the essence of that kind of acting, for a lot of it had to be made up on the spot, to take account of deficiencies in the stages and props available to the actors. They provided their own costumes when necessary. So my father was able to use his uniform from the First World War when he played the part of a Black and Tan officer in *The Informer*, by Liam O'Flaherty. Indeed he was so good in the part that he came close to being beaten up by the locals in the pub in one village, the day after a performance. They were sure that only someone who had actually been a Black and Tan could have played that part so realistically. He somehow managed to convince them that he was only a harmless thespian and he swore that thereafter he would play only the part of 'Gippo' Nolan, the informer, who has the good fortune to be shot on stage.

As well as *The Informer*, which had been stolen and freely adapted from John Ford's 1935 film, I remember seeing such gems as *Little Old New York, Peg o' my Heart* and *Maria Marten or The Murder in the Red Barn*. But I recall best of all *East Lynne*, because I appeared in it, playing the part of Little Willie, the child who died nightly to the combined sobs of his mother and the grief-stricken audience.

I don't remember now the finer details of the drama, which had been created for the stage from the Victorian novel by Mrs Henry Wood, except that the single line for which the play is best remembered was not written by the author, but by the impresario who adapted the book. This is how the big scene ended, with not a dry eye in the house.

Lady Isabel Carlyle, the mother of Little Willie, comes to visit her dying child but she is disguised as Madame Vaine. (This is Victorian melodrama, after all.) The poor little fellow, dressed in a green and yellow satin suit – oh! I recall it all so well – raises himself painfully and asks in a weak voice 'Will it be long before I die, Madame Vaine?'

She collapses, weeping, across his bed of pain and by the time she manages to gather herself together, the little chap has left this vale of tears. She throws herself across his bed once again, still sobbing and uttering the immortal line, 'Dead! Dead! And never called me mother!'

The curtain was rung down slowly and after a decent interval for grieving by the tearful audience, we artistes took our bow and went back to our humble theatrical digs. It must have all been very convincing, for my little sister used always rush round backstage to confirm that I was indeed alive and would be able to come out to play next morning.

But soon school beckoned, putting an end to my role as Little Willie and a great career on the stage. The role, together with the green and yellow satin outfit, then passed to that same little sister and the audiences continued to weep buckets every time *East Lynne* was presented.

RICHARD GANLY
Sheila Gorman

The death of a seven-year-old boy, Richard Ganly, who had once surprised his father with a handful of bees, was marked by a couple of paragraphs in *The Irish Times* and a notice in the obituary column.

The story has been in my family for as long as I can remember. The little boy shot, supposedly by a stray bullet, while playing in the field at the bottom of the garden. Several children were there at the time, under the care of their nanny, when they were suddenly ushered into the gazebo. They were subsequently rushed into the house – no explanations were offered. It was never really explained to the children what had happened but they had never seen their brother Richard again.

He had been playing in a tree when the bullet hit. Perhaps they thought he had fallen and they'd shouted, laughing, at him to get up. He didn't. A shooting party, in civilian dress – target practice they said – were in an adjacent field. No one was held accountable. It was 1922.

He was taken to the Meath Hospital where a bullet was removed from his head. Death was due to laceration of the brain, they said. The jury found in accordance with the medical evidence, adding that target practice should not be permitted where it endangered public safety.

I wanted to place that small boy back into the family. To give back the memory. To locate him in history. To remember him. To recall him for those who never knew him because he died so young. It seems he had a way with bees. The one memory we do have recalls him, unafraid, cupping and closing his hands over a bundle of bees, running to his father and releasing the bees under his father's chin.

Anyway, we were given a map of the cemetery by the clerk in the office near the chapel. The plots were indicated by dotted lines. Certain plots were cut off by the perimeter wall.

My twelve-year-old son and I found his headstone. The single plot holds layers of dead. Grandfather, fathers and sons, including one of Richard's brothers, David, who was only one year old at the time of Richard's death. David lived for another sixty-eight years. It was reassuring to find him in the same plot as his young brother even though he couldn't have remembered him.

They all lie together, one on top of the other, in a dusty graveyard within the sound of heavy traffic. They lie in a sandwich of earth, soft wood, coffin handles, and bones marked by a white marble headstone, facing away from the path.

The graveyard is filled with fallen and broken slabs, stone urns, draperies and angels. Quotations about dawns, angels and resurrections. Words of questionable comfort. Pathways and bones. Family vaults and plots. Elaborate headstones. Map supplied. On a summer afternoon colourless and dusty, overgrown and yet not green.

On our way out we watched a woman crying quietly. Perhaps recently bereaved. As we walked further down the avenue, lined with yew trees, we encountered a cortège on its way in. The flowers in the hearse being the only colour I had seen all afternoon. There was a mourner who wore a bowler hat. A bell tolled. We continued on towards the gate.

The stray bullet that entered the young boy's head that afternoon over seventy years ago could have hit any of the children who played together. One of those children was my mother. She was four and Richard, her brother, was seven and a half.

I went looking for my history in his history. Looking for answers in his questions.

Family bones intermingle in that plot. It is said that as long as a person is remembered then they are not really dead. They live on in others' memories. My mother is the last of that generation. She is the only person left who remembers her brother and the day of the shooting. Her memory is fading. Will that young boy be gone when she can no longer remember? Or will he live on as a second-hand memory of mine and as a third-hand memory of my son's?

THE ENAMEL JUG
Peter Jankowsy

In winter the playground of the kindergarten was reduced to a few grassy square metres rising, just about, over low-lying ground which, from autumn onwards, turned into a morass, the remnant of a number of allotments, now devastated by war action. All around the mud loomed the typical four-storey houses of Berlin, many of them now in ruins. A group of children were playing on the little patch of green, five-, six-year olds, a single boy and half a dozen girls. It wasn't peaceful play, it consisted of chases and scuffles, the girls nagging the boy, he making them scream by pulling their sleeves and their hair – all bitterly enjoyable in the dim November light of the first winter after the end of the war.

Unnoticed by the playing children, another boy had appeared on the scene, like an emanation of their grim surroundings, a tall, scraggy lad of maybe fourteen years, poorly dressed in something uniform-like that hung down from his shoulders, as did his long arms. His right hand clutched the handle of an enamel jug, the kind you would take to a field-kitchen for a ladle-full of soup. He stood there motionless, watching, his pale face without expression.

The little boy had just burst into a wild dervish dance, making the girls scatter and scream, when the din was cut as if by a knife, by the tall boy's voice.

'Look away!' he ordered the girls calmly. The children all froze and looked at him. The small boy stood in front of the tall one, looking up at him. He saw him raise his right arm slowly, the handle of the chipped enamel jug clenched in his fist, he saw him swing his arm back as far as he could. And then the stranger, with all his might, brought the pot down on the little boy's head, hitting it just above his right eyebrow and cutting down to the bone. They all could hear the short, hard knock, as if on wood, the little boy heard it from within. Blood spurted out promptly, then after a moment of silent shock, came a howl, more of horror than of pain. Fingers covering the violated face were flooded with blood and tears and saliva. He stumbled forward, calling for the kindergarten nurse, the girls fluttering all around him, now screaming with genuine terror. They completely forgot about the tall boy who had vanished, unseen, back to from where he had first appeared, the ruined city. The bleeding boy was brought to a first-aid station in the neighbourhood. The wound needed a few stitches and with a big bandage, like a turban, he was delivered home into the arms of mother and grandmother.

And that's where that day ended for me – in a nest of warmth and nourishment and care. Where did the tall boy go? Where had he come from? For half a century now his darkly looming figure, his right arm swung back, has been a regular visitor to my sleepless hours. Why had he wanted to erase me from his world? For that had been his intention, no doubt about that, had he had an axe instead of that enamel jug, he would have used it, such was his ferocity. Over the years I have brooded over every one of the few details I can remember. Those uniform bits, for instance. Had he perhaps been one of the unfortunate teenage boys the Nazis had drafted in at the very end of the war, had taught to kill, to be heroes, to defend their mothers and sisters? Had he, in his confused mind, wanted to rescue those little girls from their tormentor? Even then I had felt that jealousy had been a motif, not so much of me being with girls, but of me not being alone.

And that pitiful enamel jug – had he no one to feed him, were his parents dead, maybe still buried under the rubble? Was he just roaming around, homeless, gone feral, after all he had seen, all he had lost? Was he, when we met, as impregnated with death and killing as I was as yet untouched by it? I will never get the answers to these questions, but over a lifetime they have brought him ever closer to me, my would-be executioner, my older brother Cain.

A SOCIAL EXPERIMENT
Maureen Keane

In a little town of Ushaia, on the southernmost tip of Argentina in South America, there's a shop called Jemmy Button's. When I first saw it I was puzzled by the name, then it clicked. Jemmy Button was a participant – not a very willing one – in a social experiment over one hundred and sixty years ago.

In 1830, Captain Robert Fitzroy was in command of the sailing ship, the *Beagle*, on a coastal survey of South America for the British Admiralty. The vessel put ashore in the desolate region known as Tierra del Fuego, about as far south as you can go. The name, Land of Fire, was given to the area by early seafarers who from their ships saw countless little fires across the land. These belonged to the natives, who were mainly nomadic and carried their fires with them wherever they went. Embers were wrapped in wet moss and clay and came to life when needed. The natives were a hardy lot, almost naked, but smeared with grease to repel the cold. The women spent hours in the sea, diving for mussels, while their babies rocked on cradles of frozen kelp leaves.

To the white sailors these natives seemed hardly human, and Captain Fitzroy, a committed Christian, was horrified by their condition. When, therefore, a party of natives stole some of Fitzroy's property, he took four of them hostage and brought them back to England with him. His motives were of the highest; these four would be turned into Christians and then sent back as missionaries to their benighted brothers and sisters. One of the four died, probably from smallpox, but the other three – Jemmy Button, York Minster and a girl, Fuegia

Basket – arrived safely in England. They were put in the charge of the Church Missionary Society and soon became minor celebrities. They were even presented at court where King William IV was most intrigued. He asked many questions and his wife, Queen Adelaide, gave generous presents to Fuegia Basket. Jemmy Button was the most popular of the three Fuegians. He had learned English very quickly, was both respectful and friendly, and cut a fine dash in his tailcoat and breeches.

In 1831 the three hostages set sail again in the *Beagle*, this time homeward-bound. The young naturalist, Charles Darwin, was on board and watched scornfully as the goods provided by the Church Mission Society for the Fuegians new life were unloaded. Tools, seed, timber, these were essential, but what use were wineglasses, soup tureens, fine white linen and chamber pots? Indeed Darwin, too, was appalled by the sight of the wild men and women and wondered how these strange beings could have come from the same stock as the three kinspeople who were now disembarking. However, he took comfort from the fact that the three Fuegians who had spent the year in England had learned civilized behaviour. Their good example would inspire others.

The *Beagle* sailed away back to England, leaving behind York Minster and Fuegia (who were now married) and a disconsolate Jemmy Button. Fifteen months later, the *Beagle* returned. There was no sign of a settlement, the huts were deserted, the gardens trampled and overgrown. Then a few natives appeared in canoes, and one particularly savage looking one, with wild hair, almost naked, gave a perfect naval salute. It was Jemmy Button. He was invited on board and entertained to dinner. His English was still good as were his table manners, but otherwise he had totally reverted to his native state. He was perfectly happy and contented, with he said 'plenty birdies' and 'plenty fishies' to eat. With that he said 'good bye' and returned to his canoe where his pregnant wife awaited him, and rowed off into the night.

So much for the great evangelical experiment. It was, as Fitzroy conceded, a total failure. However, more organised missionary endeavours followed in later years, and the primitive life of the Fuegians disappeared under the onslaught of Christianity. Now all that is left of Jemmy Button and his companions are a few artefacts in a museum and a name on a shop front, in the town at the end of the world.

HORSLIPS AND LOBSTERS
Cyril Kelly

In August 1970 the band Horslips came to the Western Ballroom in Dingle and I was there. With a few preparatory pints in Foxy John's to begin with, we arrived in the dancehall to witness Dingle leapfrogging thirty years from the forties straight into the seventies. I can still feel the excitement, shored up for almost a month, bursting like a wave over the crowd that night when the band appeared on the stage and we saw that the fiddler had a blue fiddle to mesmerise us, not only with colour, but also with a revolutionary, Celtic sound. None of the auld lads that I had seen back in Feoghanach and Baile na nGall had ever played a blue fiddle. So I was there with the youth of West Kerry; all the lads tingling with Old Spice, the only scent known to Homo Sapiens at the time, and for the girls the Mary Quant miniskirts which, having crossed the bridge at Blennerville, had arrived to claim a place in the folklore of Corca Dhuibne. We were all there for that almost delirious night.

I got home to Baile Bhóithin at 3am that morning and at half five Mom was waking me again because Liam was outside in the car. Before I knew what was happening, I was halfway down to Barr a' Duinín, struggling into the second polo neck jumper and reeking to high heaven of fish. Even when Liam aimed the prow of the *naomhóg* out of the harbour and headed for the lobster pots, the Western Ballroom was still buzzing in my head. The sun lay behind Brandon and my senses were in a whirl; the smell of diesel and fish tangled with the tinctures of perfume still in my nostrils and in my ears Horslips played to the beat of the two-stroke outboard motor. Liam cut the engine and the *naomhóg* skated across the polished sea. In the ensuing silence we had dropped back to the dawn of time when Stone Age man first began to harvest food from the sea.

The rim of the sun appeared above the dark mass of Brandon as we began to haul the first pot. Rocking on the ocean, the blue-black cliffs hanging over us, we were dwarfed. With every heave we gave, the rope serrated across the gunnel and the sound was like a saw cutting through the silver layer of silence that stretched over the sea. A pot could be 20 fathoms deep with a half a cement block anchoring it, but the struggle was worth it when the pot broke the surface and that blue 4lb beauty, encrusted with a few barnacles, jabbed out at me.

I had the bicycle tube cut into rings at my feet. Holding the lobster between my knees, I snapped one rubber ring around the big claw and wound another ring three times around the small claw. At the front of the boat I had made a yellow corral with the oilskins and the lobster was deposited in there. Liam dipped the blades of the oars lightly to nudge us into a glide. The mauves and pearly pinks had drained from the sky. I took off one of the polo necks and the mobbed sensation of the Western Ballroom fell away. The expanse of the ocean stretched out beyond An Fear Marbh and the Blaskets towards the haze rising from the horizon. The sun was now a blazing ball balanced on the summit of Brandon. A new day had begun. We dropped the day's catch in the storepot and headed for shore.

There was little talk on the boat. Liam was the skipper. I was glad of the job for the summer. Mom was praying that when the Leaving results came out I would get a call to the Training College. With the cockiness of youth, I didn't see why not. I'd heard that in Dublin you could see Horslips every week.

THE SECRET ROOM
Patricia Moorhead

I grew up in a house that had once belonged to my great-grandfather. There was a room in the basement that was always kept locked and my father would tell my sisters and me ghost stories about the secret room, as we called it, to stop us wanting to go inside. It had the opposite effect. Our favourite childhood game when my father was safely out at work was to get the key from his pantry, unlock the door and go inside. The room with its shutters tightly locked against the daylight was like Aladdin's cave to us children.

Amongst the toys held in this time-warp were skipping ropes, whipping toys, toy drums, sets of metal toy soldiers and a wooden rocking horse, its mane tugged bare and its once shiny legs scuffed from endless races. Trunks full of old fashioned clothes were pulled out for dressing up games and charades.

There was an assortment of old-fashioned dolls and dolls' prams bought over forty years for three generations of little girls. Cane basket-weave prams bought in 1908 were much more exciting to us that our own dolly prams of the 1940s. On wet winter afternoons we played school in the secret room, my eldest sister being the teacher while my other sister and I sat in two school desks and scribbled into old copy books with pens and crayons. Inside the desks were exercise books filled with my father's copper plate handwriting.

There was a high chair which had been bought at an auction in 1902 for my father's first birthday, and used by him, his baby sister and his stepsister born years later in 1922. It came back into service in the 1930s when my sisters and I were born. It had a semi-circular tray that you brought down over the child's head. The seat was made of cane and the chair could be lowered down and made into a rocking chair and lifted up again to its full height for mealtimes.

Still carefully packed in boxes was a train set given by my great grandfather to my father on his seventh birthday in 1908. He had kept his trains hoping one day to give them to his son, but he had three daughters instead. I don't remember being allowed play with the trains when I was a child. But my children who grew up in the house in the 1960s were allowed to set up the trains in their bedroom and my son and his Grampa spent many happy hours lying on the floor of the bedroom playing trains. Years later my father presented his train set to the Museum of Childhood in Palmerstown Park in Dublin.

In 1975 my father cleared out the secret room and apart from a few things I managed to save, all those treasures went one day to a junk man. My father hadn't wanted anyone to see what was inside the room. Perhaps because of his memories of a lonely childhood in his grandfather's house surrounded by adults, the death of his mother when he was just four after the birth of his baby sister, followed three short years later by the death of that little girl. He didn't realise that what we had was our own Museum of Childhood, right there in our secret room.

THE DAMASK TABLECLOTH
Melosina Lenox Conyngham

In my family, there is a miniature of an eighteenth century lady with a turned-up nose that is passed down from eldest daughter to eldest daughter. With the miniature alas, I have also inherited the nose, which is not an endearing button beloved by romantic novelists but a proboscis that one could hang a hat on, as one of the in-laws unkindly remarked.

There are no emerald tiaras or diamond necklaces amongst our other family heirlooms, though at one time there was a brooch that, in a will dated 1873, was described as 'set with two of my godmother's teeth which only fell out at the age of eighty-seven years' but fortunately it has either disappeared or is treasured by some other branch of the family. We are not sure if the lion's claw set in gold should be an heirloom or not, for no one is certain if it is the claw of the lion that ate Cousin George in Zululand at the beginning of the century and we don't like to revere just any old lion's claw.

But our most venerated possessions are a white damask tablecloth and twelve napkins, all much stained, which came to us in the following way:

My great-great-grandfather was a humble curate in the cathedral town of Lichfield in Staffordshire. He was in love with the Archdeacon's daughter, but her family considered that he was her equal neither in birth nor fortune and bitterly opposed the match. Also in Lichfield lived an elderly lady, Miss Lucy Porter, the step daughter of Dr Johnson, the writer of the Dictionary. She was very fond of great-great-grandpapa though once when she was opposed in conversation by him, she said, 'Why Mr Pearson you are just like Dr Johnson, I think. I do not mean that you are a man of the greatest capacity in all the world like Dr Johnson, but that you contradict every word one speaks just like him.'

She also used to tell him that on her death, he would not be forgotten, which he took to mean some little keepsake, but when the will was read it was found that she had left him a house, a great deal of money and a number of relics of Dr Johnson. These included the manuscript of the dictionary, a bust of Dr Johnson taken after his death, his walking stick and an enormous tablecloth with twelve huge napkins.

Now that my great-great-grandfather had inherited a fortune, the Archdeacon had to withdraw his opposition to the marriage of his daughter though the bride's mother was so annoyed about the nuptials, she stayed in bed all their wedding day.

The couple lived happily ever after, though I am ashamed to say they did not take the care of the Johnson mementoes that they should have. My great-great-grandmother said Dr Johnson was 'a gross old man and a dirty feeder' and she tossed the things up into a loft. Sometime later an American came and offered a thousand pounds for the manuscript copy of the dictionary, which caused her to scurry off to look for it, but alas the rats had already found and gnawed through most of it. The bust of Johnson was put on a shelf from which it fell and was shattered into little pieces when someone slammed the door in a huff. The walking stick was burnt in a house fire, so only the tablecloth and napkins remain.

Nowadays the stains are the most interesting part of the tablecloth. Is this where the Great Cham of Literature slopped his chocolate when he topped it up with cream or melted butter? Is that the mark of a leg of pork, boiled till it dropped off the bone? The very dark stain is probably the outside cut of a salt buttock of beef or is it where the veal pie with plums and sugar was spilt? For all of those were Johnson's favourite dishes and they say you can tell a man by what he eats.

ANIMAL ANTICS IN ANCIENT IRELAND
Seamus McCluskey

Without a shadow of doubt, the most amazing animal ever born in Ireland was surely the Dalkey Island cow which first saw the light of day in the year 727. According to the early Irish annalists, this remarkable creature had one head and neck, two bodies, six legs and two tails. And the lucky Dublin farmer who owned her got milk three times a day. No trouble there reaching his milk quota.

The east coast also had an unusual visitor in the year 739, when a remarkable whale was thrown up on the strand at Carlingford in County Louth. When opened up, this huge sea mammal was discovered to have three gold teeth, each weighing forty ounces. I wonder who was her dentist!

But animals hadn't matters all their own way, and the birds also figured prominently in early Irish history, that is if we are to believe the authors of *The Annals of the Kingdom of Ireland* who recorded that in 945, the birds of the sea went to war with the birds of the land at Limerick, while over in Waterford, there was a battle royal between the ravens of Munster and the ravens of the West, with the Munster birds coming out on top.

But the birds of the south and west were nothing compared to the birds of Leinster. According to the *Four Masters*, a steeple of fire was seen for five hours over Durrow in 1054. Innumerable black birds were seen passing in and out of it. There was one very large bird in the middle, and the little birds went under his wings and into the steeple. Then they came out again and, between them, raised up into the air a greyhound that was in the middle of the town. Then they let it drop and it was killed when it hit the ground. But the birds weren't satisfied. According to the annalists they then took up three cloaks and three shirts and let them drop to the ground as well. The wood on which these remarkable birds perched fell under their weight and the oak tree shook to its roots in the earth.

Back to the animals and fishes however, and the *Four Masters* recorded that a monster salmon was caught at Clonmacnoise in 1113, which was twelve feet in length, twelve hands in breadth without being split, and three hands and two fingers the length of the fin on its neck (a real 'fisherman's tale' if ever there was one) while for the year 1355 they tell us that a sheep produced no less than ten lambs in the one year. But the best description of all comes under the year 1472. It reads:

'A wonderful animal was sent to Ireland by the King of England. She resembled a mare, and was of a yellow colour, with the hoofs of a cow, a very large head, a large tail which was ugly and scant of hair. She had a saddle of her own. Wheat and salt were her usual food. She used to draw the largest sled-burden by her tail. She used to kneel when passing under a doorway, however high, and also to let her rider mount.'

An Irishman's description of a camel, on seeing one for the first time. I wonder how he would have described a hippopotamus!

LACEY'S CROSSING
Jacqueline Morrissey

At a crossroads in county Waterford stands a small pub. A long, low, cottage-style building, it sits discreetly into the side of a hill. Its roof is of corrugated iron, but it must once have been thatch. Although small, it does a busy trade, snagging customers as they converge from the various branches of the crossroads to travel the Waterford city road. One hundred and fifty years ago it was attracting travellers on the same journey, when it served as inn and stage coach station, and was known locally as Lacey's Crossing.

It was here in the black years of the 1840s that two of my ancestors met, in a soup kitchen set up at the Inn to feed the hungry victims of the potato famine. During the grim summer of 1847, John Tobin arrived to help with the relief effort. The son of a hedge-school master from the Comeragh Mountains, he too held classes in the kitchen of the cottage he shared with his elderly father. Many of the local Irish-speaking population acquired their basic education at his turf fire. By day, however, he worked on the estate of one Captain O'Shea, a local Catholic landowner. It was in this capacity that he arrived to help the relief effort.

Waterford was not as badly hit by the Great Hunger as were many other areas. Parts of the county escaped almost unscathed, but to the west, and up in the small villages that dotted the Comeragh Mountains, starvation, disease and death were common.

There is a road, high in the mountains above Kilrossanty, which leads nowhere. In the harsh creed of the mid-nineteenth century, it was never acceptable to feed people merely because they were starving. Work had to be created to justify famine relief. The lonely mountain road was the result. Many of the people who built it died along the way, weakened by hunger and exhausted by the labour. For them, death was the only relief from famine. The population which might have used the road was soon dead too, or in exile. Some made their way down from the mountains and in towards the east of the county, seeking the institutional aid of the city poorhouse or the temporary relief offered by makeshift soup kitchens.

Lacey's Inn was one such place of relief. Here at the age of thirty, John Tobin met Catherine de Lacey, the landlord's seventeen-year-old daughter. Working together in the midst of such catastrophe must have created a considerable bond. In the midst of the squalor and starvation of the time, a romance developed. The oddly matched pair went on to marry. Amongst the children born in the years that followed was my great-grandmother, Cáit.

Greek mythology had it that three sinister women were responsible for spinning the threads of human destiny. One carried a scissors with which she would snip an occasional thread, thus ending a life. Her shears were certainly busy in those grim famine years, slicing through the fabric of rural Irish society, leaving ragged edges of death and destruction in their wake. Amongst those broken threads and ended loves, it is hard to imagine that a new link could have been formed. To me it seems almost more surprising that now I can still trace that fragile connection, through family reminiscences and oral tradition, back into the dim, frayed, tapestry of time.

FRAGMENTS OF MEMORY
Marie O'Nolan

My mother taught the piano and she died when I was a child. The trauma of her early death turned her, for me, into a defensive, hazy memory. Even now I cannot picture her fully. There are only unrelated fragments that I fear will never make a whole picture. I chiefly recall her hands. I also remember a long, narrow, flat, padded cushion with which she covered the keyboard of her piano when not in use and, above all, I recall something that I found later, hidden in her prayer book.

Her hands, I remember, were firm, thin and shapely, the rings loose enough to twist on her fingers. They looked mostly at home when they were moving on the keyboard. Her manual skills however did not extend to sewing although she did make a pink silk cover for the flat cushion that was spread over the black and white keys; its stitches were clumsy and visible and at one end they had come undone and were never mended.

Other memories are less defined but I do recall the days when pupils came to the house for lessons. That meant that the house would be filled for hours with the vibrations of scales and sometimes a short hesitant study or piece. There would be gaps during which I would hear just her low voice, admonishing and advising, then the music, if such a painful struggle between talent and patience can be so called, would start again. I have no personal memory of my mother's teaching simply because she decided not to try to teach either me or my brother. She passed that task on to an aunt.

When she did play for her own family it was indeed music and we children often fell asleep to the strains of the *Moonlight Sonata* or woke to the ripples of the *Rustle of Spring*.

She was also employed sometimes to play at the silent cinema from which my father would collect her each night at the end of the performance to escort her home. Quite often she was called upon to accompany singers at local concerts. I have a vague memory of someone, who could have been she, once accompanying Jimmy O'Dea during a comic song but she laughed so much she could hardly keep on playing. It must have been she because she was wearing my mother's satin and lace wedding dress which had been dyed a deep midnight blue for the occasion.

Although my parents lived through a period of political turmoil in Ireland, I never remember politics being discussed or sides of the Civil War divide evaluated. They were gentle, domestic people and both of them, it was obvious, hated conflict of any kind. This made it all the more surprising that I should have found what I did in my mother's prayer book.

It was very many years later, after my father's death, when the small suburban house where we had once lived was being sold. Corners of family history that had not been touched upon for years came to light. In a box in the attic I came across my mother's old prayer book. I took it out and dusted it reverently. It was worn and well-used. As I idly turned the pages that bore marks of her thumbs, something fell out onto the floor. I bent down and picked it up. It was a faded snapshot of a tall, handsome young man in Irish army officer uniform. I did of course recognise the face but even if I had not, on the back of the picture there was a name, a date and some letters, written in my mother's handwriting:

> Michael Collins, 1922, R.I.P

THE DANCE CARD
Madeleine O'Rourke

The music was loud and the darkness was punctuated by multicoloured shafts of light which were flashing high from one corner, blinding you, so that the approaching figure was a silhouette looming out of the smoky darkness.

The man's voice raised over the pulsing music asks 'Are you coming up?'

A hand comes forward and guides you through the mass of heaving bodies, finally a small space appears and for the first time you face your dance partner and through the dim light try to make out his features. Would this be just the one dance or perhaps more? Not being able to communicate verbally was a great disadvantage in your assessment of the possibilities.

The first spark of romance has great difficulty in igniting in such hostile conditions with smoke in your eyes and elbows in your ribs, and that glass ball constantly revolving above your head.

That's my abiding memory of the dance floor during the Saturday night hops at rugby clubs in Dublin in the late 1960s.

The clip clop of the horses' hooves resonated off the cobbles as the carriage drew to a halt outside the building. As the driver pulled on the brake, the young ladies resplendent in their long flowing ball gowns were starting to step down from the carriage, the gentlemen assisting their passage.

This is how you would have arrived to a dance in 1875, and this picture of the past came to mind as I held in my hand a tangible link with a romance of the past – a keepsake of my great grandmother, a memory of her first meeting with her future husband.

It was a dance card – a dance card for the Third Annual Ball of the Clan Na Gael. Clan Na Gael was an Irish-American organisation set up after the defeat of the Fenian rising in 1867. It was more than likely this ball was held as part of their fund raising activities in Ireland at that time. The dance card for the ball was circular in shape, and half the size of a postcard – the cover was padded silk with a paper lace effect trimmed in gold, with four pages inside – a cord was attached to the top of the card and had a white pencil with a tassel at the end. This allowed the dance card to be slipped onto and worn on the lady's wrist as she danced.

The inside pages listed the order of dancing – polkas, waltzs, quadrilles and marches were amongst the list of thirty five dances that evening before the Grand Finale and 'God Save Ireland'.

On the back page of the dance card was a poignant verse:

'Far from the hills of Innisfall, we meet in mirth to-night.
Some of the scattered Clan Na Gael, with spirits warm and bright.'

As I held the card in my hand I could just imagine the scene, on that night of January 11th 1875, when they met at Ferrero's Assembly Rooms in Dublin. As Gilmore's 22nd Regimental Band was playing stirring melodies in the background, did their eyes meet across the dance floor and with the formalities of first introductions observed, would she have removed her glove to receive a kiss as they consulted the card and agreed on their first dance and the start of their romance together?

This first meeting between the handsome twenty-five-year-old Frenchman and a sixteen-year-old Irish girl was set against the turbulent background of an Ireland searching for political stability and Home Rule. Both merchant families were involved in the political movements of the time, and were supporters of Parnell.

So this dance card is a tangible link with a time and customs long gone and is one of the few keepsakes of significant events in my ancestors' lives which have miraculously survived, having been passed down through the family, to be rediscovered a century later at the bottom of a wardrobe, in a small dust-covered leather case.

THE LONG HANDLED PEN
William Wall

My father used to say that his pen had a long handle, meaning that his work was with long-handled hoe and hayfork rather than with pen. The saying always reminded me of those long-handled pens we used to have in national school. The paraphernalia of childhood education has altered beyond redemption – for the good of course – and the language and imagery have gone with it. Children have parers now, whereas we used to have toppers and before that we even had blades. They have biros instead of pens. I have even heard a child of my own referring to the rubber as an eraser.

The old high-ceilinged schoolroom in Whitegate National School in the 1960s, where I spent what should have been my formative years, was far simpler than its modern counterpart, and yet, in a way it was more complicated too.

Instead of desks we had benches – long wooden benches with fixed seats and sloping tops and a little ridge to keep the pens from rolling down. We used to sit eight to the bench. Then beyond the benches in the master's realm was a black pot-bellied stove. Providing sticks or kindling to light the stove was a duty taken in rotation by each boy or girl in the class. You were expected to bring a single newspaper and a bundle of sticks. One of the things you were taught in a country national school in those days was how to twist paper to exactly the right density so that it would catch fire but not burn out before the sticks took on.

Snatches of rhyme, rarely wholesome, initials and declarations of love and war were all carved deeply into the surfaces of the benches. Every two places there was an inkwell – a small, white, chipped ceramic pot, fitted into a circular hole in the desk. One of our favourite occupations on a dull afternoon was stuffing bits of paper into the well. Then, when you stuck the pen in you could wriggle it in the glutinous mass at the bottom and the nib would come up clogged with black sodden gunge. Of course, ink meant blotting paper, and many a happy hour I spent watching ragged blots spreading over the pristine surface of a sheet of blotting paper in all sorts of fantastic shapes under a dripping nib. Louis le Brocquy, the artist, has almost made a career out of that kind of thing, but as the saying goes, we were there before him.

In those days we learned joined-up writing almost from the word go. Unlike the modern schoolchild, who imagines letters as unconnected things, bits of the alphabet without any friends or relations, we saw every letter as a member of a tightly-knit community of other letters, all joined by frail lines and curls.

We used to enter handwriting competitions which always seemed to have first prizes of Fountain Pens with Platinum Nibs. Nobody ever won anything, not in our school anyway, but it wasn't for the want of trying. None of us even knew what platinum was, not to mind a platinum nib, but we were entirely convinced that good handwriting and fancy fountain pens went hand in hand. To this day I can't look a fountain pen in the eye without reflecting that whatever the Irish education system of the 1960s did for me, it failed miserably, despite all that practice, in the handwriting department. My father used to say that my writing looked like the wanderings of a drunken spider. Coming from a man whose pen had a long handle, that was a devastating description.

THE KEY
Anne Sharpe

When we discovered the old lodge six years ago, it felt at once like somewhere to live. This would be a place to grow into, allowing the atmosphere of all the accumulated doings of over two hundred years to seep, in turn, into our present lives. We could be staking our own claim to history by fronting the future with the refurbishment of this old hunting lodge. We would be giving it, in turn, its continuity into the early reaches of the twenty-first century. In this instance, we humble mortals were the link between past and present. Guns had once been laid down in that lodge and carcasses stored there, but feasting and merriment must have had their place at the wide fireplace as well. We would extend it all even further, pushing out old boundaries, opening the whole thing out to the expansive light of the present. Though we would try to keep whatever essence the shell still possessed.

But our plans went awry. As it turned out, only the sandstone walls were sound enough for preservation, for foundation and roof were beyond repair. Sadly, the dream quickly faded and a modern house was built on the site instead. At last, all that was left of the lodge was the large key of its former door. This was a formidable metal object of no mean weight that we placed on the dining room mantelpiece of the new house. I can't say exactly what made us display it like that. But it remained upright against the bricks, black and unrusted, the only link with what had been so decisively abolished.

When, months later, a visiting friend recently returned from New York dropped in, she made straight for the key.

'That's it,' she said. 'That's just how they placed them... against the wall like that', lifting it up and weighing it in her hand.

It turned out that when the nineteenth century Irish emigrants had arrived in New York, they all still carried their front door keys with them, if they had a front door at all. This was so, no matter how impoverished the dwelling nor how slim were the chances of returning. That key held pride of place in their apartments, long years after any pretence at return had faded and they were well settled in their new continent.

And nowadays, various museums still hold the range of keys, line after line of them, still black and purposeful looking, still ready for use, protected against cobwebs, holding their own.

FROM MONET TO MURDER
Nuala Smith

I floated out of the Monet exhibition in London, my eyes full of turquoise lily pads. I'd spent too long in the gallery shop where eleven cash tills murmur the public's appreciation. Now I had a Monet umbrella, a Monet mug and a mousepad of Giverny. Outside, more wonders beckoned; across the street, Fortnum and Mason – Grocers to the Queen. Dodging through black taxis, I was in.

Chandeliers, knee-high carpet pile in ruby, food. Food for kings, oil barons, heiresses, quail in aspic, starfish paté.

I glided round, fingering essence of vanilla, distilled in Aruba – two-inch bottles the price of a shirt. Mustards in blue and white jars that you'd certainly plonk in the middle of the damask, price label underlined. From obscure vineyards, vinegars you could have a damn good party on.

I waltzed with the wealthy to the bakery section, led by my nose. Florentines winked cherries through revealing shifts of chocolate, currants watched from damp iced strudels. A girl – no, a Claudia Schiffer – in uniform, transformed wax paper into protective clothing for meringues, bagged them in paper carriers with those stiff handles, surrendered them to aristocrats in cashmere.

I did a side-step to the fruit and veg. To the assistant's credit, he sold me one green apple without a flicker. As he wrapped it, I read a notice on a gilded easel: 'Fourth Floor Exhibition – Table Wear of the Russian Czars.'

The lift expelled me onto dove-grey carpet. Russian coats of arms on tissue-fine porcelain, basket-cut fruit bowls, candlesticks, crystal. Royal blue dinner plates edged in gold, huntsmen pursuing stags across soup tureens big enough to bath a child in.

And then I came to it and my throat contracted. At the front of the last display, a tiny china tea set; apple green, edged in gold with an inner rim of rosebuds. Two small cups on saucers, a little jug, a sugar bowl with a lid. The set stood on a dainty tray, maybe eight inches square. The card said 'Tea set of Czarevich Alexis, only son of Czar Nicholas II'.

Underneath, the boy's dates: 1904 to 1918. I imagined him in a sailor suit, sitting on the floor in the palace, having pretend cups of tea. With four big sisters, he'd have been in on a lot of tea parties. A beautiful child with large grey eyes but so delicate that he was seldom able to go out to play. So many times in his short life, a slight bruise escalated into coma and the brink of death. Yes, anything that was fun, indoors, must have been a gift.

The hot display lights shone down and I thought how the little boy must have passed that tray to Nagorny, his ever-present bodyguard. Nagorny, who in the end wasn't there when Lenin gave his orders and the newly hated monarchy was shot to bits.

INCLINED TO RHYME
Thomas F Walsh

'They are not long, the weeping and the laughter,
Love and desire and hate:
I think they have no portion in us after
We pass the gate.'

Ernest Dowson's old poem comes to mind as I drive by the gate of the ivy-covered thatched farmhouse where I grew up. In this fine weather there should be people saving hay, but now,

'The silence of unlaboured fields
Lies like a judgement on the air.'

Poetry always reminds me of my mother. I can see her now, bringing tea and soda bread out to that high meadow on a hot June day. My father is castigating a labourer who had failed to show up to help us with the hay. The labourer was a drunkard and a waster, we all agreed. All except my mother, that is.

'Who steals my purse steals trash,' she says quietly,
'But he that filches from me my good name
Robs me of that which not enriches him,
And makes me poor indeed.'

Well that shut us up, alright. Not for the first time, my mother could make the words of the poets fit the world. She never went beyond primary school and yet she could quote from Shakespeare's plays and Milton's *Paradise Lost*.

She was not unique in this respect. When my parents and grandparents learned poetry, they committed it to memory, and such learning enriched their lives as well as ours.

Gray's *Elegy* and Goldsmith's *Deserted Village* were the people's favourites.

> 'Full many a flower is born to blush unseen
> And waste its sweetness on the desert air'

she would say wistfully, or maybe

> ' ...of all sad words of tongue or pen
> The saddest are these: "It might have been!"'

It was pure wisdom packed tightly into verse, lines from the old Lesson books that everybody seemed to know but it was not all pragmatic. I remember a July evening, coming from the well, when we watched the sun set behind the islands of Lough Corrib and Gerald Griffin's poem sprang to her lips,

> 'On the ocean that hollows the rocks where ye dwell
> A shadowy land has appeared as they tell,
> Men thought it a region of sunshine and rest,
> And they call'd it Hy Brasil, the Isle of the Blest.'

Poetry belonged to the people then, not to a chosen few. It lay lightly on the spirit.

Small wonder, in those green summers, that we, as children, were inclined to rhyme too.

The aforementioned labourer who was given to drink wandered into our house one night and fell asleep on the hearth. During the night he felt the cold and put two sods of turf, as he thought, on the fire. In the morning my father found his new shoes burnt to a cinder.

As Homer's ghost whispered to Patrick Kavanagh,

> 'I made the Iliad from such a local row.'

The next day, as we crept along the drills thinning turnips, we composed our own epic in hushed voices.

> 'The night Pat Forde was on the booze,
> He burned my father's Sunday shoes.'

Last year when my mother died I found among her papers a little book that I had never seen. It had a worn cover stitched on with white thread. It was Blackie's English Classics edition of *The Deserted Village*. On the fly-leaf, her name, in fine curved copper plate; Anne Lee, Fifth Standard, July 12th, 1918.

As I looked out at the overgrown fields where we made hay, I didn't have to read the lines she would have quoted;

> 'Ill fares the land to hastening ills a prey,
> Where wealth accumulates and men decay.'

SHIPWRECK WITH ORANGES
William Wall

When the White Star liner *Celtic* went aground on the Cow and Calf rocks off Roches Point on December 12, 1928, my father saw his first orange. Such are the minutiae of history. The story of the wreck of the *Celtic* is told in all its stark simplicity in that excellent piece of local history *Down Paths of Gold*, a product of the historical society of the little Cork harbour village of Whitegate. My father's oranges, of course, do not get a mention. A young farmboy of fifteen coming face to face with the realisation that there were fruits with exotic skins such as could not be grown in his father's orchard, is surely too tiny a ripple to bear any relationship to the great current of history.

Yet it is part of that current, and connects with other ripples in the way that we are told the beating of a butterfly's wings relates to the great currents of the air.

The liner *Celtic* was the largest vessel ever built anywhere in the world in 1901. Fast and elegant, the very epitome of the luxurious transatlantic liner trade. By 1928 she was an ageing queen, still powerful, still elegant, but fading fast.

She seems to have been hove to, awaiting a pilot on the night of the disaster, too close, as it happened, to the lighthouse and the rocks. A tremendous gale was blowing, but that should have been a minor matter to those enormous steam turbines. At any rate, a huge wave, a gust of wind, and she was lodged firm and fast on the rocky pinnacles of the Cow and Calf. She was in no danger of sinking and the passengers were actually served a hot breakfast to fortify them for the rigours of rescue and a long tram journey.

There was no unseemly panic and all hands behaved with dignity and professionalism.

She was never refloated though, and in due course she broke up in the usual gales of the winter months on that coast, contributing, in the process, a great deal of wrack and salvage to the local community. My father 'salvaged' a considerable amount of fine timber and had the foresight to bury it under a new concrete floor in the dairy because shortly afterwards the Civic Guards arrived searching for the plunder.

It was often said that there were teak deckchairs in houses that had never heard of a deck, and a substantial beam of timber supports the ceiling of a local pub. Just recently I saw a man adding two beautiful mahogany doors to the cabin of a boat. When I enquired he told me they were salvaged from the *Celtic* and kept stored in an outhouse over the years. No doubt the family was waiting for the hue and cry to die down.

As for history? Well, plundering wrecked ships was a staple of all shoreside communities once. And my father's oranges and the teak planks? What else were they but a part of that ancient tradition.

THE HUT
Lydia Carroll

The hut stood alone in the meadow with the panorama of the city in front and the bulk of the Three Rock Mountain behind. It was separated from its neighbours in the next field by a high mixed hedge and a dyke. All of the huts were of similar design, solid wooden structures with felt roofs, and their equivalent could have been found in many areas on the outskirts of Dublin in the 1950s. The huts had something else in common besides their design – they were all built by city dwellers, summer migrants who looked on these shacks as a sort of Shangri-La to which they escaped from the drudgery of city life.

The few items of furniture were usually rejects from city homes. Ours had big brass beds, then considered old-fashioned, to which I can unfortunately remember regularly sticking my chewing gum. Our simple meals were cooked on a primus stove, a temperamental appliance, and the only thing I ever knew that caused my father to use bad language. Sanitation was provided by Elsan chemical toilets, the disposal of whose contents was a strictly male preserve and, for all I know, may even have had an initiation rite. Certainly, the disposal ceremony, which took place under the cover of darkness, and from which all females and children were excluded, had all the marks of a secret society. Hidden in the bushes, we would watch as a dignified and silent procession wended its way, laden with metal canisters, to the cesspit in the far corner of the field. In idle moments I often wonder if some luxury house in the Dublin mountains has a particularly fertile corner in its garden, and hope they never find out why.

The men, for the most part, had the worst of the bargain, for these were ordinary working men, who continued working throughout the summer months, while their wives and families reaped the benefits of their summer retreats. Some only visited at weekends, while others, like my father, travelled by bus or bicycle into the city at first light, returning wearily at sunset. He had his moment at the weekends when, monarch of all he surveyed, he organised impromptu cricket matches for visiting relations from the city.

Our mothers fared somewhat better, for who would not rather drape clothes to dry over scented hedges rather than on grimy city washing lines, or buy milk and eggs straight from the farm instead of from the huckster's shop on the corner? And after the simple chores were done, being able to sit in the sun in a carpet of lush grass dotted with clover and buttercups, with the smoky haze of the city far, far away in the distance.

But above all it was a child's world. For three wonderful months, the mountains were our playground, to gather wild berries, dam streams, help the farmer's wife look for eggs, roll down hills till we were dizzy, catch frogs among the bulrushes.

The idyll came to an end with the approach of the sixties, when land for houses became more valuable than land for huts, and the city came to the mountain.

But I was reminded of it some time ago, as my daughter and myself wandered through one of Dublin's most exclusive stores. There, in the furniture department, at a suitably exclusive price, was a brass bed identical to the ones we had in the hut.

'We used to have one of those in the hut,' I told her.

My daughter looked at me in amazement and admiration, and I could see that I had gone up several notches in her estimation as she said, 'You had one of those in your holiday home? You must have been very rich.'

I was about to deny it when the memories came flooding back.

'Yes,' I said, 'we were.'

LIST OF CONTRIBUTORS

Gregory Allen 78, 197
Former member of the Garda Siochána. Sometime curator of the Garda Museum.

Paul Andrews 3
A Jesuit Priest from Omagh. Teacher, psychologist and therapist. Currently Rector of Manresa Retreat House, Dollymount.

Ken Armstrong 79
Writer for theatre, radio and film. Five radio plays produced. Winner of the 1994 London Radio Playwright's Festival. Writer-in-residence for Claddagh Films.

Mary Arrigan 81
Writer of teenage and children's fiction. Illustrator of books for younger children. Many awards include the Hennessy Award 1993 and the Bisto Merit Award 2000 for illustrated books.

Ivy Bannister 42, 133, 161
Writer and lecturer. Awards include the Francis MacManus Award and the Hennessy Award. She is the author of Magician, *a collection of short stories.*

Richard Beirne 83
Born in Roscommon. Broadcaster in RTÉ Radio and co-creator of the series 'Gumgoogly'.

Annette Black 4
Lives in Wicklow. She is a teacher and writer for magazines and radio.

Denise Blake 163
Lives in Letterkenny. Writes poetry and short stories and has been published in Poetry Ireland. *Short-listed in the Sunday Tribune/Hennessy Awards.*

Pat Boran 7, 84
Ten books of poetry, short fiction and non-fiction. Regular contributor and reviewer to Sunday newspapers and RTÉ radio programmes.

Denys Bowring 164
Worked as social worker in England. Now lives in Connemara. Is currently revising a novel. Reads his short stories and verse on local radio.

Larry Brassill 198
Retired Borough Engineer of Dun Laoghaire. Part-time Consultant. Eight grandchildren keep him fully occupied.

Tony Brehony 87, 199
Short story writer, historian, novelist. First radio story accepted by Francis MacManus in 1949. Regular contributor to Sunday Miscellany since 1977.

Matthew Byrne 44
Priest, broadcaster, writer. Formerly producer, presenter with BBC and RTÉ. Books include Heaven Looked Upwards, *published by Townhouse.*

Seán Canning 202

Born in New York, spent much of his youth in the West of Ireland. Was a construction worker, salesman and telephone operator. Now a teacher.

John Carmody 171

Artist-in-residence at Arthouse, Dublin. Involved in community-based work in Limerick. Working on a collection of poems.

Lydia Carroll 232

Lives in Raheny, Dublin. Works as an Executive Officer in Trinity College.

Maureen Charlton 204

Contributor to various RTÉ radio programes. Has written drama for the stage and radio. Published work includes Selected Fables of La Fontaine *(Irish nomination for a European Translators' Prize).*

Neil Cleminson 8

From North-East of England. Producer and director of ward-winning documentaries on wildlife, botany and green issues for Channel 4 and the BBC.

Fiona Coyle 129

Born in County Armagh. A former teacher, now living in Belfast with her husband and teenage son.

Richard Craig 154

Born in Glasgow. A Graduate of London, Leeds and Strathclyde Universities. Now lives permanently in West Cork.

Rita Curran Darbey 88, 165

Born and educated in Dublin. Writes regularly for radio. Currently writing a novel.

Gordon D'Arcy 10

Born in London in 1947. Works as environmentalist/educator/artist/writer in the Galway region.

Pat Donlon 12

Director of the National Library of Ireland from 1989-1998. Member of the Royal Irish Academy and the Heritage Council.

Frances Donoghue 13, 134, 143

Dublin-based. Worked as a teacher, guidance counsellor, social researcher and part-time writer. Regular contributor to various radio programmes.

Mick Doyle 38

Born in Athy, Co Kildare and spent several years abroad. Has been writing poetry and prose for over ten years. Currently writing a novel.

Norrie Egan 40

Taught for several years in the North. Has had stories and plays broadcast.

Shane Fagan   167

Retired Maintenance Supervisor. Writer of variety show scripts, prose and short stories.

George Ferguson   205

Retired Methodist Minister living in Dublin. Now teaches Creative Writing to adults.

Sean Fitzgerald   207

Now living in Blarney. Worked in telecommunications. Interested in amateur drama, sailing, astronomy and reading.

Maeve Flanagan   170, 208

Currently working as secondary teacher of English and French in a South Dublin girls' school. Author of a memoir and a novel.

Tony Flannery   89

Native of Athenry, Co Galway. Member of The Redemptorists. Has written two books and articles for many publications.

John Fleetwood   93

Author of several books, including The History of Medicine in Ireland, *and of five pantomimes. Regular contributor to various radio programmes.*

Bryan Gallagher   94, 160, 172

A former headmaster, took early retirement in 1997. Author of There'll not be a Crowd till the Crowd Gathers.

Madeleine Going   46

Took up writing after living all over the world and raising a family. Has taught in Africa. Now lives in Greystones.

Ted Goodman   211

Born in Co Louth in 1932 and grew up in Newry, Co Down. Worked as an Inspector of Taxes with the Irish Revenue from 1955 to 1995.

Sheila Gorman   15, 212

Lives and works in Dublin. Short stories and poetry published internationally and broadcast by both RTÉ and BBC. Working on a collection of short stories.

Marian Gormley   98

Contributor to The Evening Press and several Irish magazines. Has awards for short stories, limericks and poetry.

Vona Groarke   157, 175

Her second collection of poetry, Other People's Houses *was published in 1999 by The Gallery Press.*

Michael Harding   39, 176, 189

His plays have been presented by The Abbey Theatre in Dublin. Has received numerous awards, including The Stewart Parker Theatre Award, the RTÉ/Bank of Ireland Award for Excellence in the Arts and a Hennessy Award for Short Stories. Shortlisted for the Irish Times Literature Awards.

Francis Harvey 137, 139

Born in Enniskillen but has lived in Donegal for most of his life. Poet and playwright. New and Selected Poems *to appear next year.*

Bill Hammond 99

Has written short stories, plays and articles as well as eight books, including the bestseller Footsteps on Blarney Street. *His latest novel is* The Poacher's Daughter.

Nuala Hayes 18, 49

An actor, broadcaster and sometime storyteller. Founder of the Two Chairs Company. Director of Scéalta Shamhna, Dublin's annual celebration of stories and music in November.

Don Heenan 11

Born in Shropshire, he also lived in rural Warwickshire. He moved to Ireland in 1979. He runs a small farm near Rathvilly.

Monica Henchy 138

Retired Assistant Librarian (TCD). President of the Dublin Spanish Society for several years.

John Heuston 75

Has worked on oral history projects in Ireland, Australia and the US. He is currently Communications Officer with a semi-state agency.

Judith Hoad 50

A planetarian and widow of the landscape painter, Jeremiah Hoad. She is now living in Co Donegal, teaching native European herbalism, writing two regular columns, and planning another book.

John Horgan 52

Professor of Journalism at Dublin City University. Former journalist with The Irish Times. Thirteen years in politics as a senator, TD and MEP.

Peter Jankowsy 19, 177, 214

Born in Berlin in 1939. He has lived in Dublin since 1971. He is a language teacher at the Goethe Institut, an actor and poetry translator.

Brendan Jennings 85

Writer, contributor to Sunday Miscellany.

Michael Judge 100, 124

Born in Dublin. Has written extensively for stage, radio, TV, screen drama and multimedia shows.

Maureen Keane 53, 215

Lives in Sutton, Dublin. Has written two biographies, Mrs S.C. Hall, *and* Ishbel, Lady Aberdeen.

Bill Kelly 54, 180

Former member of Garda Siochána. Articles published in magazines and newspapers. Book of short stories Searching for a Place *published (1992). Spent ten years with the United Nations on peace-keeping assignments.*

Cyril Kelly   101, 140, 217

Born in Listowel in 1945. At present teaching in Artane, Dublin.

Anne Kennedy   20

Born in Los Angeles, California. As a student, she recorded conversations with Jazz musicians. This material is part of the Duke Ellington Archive in the Smithsonian Museum of American History. In 1977 she moved from Washington to Galway. First book of poetry Buck Mountain Poems *published in 1989. Second book* The Dog Kubla Dreams of my Life *in 1994. She died on the 29th September 1998.*

Thomas J Kinsella   181

Writer, contributor to Sunday Miscellany.

Chuck Kruger   16, 22

Grew up in upstate New York. Has worked as secondary school teacher of Literature, Philosophy, Psychology and the Humanities in Switzerland. Writes poems and stories, reads for radio and organises storytelling events.

Gerard Lee   103

Actor and writer. He has previously been published in Poetry Ireland Review *and has co-scripted work for the stage with Peter Sheridan.*

Melosina Lenox-Conyngham   104, 219

Born in Ceylon on a tea estate. Her family came from Co Louth and she now lives in Co Kilkenny. She is the editor of an anthology, Diaries of Ireland.

Mae Leonard   23, 132

Lives in Naas, Co Kildare. Best known for scripts on memories of growing up in Limerick. An award-winning poet and short story writer. Writer-in-schools for Co Kildare.

Brian Leyden   5, 25

Lives in Co Leitrim. He is the author of the short story collection, Departures *and the novel* Death and Plenty.

Nicola Lindsay   107

Author of a published collection of poems, Lines of Thought, *an illustrated childrens' book* Batty Cat *and a novel* A Place for Unicorns. *Reads her work on radio both in England in Ireland, and at various public readings.*

Brenner Lynch   26

Born in Dublin in 1947. A prolific short story writer, his work has also been broadcast. Has received awards for his poetry.

Enda McAteer   109

A civil engineer with the civil service. Writes in his spare time.

Matt Mc Ateer   126

Retired teacher. Won the 'Bard of Armagh' competition in 1996 and the 'Jester to the Kingdom' title at the Kerry Arts Festival 2000.

Sam McAughtry 110, 168, 185

Author of nine books: autobiography, travel, short stories, novel, radio playwright. Columnist for The Irish Times 1981-1987, Irish Columnist of the Year 1986. Seanad Éireann 1996-1997.

Bríd McBride 27

Freelance journalist, arts critic and broadcaster. Reviewer of arts happenings for 'The Arts Show' and 'Rattlebag' (Radio 1, RTÉ). Adjudicates drama festivals at home and abroad.

Ann McCabe 61

Lives in Delgany, Co Wicklow, where she is a teacher of French, English and Creative Writing.

Áine Mac Carthy 141

Teaches art at Coláiste Choilm, Ballincollig, Co Cork. She has published a textbook called Art History – Revision for Leaving Cert *(Gill & Macmillan).*

Seamus McCluskey 220

Retired schoolteacher. Has published three local histories and three GAA histories. A regular broadcaster with a local radio station, 'Northern Sound'. Wrote a weekly column for the 'Northern Standard', a Monaghan newspaper.

Marguerite MacCurtin 43

Born in Co Galway, and travels extensively.

Kevin Mc Dermott 62, 105

Born in Dublin, where he now lives with his family. He is a teacher and writer.

Niall McGarrigle 142

Prizes include the O.Z. Whitehead Competition for Stage Plays and RTÉ's P.J. O'Connor Competition for Radio Plays. Also a scriptwriter on RTÉ's TV soap Fair City.

Padraig Mc Ginn 96, 111, 145

A retired headmaster, living in Carrick-on-Shannon, Co Leitrim. His stories have been published in The Leitrim Guardian and First Cut.

Joe Mc Gowan 63

A fisherman/part-time writer living in Mullaghmore, Co Sligo. He won several awards for his short stories. Has published two books on local history.

Leo McGowan 66

A Dubliner who teaches Management at NUI, Galway. In addition to creative writing, his hobbies include swimming, acting and dog-walking.

Barbara McKeon 65, 148, 209

Born in Dublin, has published and broadcast numerous short stories and many radio and TV dramas. Associated with The Irish Press for years, she now lives and writes in Galway.

Norma MacMaster 113

Born and reared in Bailieboro, Co Cavan. Trained as a Psychotherapist in Montreal where she lived for a number of years. She currently resides in Skerries.

Anne McSherry   149

Born in Dublin and studied biological sciences in UCD. She taught Science in secondary schools in Dublin for fourteen years.

Marie MacSweeney   150

A Kerrywoman born in Dublin and living in Co Meath. As well as Sunday Miscellany pieces, writes radio plays, short stories, articles and poetry.

Aodhan Madden   146, 183

A Dublin-born, award-winning playwright, fiction writer and journalist. Several of his plays have been staged by The Abbey Theatre and broadcast on RTÉ and BBC. Screenplays include 'Night Train'. Film 'Skerries' is in production.

Martin Malone   56

First novel, Us was published in April last, (Poolbeg Press). A soldier who has made extensive trips abroad.

Geraldine Mitchell   30

Taught and was a journalist for many years in Algeria, France and Spain. Now living in Co Mayo. She is the author of two novels for young people and of a biography Deeds not Words: the Life and Work of Muriel Gahan (1997).

Patricia Moorhead   218

Born in Dublin. A professional genealogist, she has written several stories about her own family which have been published in family history journals and magazines.

Gerry Moran   114

From Kilkenny where he is Principal of St Patrick's Boys Primary School. His work has featured in a variety of publications.

Jacqueline Morrissey   222

Lives in Dun Laoghaire. She works as an Associate Lecturer for the Open University.

Rita Normanly   187

Lives in rural South Sligo with her husband and three children.

Mary O'Donnell   47, 59

Novelist, short-story writer and popet. Three novels published, most recently The Elysium Treatment (Trident Press), also three collections of poems and a book of short stories. Scripted and presented three series of poetry programmes for RTÉ Radio 1 and is a frequent contributor to national radio.

Molly O'Duffy   58

Primary teacher and adult education trainer. Has spent five years living in Central America and currently works with the disability movement.

Tadhg Ó Dúshláine   69, 91, 117

Senior lecturer in NuaGhaeilge, NUI Maynooth. Director of the Frank O'Connor project. Writer-in-residence with Cork Corporation and the Munster Literature Centre, 1999-2000. Trí chnuasach filíochta agus dhá leabhar critice foilsithe aige.

Marie O'Nolan 223

Born and educated in Dublin. She published a collection of short stories in 1997 under the title Tales of a Long Dry Summer. *She is currently working on a novel.*

Hugh Oram 70

Author, broadcaster and journalist. Based in Dublin. Has contributed to many RTÉ radio programmes over the past twenty years.

Thaddeus O'Regan 68, 115

Born in Rosscarbery, West Cork in 1951 and studied English and Geography at University College, Cork. He works as a secondary teacher and lives near Carrigaline, Co Cork.

Patricia O'Reilly 29, 32, 118

Writer, lecturer, researcher. Author of several non-fiction books, including Writing for the Market *and* Working Mothers. *First novel* Once Upon a Summer *published summer 2000.*

Madeleine O'Rourke 224

From Dublin, and currently freelances as a radio-feature maker.

Ger Petrie 120

Lives in Dublin and Wicklow. Having retired as full-time mother and home-maker, now writes the stories she has been narrating for years.

Michael Reeves 72

From Limerick, he now lives in West Clare. A former teacher, he has had poetry published in Ireland and Britain. He paints, sculpts and is a keen photographer.

Tom Rowley 121

Has worked as a journalist since 1972, primarily with the Irish Independent. He is currently press officer for the National Millennium Committee.

Mary Russell 156

A writer and traveller. Her work appears in The Irish Times and one of her short stories won first prize at the Listowel 2000 Writers' Week.

Sylvia Sands 136

Has spent twenty-nine years in Belfast, involved in peace and community work. She has written two books and broadcast regularly for BBC radio and occasionally for RTÉ.

Bernard Share 151

A writer and editor, formerly of 'Cara' magazine for Aer Lingus and 'Books Ireland', which he edited for 12 years from its inception. His books include novels, travel and social history. Working on a study of Irish nomenclature.

Anne Sharpe 227

A psychologist, she has had a number of stories published by Blackstaff, Attic and other outlets. At the moment, she is writing a novel.

Carol Slowey 2

Born in 1954 in Donaghadee, Co Down. She studied Irish and Irish Folklore at University College, Dublin. Now living and working in North Antrim.

Nuala Smith   188, 228

Has worked as a freelance journalist, an airhostess, manager of a restaurant and has taught computers.

Adrian Smyth   192

A freelance broadcaster and programme maker. Has made a number of documentaries for RTÉ Radio 1 and presents a music programme on independent local radio. Also lectures in the production of community radio.

Sheila Smyth   153, 196

Taught for thirty years in London. Retired to Co Waterford. A regular contributor to SQ magazine and Ireland's Own. A Touching of Spirits, *one of her short stories, broadcast by RTÉ.*

David Sowby   33

Practised medicine in Canada and then served as Scientific Secretary of the International Commission on Radiological Protection. On retirement, returned to Ireland. Has spent the last year writing his memoirs, Man Ages.

Dolores Stewart   201

First collection of poetry In Out of the Rain *is published by the Daedulus Press, 1999.*

Richard Stokes   123

Worked for most of his career in the Department of the Taoiseach, dealing for many years with arts and culture. Member of Arts Council, 1973-83.

William Wall   226, 231

Author of Alice Falling *(Sceptre, 1999), and* Mathematics & Other Poems *(The Collins Press, 1997). He lives in Cork.*

Thomas F Walsh   193, 229

Compiler of the series Favourite Poems We Learned in School, *published by Mercier Press. He was formerly a primary school headmaster and is a regular contributor to Sunday Miscellany.*

Kevin Whelan   191

Published two books, Izzy Baia: Autism, Life and Other Unsolved Mysteries, *and a novel,* A Wonderful Boy: A Story of the Holocaust *(both Marino). He has recently completed* The Blue Crystal *and* Cutting Loose. *He lives in Galway.*

Biddy White Lennon   127

A freelance food writer, journalist and broadcaster. Her father Tommy Lennon was one of Dublin's well-known 'literary landlords' (in The Abbey Bar where the Abbey Theatre now stands).

Peter Woods   74, 80

Born in London, brought up in Monaghan. Now lives in Dublin.

Susan Zelouf   34, 186

American writer and performer, she has lived and worked in New York, Rome, Los Angeles and Belfast before settling in Co Laois. She has appeared in clubs internationally, and is a frequent contributor to RTÉ radio programmes.